HE WAS ALWAYS SUCH A QUIET BOY . . .

Padding softly up behind his mother, Oliver snaked out a muscular arm, trapping her neck in the crook of his elbow, and squeezed. Mother and son thrashed furiously, Oliver desperately trying to maintain his chokehold while his mother wildly flailed her arms and legs.

With the shotgun only a few feet away, the husky youth began to drag the furiously struggling woman through the doorway. Releasing his hold on her, he grabbed for the weapon. Gasping for air, Anna rolled to her knees and groped for the table, trying to pull herself to her feet.

She was too late. Oliver was already cradling the shotgun in his arms. Shoving the barrel against the base of his mother's skull, he pulled the trigger. . . .

D1390908

Clifford L. Linedecker

KILLER KIDS

SHOCKING TRUE STORIES OF CHILDREN WHO MURDERED THEIR PARENTS

ROBINSON

LONDON

Robinson Publishing Ltd
7, Kensington Church Court
London W8 4SP

First published in the USA by St Martin's Press 1993
First published in the UK by Robinson Publishing Ltd 1994

A copy of the British Library Cataloguing in Publication
Data for this title is available from the British Library.

ISBN 1-85487-253-2

Typeset by Hewer Text Composition Services, Edinburgh
Printed by HarperCollins, Glasgow

10 9 8 7 6 5 4 3 2 1

Acknowledgments

I've had the good fortune to be supported and assisted by many individuals and organizations in the preparation of this book. My thanks to each and every one, but especially to my friends and colleagues Bob Abborino, Billy Burt and Donald Vaughan.

Contents

Introduction   1

Chapter 1 .... Mom's Beer Party   10

Chapter 2 .... Mom, Dad, and the Axeman   37

Chapter 3 .... A Hollywood Tragedy   60

Chapter 4 .... Daddy's Precious   86

Chapter 5 .... The Girl in the Closet   107

Chapter 6 .... A Family Tragedy   133

Chapter 7 .... Hell House   162

Chapter 8 .... Hit Man for a Cheerleader   192

Chapter 9 .... Ten Faces of Evil   229

Chapter 10 .... Lethal Lovers   255

Lizzie Borden took an axe
And gave her mother forty whacks.
When she saw what she had done,
She gave her father forty-one.

—Children's ditty

Introduction

Parricide, the murder of a parent—or the more specific patricide for the murder of one's father, and matricide for the murder of one's mother—are ugly words for ugly acts.

Until recently, parricide was an almost unheard of crime, deserving of prominent mention only in Greek mythology, where the tale of hotheaded Oedipus's unwitting murder of his father and marriage to his mother provided the father of psychoanalysis, Sigmund Freud, with a name for a favorite complex.

In real-life America, the most notorious accused parent killer in criminal history is Lizzie Borden, the Fall River, Massachusetts, spinster who was charged with using an axe to chop to death her father and stepmother on a stifling hot August day in 1892. Although Lizzie was exonerated following a sensational jury trial, today, a century after the dreadful double murder, crime historians still disagree about the identity of the axe murderer. Lizzie's older sister, Emma; a housemaid; and a mysterious tramp have all at one time had a finger pointed at them as the possible killer. But many, perhaps most crime buffs who have studied the case, are convinced that Lizzie did, indeed, murder her parents.

What could have led the thirty-two-year-old Lizzie to commit the horrendous act? Suggested motives have run the gamut from her admitted jealousy and dislike for her stepmother, to her father's miserly ways and threats to disinherit her, to a quarrel over her embarrassing spinsterhood, to premenstrual syndrome, and a torrid lesbian love affair.

Whatever the motive, and whoever the real killer may have been, the grisly double murder that shattered the peace of Fall River a century ago has become a dark piece of American folklore. And the one-time local mainstay of the Women's Christian Temperance Union, and devoted churchgoer, even has her own Lizzie Borden display in Fall River's Historical Society Museum. She is indisputably the town's most famous citizen.

One of the reasons that the Lizzie Borden case attracted so much attention a hundred years ago was because parricide was such a rare crime. It wasn't that savage, brutal murder was unknown in the United States then, but the killing of one's parent or parents was almost unthinkable.

Unfortunately that is no longer true. Today parricide is no longer a rare crime, and it's unlikely that accused killers of parents will be remembered with historical displays in their hometowns. Parricide is spreading like an out-of-control virus. Parents are being murdered by their progeny in alarming numbers over such seemingly trivial factors as disagreements over domestic chores, boyfriends and girlfriends, other dating restrictions, curfews, spending money, and driving privileges.

In Colorado, a fourteen-year-old boy beat his hardworking single mother to death with a barbell after she refused to buy him a waterbed. A ten-year-old boy in Houston, Texas, picked Mother's Day to shoot his father to death and fire four shots into his mother because she wouldn't let him play outside. In Wolcott, Kansas, a hulking 310-pound high school honors student calmly shot his father, mother, and sister to death. Then he explained to authorities that he was practicing to become a professional hit man in Chicago.

These are simple, obvious motives and explanations most quickly and easily discernible to investigators and shocked relatives, neighbors, and friends. But they don't always tell the entire story.

The underlying motivations are sometimes complex and evasive. And a child whom it seems suddenly and inexplicably erupts into a rage and bludgeons his mother to death because she won't buy him a waterbed, has likely been nursing other more deep-seated resentments for months or years. Law enforcement authorities, sociologists, and mental health professionals agree on some of the underlying causes, and disagree on others. The family background, emotional history, and intelligence of each child who kills a parent is different. And parricide is a crime, as well, that spans both racial and socioeconomic lines.

In my own research I have found that most children who commit parricide fit into one of five major categories:

- Children who have been exposed to sexual, physical or emotional abuse and violence in the household. Most often when violence occurs it is directed from the father toward the mother and the children. But in some households everyone fights. It is a short step for a child who grows up surrounded by violence and abuse, to perceive violence to be a proper way to deal with problems.

- Sociopaths. Sometimes children, those from privileged families as well as the underprivileged, simply seem to grow up without a conscience. They are cold, uncaring, and have a total disregard for the needs, rights, and welfare of other people. It is a term that no one likes to use, but it seems that some children are simply "bad seed." They are born to evil. In Colorado a teenager was charged by authorities with enlisting three friends in a bizarre plot to murder her mother, after a mechanic tipped off the woman that someone was trying to kill her. The three girls and a boy were accused of lacing the woman's coffee with nicotine, sabotaging her car in an effort to blow it up, and scheming to strangle her or beat her to death with a hammer. A sheriff's detective said that the nineteen-year-old simply didn't like her mother. And in perhaps the nation's most horrific case of parricide, Jack Gilbert Graham hid a bomb in his mother's luggage to blow up an airliner shortly after it left Denver. Graham's mother and forty-three other innocent people were killed as part of the depraved insurance scheme. The bomber was executed.

• The mentally ill. This can but need not include those who have deliberately burned their brains with LSD and PCP or softened their minds with other damaging drugs. Sometimes it is a combination of both. The mentally unstable turn to drugs, which complicate already severe problems and send them off into a terrifyingly capricious world of delusions, paranoia, and violence. They may hallucinate or hear disembodied voices that command them to kill.

One of the more notorious cases that fits into this category drew wide attention from the press because the killer was the son of then President Ronald Reagan's personal attorney, Roy Miller. Michael Miller was described by his own defense psychiatrist as one of the "most severely mentally ill individuals I have had the opportunity to examine," after the tragic twenty-two-year-old beat his fifty-two-year-old mother, Marguerite, to death with a club. Miller was convicted of first-degree murder, but the judge ruled that he was insane at the time of the crime and committed him to a state psychiatric hospital in California. Young Miller was declared not guilty of raping the victim, who was found nude and bludgeoned in the master bedroom of the family's exclusive Palos Verdes Estates home in March 1983.

- Children who have become dangerously involved in devil worship, blood cults, or obsessed with certain heavy metal music sometimes described as Satanic rock. Promises of power, sex, and freedom can be strong lures to impressionable adolescents who are drawn to the mysterious rituals of Satanism and other blood cults. The degree to which these desires may be supported and nourished by the arcane metaphors and symbolism of the lyrics and music of some heavy metal—or by the popular intellectual fantasy game Dungeons & Dragons—is controversial. But there is no question that police have found quotes from rock lyrics referring to Satan, blood, and human sacrifice in diaries or other journals kept by certain young parricides. And some ritual killers have talked openly to police and to psychiatrists of messages from Satan in heavy metal or punk rock lyrics. Even before the advent of heavy metal, Charlie Manson and his freaky family of flower children were convinced that the Beatles had hidden secret messages in some of their lyrics.

- Children who kill for greed. In most instances these parricides, like Jack Graham, are adults or are near enough to adulthood to qualify for inheriting the estates of their parents with few strings attached. Some of the more notorious cases, which have been chronicled elsewhere, include those of New York socialite Frances Schreuder, who dispatched her son to murder her father, a multimillionaire and hardworking auto parts dealer in Utah; Steven Wayne Benson, who blew up his wealthy tobacco-heiress mother and her adopted son with a pipe bomb in Florida; and Cynthia Campbell Ray, who conspired with a former lover to kill her lawyer father and her mother in Houston.

Incredible as it may seem, children convicted of killing parents sometimes walk out of mental hospitals or prisons after a few months or years and inherit the estates of the victims. In Indiana, survivors reacted with outrage when an appeals court ruled that a Greenwood man who shot his parents to death when he was nineteen was entitled to his inheritance from them, as well as a share of a life insurance policy on his mother.

There was similar public reaction in Wisconsin when a teenager who stabbed, slashed, and shot to death his foster parents and foster brother in their rural Mineral Point home when he was fourteen filed claim for their near $400,000 estates. The claim was filed a month before his scheduled release from a boys' school when he reached the age of nineteen, in accordance with the juvenile court statutes he was sentenced under. And in California, a sixteen-year-old boy who stabbed his mother and sister to death, then burned down the family home to hide the grisly crime, was freed after five years and paid $21,500 in Social Security benefits because he was an orphan. Another fourteen-year-old California boy who fatally blasted his father with a shotgun, was freed after four years in custody and collected $8000 in Social Security survivors pay.

Most states now allow minors to be tried as adults on charges of murder, but obtaining convictions can be difficult. Juvenile killers know how to take advantage of their innocent appearance, and prosecutors can have trouble convincing a jury of adults that a sobbing or frightened boy or girl willingly committed such a horrible crime as parricide. Dead parents can be accused of physical or sexual abuse, or of dreadful emotional bullying, and there is no way they can be called on to refute the testimony.

Even when convictions are obtained, judges can sometimes be reluctant to sentence teenagers or preteens to adult prisons, where they can face terrible sexual abuse or at the very least spend their time sharpening their criminal expertise in anticipation of an early release.

One of the alternatives is dealing with the child through the juvenile system of the individual states. But murder, especially the murder of one's parent, is a horrendous crime that in most instances justifies severe punishment. And punishment is a valid response by society to violent crime, even when the offender is not yet an adult. But punishment available through juvenile court action is severely restricted in every state, and less than five years in a boys school—the punishment for the rural Wisconsin youth—hardly seems adequate for the cold-blooded slaughter of three family members.

A recent study indicated that the average time served by youngsters sent to California Youth Authority lock-ups for first degree murder was less than four years. Not only law and order hardliners, but others who are concerned about the rising tide of violence, question if less than four years of CYA supervision for murder is proper punishment to fit the crime.

There's no question that the best course in dealing with the shocking increase in parricide and other family violence is identifying causes and attempting to prevent the crime from occurring. Sociologists are quick to point to the breakup of traditional families, single parent households, latch-key children, and the lack of affection and participation by parents in the lives of their youngsters, as contributing causes to violence. But it appears highly unlikely that any major changes in the situation are about to occur soon. And it is not only the United States that must deal with the breakdown of traditional family structure and violent behavior.

A lack of affection and emotional support by the parents of a fourteen-year-old boy was blamed in Japan, where murder is almost unknown compared to the United States, when he exploded in an orgy of violence, killing his mother, father, and grandmother. After the massacre, the teenager's mother was widely condemned in the national press for being a *kyoiku mama,* an education-obsessed parent who was so intent on getting her son into the proper schools that she constantly badgered him to study for tests. She reputedly never eased up on the boy for a moment. The press criticized his father for being a classic Japanese workaholic husband, who devoted so many hours to his job and to socializing with clients and business associates that he had no time for his son. One night after both his mother and father scolded him for not studying harder, he stormed into their bedroom with a kitchen knife and a baseball bat and bludgeoned and stabbed them to death. Then he killed his grandmother, the one family member who had actively provided affection and emotional support, because she witnessed the crime.

The tragedy set off a round of self-criticism and examination in Japan, with the nation's newspapers, educators, and business leaders questioning the trend in their society to focus too strongly on their children's intellectual and career abilities, while neglecting their emotional growth.

The press and other self-appointed experts had clearly decided that it was the parents' own fault that they were murdered by the son whose professional future they were so diligently attempting to turn toward success. It was portrayed simply as a case of good intentions gone terribly awry. The young multiple-killer was treated as the victim.

Perhaps he was. But the parents were also victims, and so was the grandmother. Whatever the motives and the underlying causes of the parricide in Japan, and those that are occurring with disturbing regularity in the United States, they are difficult to isolate. And even when they are known, the question remains: How can the information be used to stem or slow down a continuation of the family tragedies?

Answers won't come easy, either in Japan or in the United States. Concerted efforts to find solutions must nevertheless be pursued by professionals in criminology, corrections, sociology, mental health, and other concerned methodologies.

Last year more than one million violent assaults by children against their parents were recorded by police agencies in the United States. An alarming number of the assaults were fatal.

Clifford L. Linedecker
Lantana, Florida

Chapter 1

Mom's Beer Party

It was party time at Nancy Knuckles' house!

Her daughters and the other girls were going through Nancy's belongings in her upstairs bedroom and closets, selecting clothing and toiletries they wanted to keep for themselves.

Her only son, Barton, was racing down the stairs with a gleaming new microwave in his arms. A card was Scotch-taped to the top identifying it as a present for all the kids, and a bright red ribbon lovingly tied by Nancy still encircled it.

"Thanks, Ma, for the microwave!" Bart whooped.

But Bart was even more excited when he lifted a box from a closet and pulled out an insurance policy on his mother's life. "We're rich!" he yelled.

Bart, his seventeen-year-old sister Pamela, and his fifteen-year-old sister Deborah, celebrated with their friends by breaking out beer and whiskey, putting on some rock records, and digging into additional presents their mother had been putting aside in anticipation of the approaching Christmas holiday. Both her girls found new Polaroid cameras, which they quickly loaded with film and began to use to snap pictures.

One of their favorite photographs was a shot Debbie snapped of the rest of the gang forming a human pyramid in the front room. The boys were on the bottom, supporting the girls. There was Bart; Pamela's current boyfriend, Dennis Morris; and two of Bart's and Dennis's pals, Steven Wright and David Dukes. The wobbly second row was made up of Bart's girlfriend, nineteen-year-old Cindy Caruso; a fourteen-year-old girlfriend of Cindy's; and Pamela. Another fourteen-year-old girl and Cindy's two-year-old son, D.J., were at the very top.

Nancy Knuckles was religious and wouldn't have approved of the boisterous soiree, with all the earsplitting rock music, dancing, boozing, and smoking. But even though she was right there in the front room, she had nothing to say about it. Her petite body, already stiffened by rigor mortis, had been folded up and stuffed in a steamer trunk that the kids had pulled into the middle of the floor.

An ugly ligature of strong, braided white twine deeply embedded in her neck had left her face purple and the features frozen in agony, as if she were still gasping for breath.

Only a few hours earlier, Nancy Knuckles had one hand on the front doorknob and was holding a bag of aprons in her other hand, preparing to leave the house to begin her three-to-eleven P.M. shift at the Health Oasis, a vegetarian restaurant. Her daughter Pamela had looped an efficiently formed garrote over her mother's head from behind and pulled. As Nancy felt the rope loop around her neck, she lurched around in a half-turn, and for a brief second her startled eyes locked accusingly on those of her daughter. Her lips twisted in what appeared to be a smirk, as if she were daring her daughter to kill her. Pamela responded by jerking the garrote tighter.

"Die, bitch, die, bitch!" she screeched.

Nancy was a small woman, but killing by garrote is not easy, especially when victim and slayer are about the same size. As Nancy's body slumped to the floor, Pamela dropped to her knees beside her, continuing to pull on the braided twine digging into her mother's

neck. Nancy's body spasmed and bounced as she struggled for breath, and the teenager looked desperately to
her boyfriend, who was standing a few feet away, watching the struggle.

Dennis knelt on the floor beside the struggling
mother and daughter, and leaned forward to help. He
took hold of one end of the garrote and pulled. Then he
took the other end.

Debbie was upstairs in her room when she heard the
commotion. Curious, she walked downstairs into the living room and saw her mother facedown on the floor
near the piano, with the teenage sweethearts kneeling
over the body with the garrote. Pamela turned as Debbie entered the room, and screamed for her to go back
upstairs. Obediently, the younger girl complied.

Much later, Bart would recall that he was in his bedroom when Debbie walked in and calmly advised: "Pam
and Dennis just killed the old lady."

Nancy's body was stretched out on the floor, the garrote still looped around her neck, when Bart walked
downstairs. Pamela and Dennis were breathing in short,
quick, excited gasps, and their faces were flushed as
Bart knelt and peered at his mother. He felt for a
pulse and put his hand over her heart, but couldn't tell
for certain if she was alive or not. He yelled at his sisters
to bring him their mother's stethoscope from upstairs.
After one of the girls clattered down the stairs with the
stethoscope, he pressed it to his mother's chest and listened for a heartbeat. Then he straightened up.

"Well, she won't die," he said.

He stalked into the kitchen and returned with a white
plastic garbage bag, which he pulled over her head and
tied in the back. After a few moments he again leaned
forward and pressed the stethoscope to his mother's
chest. When he straightened up, he was grinning. She
was dead at last.

Years later Pamela would recall how curious it
seemed to her at the time that her mother was still

clutching the bag of aprons. Nancy had never loosened her grip on the bag, neither as her daughter looped the garrote around her neck, nor as she slumped to the floor, nor during her dying convulsions.

Nancy D. Knuckles, a registered nurse and single mother who worked two jobs to take care of herself and her family, was deliberately and ruthlessly executed in her home by her own children and one of their friends. She was forty years old.

It was a shocking and brutal crime, even for the Chicago area, which is known for such ruthless killers as prohibition-era mobster Al Capone, nurse-killer Richard Speck, and vicious homosexual serial slayer John Wayne Gacy. But this wasn't a gangster killing, and it wasn't a senseless sex-slaying of a stranger. The teenagers had brutally and remorselessly murdered their mother.

Matricide just wasn't the kind of thing that happened in the far-western Chicago suburb of Villa Park, where Nancy had settled with her rambunctious brood a few months earlier. Villa Park was a comfortable middle-class community, presumably far enough from Chicago to insulate the hardworking residents from the runaway crime and violence of the big city. Although she grew up in the city, as an adult Nancy had been drawn to the comfort and presumed safety of the suburbs and rural Illinois countryside.

Near the end of the summer of 1984, the hardworking nurse put a down payment on a comfortable three-bedroom, red brick duplex on East Vermont Street in Villa Park. The house was in a pleasant blue-collar neighborhood within short commuting distance of downtown Chicago, yet sufficiently isolated to make it an attractive environment for raising teenagers and younger children.

From outward appearances, there was nothing about Nancy Knuckles that fit the profile of a parent likely to be murdered by her own children. Mrs. Knuckles kept so busy with her two jobs as a restaurant cook and as a visiting nurse who helped convalescents in their homes, that neighbors didn't see much of her. On the infrequent occasions when they did run into her outside the house, she was courteous and pleasant. But she never seemed to have time to do more than pass the time of day with a simple, cheery "Good morning," or a few dry comments about the weather.

When Nancy wasn't working or taking care of her domestic duties, she was attending church or participating in church-oriented affairs with fellow members of the congregation.

But the lives of the hardworking registered nurse and her teenagers weren't as comfortably normal as they may have appeared to her neighbors, prior to the dreadful event of that crisply cold late November day.

The oldest of three children and the only girl, Nancy's childhood was polluted by violence and a relative's mental illness. There were terrible fights, and a family member would later talk of at least one incident when Nancy was still a toddler and was the victim of sexual abuse, or attempted abuse, that was interrupted only at the last moment by her mother as she walked into the bedroom and discovered what was going on. Nancy was still in school when her parents were divorced.

Nancy seemed to handle the domestic troubles well, however, and as she grew up, she developed into an apparently normal teenager. She was a willowy blond beauty. The teenager cheerfully assumed responsibility for her share of the housework, made good grades in school, and worked after classes in the business office of a local department store. Most of the money she earned was spent on clothes.

From early childhood, religion was an important part of Nancy's existence. At first her religious life centered around the Roman Catholicism she was born into. But when she was a teenager, she left the Catholic Church and became a Southern Baptist. In 1962, shortly after graduation from high school, she took another big step toward establishing her independence and severing her strong familial ties, and moved out of her mother's house and into an apartment with a girlfriend.

Soon after leaving home, Nancy dropped her former boyfriend and began dating Robert Knuckles. Knuckles was a high school dropout who wore his slicked-back hair in an Elvis ducktail, played the guitar, and occasionally sang in country and western bars. They were married in a civil ceremony. Nancy didn't ask her mother or other family members to attend.

They didn't live happily ever after. Family members later recounted tales of Nancy showing up complaining of heavy boozing by her young husband. Somehow the couple limped through eight years of the troubled union and produced a son, Barton, and two daughters, Pamela and Deborah, before they gave up and called the marriage quits.

Nancy was hypersensitive and quick to fly off the handle, and she administered erratic punishment to her brood with screams, threats, and slaps. When Bart was about five, Nancy once flew into a rage, hurled him to the ground and kicked him. His offense? Venturing outside without a coat.

Years later, when her ex-husband was talking with a reporter about the breakup of his marriage, he didn't blame Nancy's rages. Instead, he blamed his drinking and Nancy's conversion to the Seventh Day Adventist Church for hammering the final nails into the coffin of their marriage.

As soon as Nancy was exposed to the Seventh Day Adventists, she fell in love with the Church. She became obsessed with the religious teachings, and, driven by a stubborn determination, began to rebuild her life according to her personally strict interpretation of the Scriptures and the activities of the congregation. When she began dating again, it was with a former heroin addict who was initiated into the Church at the same time she was. They dated and shared problems with each other for almost three years before Nancy broke off the relationship. He wasn't religious enough for her.

Nancy had no time or tolerance for such ungodly trivialities or venal pleasures as television, movies, rock music, dancing or alcohol. Pastries, candy, and meat were also strictly off limits for Nancy or anyone moving in her spartan religious world of stern morality and self-righteous denial.

Despite her zealous devotion to her religious faith, or perhaps because of it, the Devil began to torment her. She complained of frightening visions, and reported that Satan once stretched her mouth horribly out of shape until, after a desperate struggle, she was able to croak out the name of "Jesus." As soon as she uttered the name of the Messiah, Satan was gone and her poor, tortured mouth relaxed back into a normal position.

She told confidants that Jesus came to her rescue another time when mysterious devilish forces began taunting her by making frightful noises inside her kitchen. When she went into the kitchen to investigate, the noises stopped, but they resumed as soon as she returned to the front room to sit down. Desperate to end the ordeal, she finally shouted: "In the name of Jesus, I command you to stop." The ungodly teasing ceased for good, as mysteriously as it had begun.

Growing up in a home where devilish attacks were accepted as such a tangible and graphic fact of life, the children also began to have troubles with frightening visions attributed to the evil doings of the Prince of Darkness. There were stories of phantom figures mysteriously turning from white to black, of mystical signs appearing suddenly on the palms of tiny hands, and of a disembodied head rolling under a bed. Their mother always confirmed that it was the Devil's work, and admonished that only a strict religious life and devotion to God could offer protection and salvation.

Nancy attempted to cleanse the souls of her children by beating the Devil out of them. In a sick parody of the self-inflicted abuse of the penitents of the Middle Ages, Nancy prepared for the daily beating of her children by reciting a prayer. Then she asked the children if they understood why they had a need for punishment.

Obediently, Pamela would reply that she understood. Then the frightened child would submit to a beating with a piece of garden hose. Afterward, Pamela would sit on her mother's lap and apologize for being a bad girl, earning hugs and crooning assurances that Nancy loved her.

Bart was more rebellious, and even though Nancy would patiently explain the need to beat him to rid him of the Devil and bring him closer to God, he would sometimes stubbornly insist that he didn't know why he had to be punished. His mother beat him anyway.

Bart also fought back as best he could when his mother made him climb into a laundry bag, then dragged the bag into a closet. He ripped his way out of the bag, screaming and crying and tearing at the material with his hands. After his mother began tying his hands behind him to prevent him from ripping apart the cloth bags, he chewed his way out.

When the girls were punished by being placed in the bags, usually for being noisy, they learned to simply curl up and go to sleep until their mother let them out. When a relative once suggested to Nancy that her methods of disciplining the children might be bad for them, she replied that God had told her how to bring them up.

One time when Debbie began to take a shower, Pamela saw that her little sister's body was covered with ugly bruises. Pamela was so horrified and frightened that she ran to a relative's house for help. The relative notified authorities with the Department of Children and Family Services, the DCFS. But when an investigator went to the Knuckles home to check out the report of suspected child abuse, Nancy flew into a rage, bombarding him with accusations of interference with her right to rear her children according to her religious beliefs. Chastened, and fearful of becoming entangled in a nasty dispute over religious beliefs, parental rights, and the state, the investigator retreated. Nancy beat Pamela after he left.

Almost anything could lead to a beating in the Knuckles home during those years. Pamela was in the fifth grade when she was caught kissing a boy during recess, and a teacher at the strict church school punished her with thirty whacks. At home Nancy administered ninety more. Any punishment meted out to the children at school was tripled when they returned home.

The children were beaten for opening the refrigerator door without permission, for talking at the table, for eating meat or anything with sugar in it, making unnecessary noise, leaving hair in the sink or tub, going to a movie, or watching television at a friend's house. In accordance with Nancy's strict religious prohibitions against frivolousness or undue pleasure, there was no television in their home.

Strict timetables were established for doing household chores, homework, play, and Bible study, and the penalty for failure to adhere to the schedules drawn up by Nancy was beatings. Nancy set a timer when the children washed the dishes, and if they weren't done when the timer went off, she counted up the unfinished dishes and pieces of cutlery. Each piece left over earned one whack with the garden hose. A similar rule applied when the children returned to the house after play. If they were one minute late, they got a swat with the garden hose. Two minutes earned two swats. Ten minutes, ten swats.

Mealtimes were miserable experiences for the youngsters. Nancy dished up the helpings for the children, and if she provided them with more than they could comfortably eat, they had to clean their plates anyway. Anything left on their plate went into a bag, which Nancy tied around their neck and made them carry around with them until they gave up and finished the leftover food.

How did Nancy know if her children had disobeyed her and gone to a movie on a Saturday afternoon, watched TV at a friend's house, or accepted a fresh-baked brownie from a friend's mother? They confessed!

Nancy regularly confronted the children, and ordered them to confess transgressions. Usually they confessed if they had anything to tell, especially the girls. The guilt, and fear that their mother would somehow know that they had done wrong—perhaps through the help of God, who knew everything—was unbearable.

The punishment and violence that ruled the Knuckles home was especially bad while Nancy was enrolled in a college nursing program. She put in long, grueling hours in class and in home study, and exhaustion helped make her short-tempered. The children learned to be careful not to upset her, but invariably broke some of the rules. Nancy was so busy with her classes that she didn't have time to continue the daily beatings, so she used a note-book to keep track of the infractions and caught up with the punishment once a week.

But Nancy's overzealous efforts to raise her family with strong spiritual and moral guidelines weren't work-ing out as she had hoped. The children disappointed her and were hard to control. Her rebellious son especially troubled her with misbehavior and deliberate flouting of her rules.

Desperate to regain control of her family, and to es-cape from pressing financial problems, Nancy gathered up her brood and moved them to a Church community in Wisconsin. After a few months they moved to a simi-lar community in Michigan, then some weeks later re-turned to Chicago. Finally they trooped about sixty-five miles southwest of the Windy City to tiny Sheridan, Illi-nois.

The congregation of the Seventh Day Adventist Church in the quiet little farming community welcomed

the troubled, fatherless family with open arms. And
when Nancy disclosed that she could no longer handle
twelve-year-old Bart, who had stolen money from her
and tried to drive off with her car, they agreed to bank-
roll his stay at a farm in Nebraska where delinquent
youngsters were sent to live and work—and hopefully
mend their wayward lifestyles. Bart's move to Nebraska
and his care there cost the small congregation $300 per
month.

Even with Bart out of the way, Nancy was troubled by
the continuing responsibility of caring for her girls. She
moved again, this time shifting the family only a few
miles to Ottawa, Illinois, a larger town of about 15,000.
But the move still didn't solve her problems. With so
much to do, keeping up with her Bible studies, religious
seminars, and regular church services, she simply didn't
have enough time to spend with her daughters.

And when she was with them, her behavior was frus-
tratingly inconsistent. According to her mood, she could
be stern and distant, or warm and loving. If she was
feeling good, she would sometimes make up religious
lyrics and apply them to the tunes of popular songs,
then sing them to the girls. But if the girls didn't respond the way she expected when she wanted them to
do something, she would simply pull away, or stomp off
and leave them to themselves to do whatever they
wanted. More often than not, they were left to their own
devices.

Debbie and Pam began staying weekends with the
church pastor, his wife and baby daughter. Then they
moved in for the summer. Even after Nancy packed up
some months later and left Ottawa, the girls continued
to spend summers with the preacher's family. The
preacher also had rules he expected the sisters to ob-
serve while they were living at his home, but he and his
wife were consistent about their expectations. Pam and
Debbie thrived there.

It wasn't long before it became obvious to even the

most generously tolerant members of the church that Nancy wasn't being a proper mother to her children. And there was no question that the girls were hurt and bitter about Nancy's priorities: church first; jobs second; and mothering only if there was time left over. Nor had Bart responded well to being shunted off to Nebraska. He soon left the farm and began an unhappy sojourn of finding temporary shelter with relatives, the families of friends—and in correctional institutions.

Nancy's control of the children lessened as they grew older. By the time Pamela was fourteen, she was big enough to face down her mother and firmly reject further beatings. She not only began going to movies and watching television whenever she felt like it, but she made no secret about the fact that she ate what she wanted, and she began smoking, drinking, dating, and ignoring curfews. She dyed her hair red, plastered her face with layers of cosmetics, wore jeans so tight they almost cut off her circulation, and wobbled uncertainly around the house in high heels in open defiance of her mother.

Church members had sympathized with the need and obvious desire of Nancy's children for parental attention and love. But when two women approached the church's pastor with a suggestion that they work together to have Nancy declared an unfit mother, he reportedly vetoed the plan. Breaking up families was not something to be taken lightly.

When Nancy was living in Sheridan, she met a man who was interested in her. They dated for a couple of years, but argued about her children. He couldn't accept the way she treated them, and eventually the couple broke off the relationship. Nancy moved again, this time to Texas.

She accepted a job with a hospital to be run by the Seventh Day Adventists in Santa Anna. But the administrators were waiting for the hospital to be accredited, and there would be no salary for Nancy until it was opened for business. Consequently it was agreed that she could move into the hospital to live with her girls, and charge her grocery bills to the institution. A nineteen-year-old boyfriend of Pamela moved in with them.

Although Pamela depended on her boyfriend for emotional support, he was far from the ideal companion and protector. A friend of her brother's, he had only recently been released from a correctional institution after serving time for involuntary manslaughter for accidentally shooting his former girlfriend in the head and killing her.

The youth was extremely possessive and jealous, and he insisted on walking Pamela to her freshman classes at the Santa Anna High School every day. He strictly forbid her to talk to anyone except him and teachers who might call on her in class. There were to be no chats or sharing of confidences with classmates, not even so much as a casual hello to another girl while walking between classes.

Despite Pamela's meek acquiescence, after several weeks her boyfriend tired of the situation in Texas and abruptly announced that he was returning to Illinois. Pamela panicked at the thought of being abandoned, and swallowed a jar of pills that belonged to her mother. She vomited up the pills. The clumsy suicide attempt didn't kill her, but it helped convince her boyfriend to stick around a while longer.

It was Nancy who left. One day when Pamela returned to the hospital from school, her mother was gone. And she didn't come back that night, or the next day. She had simply cleared out, without a word to either of her daughters about where she was going or how they were expected to take care of themselves.

Debbie moved in with a clergyman's family. Pamela and her boyfriend stayed at the hospital for a few weeks more, until the grocery store cut off the credit and their food supply vanished. Pamela and the boy hitchhiked back to Illinois.

Bart had also returned to Illinois by that time and was living near Chicago, with friends. When he learned that his baby sister had been left behind he headed for Texas to pick her up and they hitchhiked back to Illinois.

It was already December when they returned, and Chicago winters can be ferociously cold. The teenagers were chilled, hungry, and miserably alone. Bart took his sister to a church he was attending, and when a woman preacher took one peek at the bedraggled girl sitting in a back pew, dirty, shivering, and with a lost puppy-dog look after a week on the road, her heart melted. She and her husband invited Debbie to move in with them. The homeless girl stayed a year.

Pamela and her sweetheart had talked about getting married, but changed their minds and moved in with her grandmother. It was about a month before Pamela caught up with her mother again. Nancy was working as a nurse in the Chicago suburb of Hinsdale, and telephoned her mother to invite her to a Christian singles New Year's Eve party.

Pamela moved back in with her mother. But she was hurt and bitter and couldn't understand why her mother would so abruptly abandon her and her sister. It was no big deal to Nancy. She explained that she was fed up because she wasn't being paid by the hospital, and decided that it was time to enjoy life for a while, unfettered by children.

Debbie finally moved back home in 1983 when her mother rented an apartment in Villa Park. But Pamela moved out at about the same time to live with her boyfriend. It was a move from the frying pan into the fire.

Her boyfriend completely took over the fifteen-year-old girl's life, as her mother had when she was younger. He didn't allow her out of the apartment unless she was with him. He forbid her to use the telephone, to play his stereo while he was away, and refused to leave food in the house. It didn't matter if she was hungry. She had to wait until he returned home from work, and then have

sex with him before he would take her out to eat. In an
eerie replay of Nancy's earlier pretentions, he convinced
Pamela, as well as her younger sister, that he could read
their minds, close up or from miles away. The girls believed him. They were programmed during their early
childhood to believe even the most outrageous asser-
tions.

On Pamela's sixteenth birthday, a few months after
she moved in with him, he brought Debbie to the apartment for a surprise celebration. Debbie succeeded in
talking Pamela into leaving the domineering boyfriend
and moving back in with their mother, who had bought
a three-bedroom town house. Bart also moved home,
and for the first time in years the family of four was
back together under the same roof.

But Nancy could no longer control her children with
fervent talk of God and the Devil, threats, fear or beatings. They were too old, too big, and the two older children had been too hardened by the years of abuse and
their nomadic lifestyle to accept either their mother's
emotional and physical bullying, her discipline, or her
advice. They simply wanted food, shelter, and the comfort of the company of their siblings who had shared
common difficulties.

So Nancy worked and paid the bills. And she ranted
and raved to her teenagers about their bad habits, un-
godliness, and sloth. She yelled at the girls to keep their
rooms cleaned, quarreled with them about their
makeup and the way they dressed, complained that they
were missing church, and sternly forbade all three of her
children—and their friends—to drink alcoholic bever-
ages in the house. But the kids did what they wanted,
and while she worked or attended church and church-
related activities, they partied at the house with their
friends. Neighbors became used to observing a steady
stream of dirty, unkempt long-haired boys, and noisy
young girls in skintight blue jeans, their faces garishly

plastered with gobs of makeup, trailing in and out of the house at all hours.

Bart had developed an interest in the occult, and also decided that he would like to become a rock music star. His pals were recruited from among young men like himself, rough, aimless youths with few goals or recklessly impossible dreams. It seemed to some that the kids were coming and going day and night. The rock music that blasted from the stereos was so loud that it could be heard outside, even with the windows closed. And the loud, raucous music didn't stop, even when Mrs. Knuckles returned home. Nancy began locking herself in her bedroom when she was home, to get away from the kids. And she often mentioned to relatives and friends that she thought it would be nice to die and go to Heaven. She moaned that she had a terrible life.

Neighbors clucked their tongues and murmured sympathetically about the poor, tiny woman who worked two jobs and carried bag after bag of groceries into the house to feed the shiftless, sometimes frightening band of teenagers.

Bart often slumped at a picnic table in the backyard for hours at a time. Neighbors could see the lanky youth with the long matted hair and drooping mustache sitting motionless, often throughout the afternoon and into the night. Sometimes Pamela sat with him in the beer-can-littered backyard, the brother and sister smoking silently and hardly moving.

At other times, neighbors complained, Pamela and her younger sister would stomp huffily out of the house screaming at local children and angrily kicking toys left on the sidewalk and in nearby yards.

Both Pamela and Bart had nasty tempers. Bart had barely moved in to join his mother and sisters before he tried one day to prevent Pamela from leaving the town house because she had been drinking too much, and she slashed him across the chest with a knife. Then she slashed her own wrist with a razor blade. Neither of the

wounds were serious, but she had made her point: Don't
cross Pamela!

Once when a bold twelve-year-old boy flirtatiously
whistled at her, she rushed at him in a fury, screaming
curses, and tried to break his wrist.

And one night when her brother, her boyfriend, and
some of their pals tangled with some other youths in a
parking lot brawl, Pamela snatched up a chain and vi-
ciously beat one of the strangers on the head. Eventually even Pamela began to worry about her sudden rages
and uncontrollable temper. She was worried enough after cutting Bart, then her own wrist, to plead with her
mother to send her to a psychiatrist for help. But Nancy
told her, instead, to drop to her knees and pray to God
for forgiveness.

Added to all the other resentment toward her
mother, Pamela was furious because Nancy had lied to
her a few weeks earlier about having cancer. After
Nancy came home and announced that she was stricken
with the frightening ailment, Pamela had been so over-
whelmed with guilt that she quit running around for a
while, prayed for her mother, and even accepted an offer to go to a Seventh Day Adventist center in rural
Michigan where she could be helped to kick her tobacco
habit. Nancy offered to pay her $100 to take the cure.
Pamela stayed about two months before returning nico-
tine-free to Villa Park, and to a new loving relationship
with her mother.

Then she learned that Nancy had lied. She didn't
have cancer, and the story was merely a cruel ruse
aimed at regaining some control over her and getting
her to quit tobacco. Pamela reverted to her old ways
with a vengeance, and their relationship became worse
than ever. The mother and daughter fought almost constantly.

Nancy's busy schedule at work and at church continued to prevent her from visiting with neighbors. When
she wasn't working or at church events, she was studying

to become an upholsterer. Even if she had wanted to, there was simply no time for casual chats or for sharing troubled confidences with neighbors.

She did talk with her friends at church about her troubles with her children, however. And on a crisply cold Sunday night in mid-November 1984, at a meeting of the Young Adults group at the Seventh Day Adventist Church in Glen Ellyn, she asked her friends to pray for her, and for help dealing with her domestic problems. She didn't offer specific information about her troubles, and her fellow church members didn't ask—they just prayed, as she had requested. But to those who knew her best, it seemed obvious that the trouble revolved around her rebellious brood.

Approximately two weeks after the prayers were offered for Nancy, police in the nearby suburb of Elmhurst recorded an anonymous telephone call. The woman refused to give her name, but advised that Nancy Knuckles had been murdered by one or more of her children. The mysterious tipster added that the body had been disposed of by stuffing it into a trunk and dumping it into Salt Creek.

Authorities in Elmhurst passed the tip on to their fellow officers at the Villa Park Police Department. Villa Park police responded immediately. While preparations were made to apply to the courts for a search warrant, a two-man detective team drove to the Knuckleses' neighborhood to put the house and its occupants under surveillance. Another team began checking up on Nancy's whereabouts and recent activities.

Investigators quickly learned that Mrs. Knuckles hadn't shown up at either of her two jobs during the last couple of days. She hadn't telephoned her employers about her uncharacteristic absence, or made any prior arrangements for someone else to fill in for her.

Another employee with the health care service she worked for told police that before leaving work Wednesday afternoon, she had been given an assignment to call the next day at the home of an elderly patient. She had agreed to accept the assignment, but never showed up.

Fellow church members who operated the Health Oasis had a similar story. She hadn't shown up for her job as a cook Wednesday night, nor did she telephone to report in sick. Nancy didn't have a telephone in her house, so the restaurant manager called church officials to ask if they had heard from her. She hadn't been in touch.

Villa Park police borrowed an unmarked car from a neighboring suburb and sent two more men to join those already watching the Knuckles residence. There was an outside chance that if the woman had indeed been murdered, that her killers, or their accomplices, might be surprised trying to sneak the body outside. But no one was observed exiting the house carrying anything large enough to hide a body.

Shortly after nine P.M., Thursday, a team of police officers from the Villa Park Police Department, DuPage County Sheriff's Department, and the Illinois Department of Law Enforcement, knocked at the door of the house and served the search warrant. Mrs. Knuckles's children and five other young people, teenagers and youths in their early twenties, were inside when officers walked into the littered living room. A vacuum cleaner was standing near the middle of the yellow carpet.

Police had barely entered the house and begun fanning out through the rooms before the younger children began to talk. Calmly and deliberately, almost as if they were repeating the plot of a murder mystery on television, they recounted the grisly story of Nancy Knuckles's death, and of how Pamela, Barton, and Dennis Morris had teamed up to kill her. And once the older youngsters were confronted with the information, they too began to talk. The complete story, eventually pieced together from their statements at the time, from court testimony, and from prison interviews and other printed news accounts, was an ugly one.

The night before Nancy's death, her children huddled together to talk about their problems. They were fed up with Nancy's constant complaints and tyrannical interference with their lives, and they wanted to take over and run the household themselves. They discussed various ways to kill her.

It wasn't the first time that the subject had come up. Both Pamela and Bart had made halfhearted efforts to do away with the contrary woman before. Pamela once put nearly fifty extra-strength aspirin tablets in Nancy's milk. But someone else saw what she was doing and poured the milk out. Years later Pamela told an interviewer that she hadn't really wanted to kill her mother with the aspirin-laced drink, just to make her sick enough to get her out of the house.

Pamela said that Bart told her he had once swung at his mother with a baseball bat, but missed and hit the door. And another time when he was even younger he slipped up behind his mother with an ice pick, but didn't have the heart to plunge it into her back.

This time as the kids gathered to talk about getting rid of the troublesome woman who was paying the bills, someone suggested grinding up glass and slipping it into one of her milk shakes. But that idea was rejected as being too messy. Another proposal to put her in the car and asphyxiate her by running the exhaust inside was turned down as stupidly impractical. The town house had no garage. There was talk of blowing her up, but they didn't have any dynamite, and none of them knew how to rig explosive devices. Another suggestion called for killing Nancy with a razor, but that scheme was also discarded as too messy. And someone proposed that she could be knocked out and killed with a pool cue.

Pamela suggested taking their mother to Joliet, a tough factory town and state prison city a few miles away, and either killing her there or leaving the body in the car after the slaying. The teenager reasoned that could deflect suspicion from the extended family, because there were frequent murders in Joliet. But they turned thumbs down on the idea because they were afraid they might be picked up by police while hitchhiking back to Villa Park.

But it was eventually decided that the cleanest and most efficient method of doing the job would be strangulation. Pamela slipped into the basement and collected four short lengths of strong twine, which she tied together to make a garrote. Then the youngsters waited for Nancy to come home.

She returned on schedule, at about eleven P.M., but no one made a move to put the murder plan into operation. When Pamela approached her mother, she made no effort to use the garrote, but instead pleaded once more for help in consulting a psychiatrist. The teenager told her mother that she was worried about serious emotional problems. But Nancy was tired and didn't want to talk about it. She shrugged off her daughter's last plea for help, and went to bed. Pamela stayed up and had a few beers, mulling over her problems. A jumble of thoughts about family, responsibility, and murder romped helter-skelter through her mind.

At about four A.M. she got up from a couch and padded stealthily into her mother's bedroom, carrying the length of twine. Nancy was stretched out under the covers, sleeping peacefully. Pamela looked at her mother's face. The taut lines around her mouth and eyes were softened in sleep, and she looked harmless and defenseless. Pamela just couldn't bring herself to drop the twine around her mother's neck, and she turned to slip out of the room. But in the darkness her foot bumped a dresser, and the noise woke Nancy up. Sleepily, she asked Pamela what she was doing in the bedroom. Pamela said she had come to kill her but couldn't bring herself to carry out the plan.

"Doesn't this prove that I need a psychiatrist?" she asked her mother. "I came up here to kill you."

Nancy stared through sleepy, half-closed eyes at her

daughter for a moment, then moved her arm and glanced at the watch on her wrist. "Pamela, it's four A.M.," she grumbled. "I have to get up for work at six."

The drowsy nurse was still in no mood to talk about Pamela's emotional problems, or about psychiatrists, so the fretful teenager turned and, with her head down, walked resignedly out of the bedroom.

It was shortly after seven A.M. when Pamela, her brother, sister, and four other teenagers staying at the house were roused from their sleep by a terrible clanging noise. Nancy was holding a metal roasting pan in one hand, banging it with a wooden spoon held in the other, and screaming that she wasn't running a whorehouse. She screeched that she was sick and tired of supporting bums and whoremongers, and everyone had to get out and find jobs to help pay their own way. It was difficult enough for the single mother to support her own three unruly children, but four of their friends had already been camping at the house for a week and had shown no indication that they were about to leave. Nancy admonished them that the free ride was over and that her boarders, relatives and nonrelatives, could no longer stay unless they helped with the house payments and food bills.

Pamela was still getting dressed when her brother locked his eyes on hers and muttered a single commanding word: "Now!"

Later the teenage girl described her response as almost dreamlike as she waited on the landing of the stairs with the garrote stuffed into the back of her jeans as her mother walked past her. Then she padded up behind her mother, who had just reached the door, and slipped the loop of twine over her neck. Pamela said she believed her mother must have wanted to die, because she hardly struggled.

The girl also remembered the relief she felt—and the momentary fear that her mother might not really be dead, that she might suddenly jump to her feet and start

screaming at them, or run to a neighbor's house to telephone police.

The youngsters in the house knew they would have to
stick together to keep their guilty secret from outsiders,
especially police. Holding their hands over their hearts,
they solemnly pledged they would tell no one about the
murder. They agreed that death would be the penalty
for anyone who broke the oath.

The youngsters decided to temporarily get the body
out of the way by carrying it into the basement. But they
knew they couldn't leave it there long, and Bart wan-
dered into the backyard after a while and halfheartedly
scratched at the ground with a shovel. The ground was
frozen, however, and far too hard to dig a grave in. The
yard was also too visible to neighbors, who might see
them dumping the body into a grave, then covering it
up. So, late in the afternoon, they stuffed the stiffened
corpse into a steamer trunk and weighted it with bricks
and large rocks. When twenty-two-year-old Dukes
stopped at the house, they showed him the body and
swore him to secrecy. Then Morris and Wright loaded
the trunk into Dukes's car and he drove to a darkened
stretch of Salt Creek behind a fast food restaurant in
Elmhurst, where his companions dumped it into about
eight feet of water in the middle of the stream.

Armed with information from the houseful of young
people, police enlisted the aid of firemen and drove to
the creek to retrieve the body. Working with portable
floodlights in the frigid darkness of the early morning of
November 30, firemen in a boat dragged the muddy bottom of the creek. After several minutes they snagged
onto a heavy object, and fished the trunk from the cold
water. The fully clothed body of the petite nurse was
bent double inside the trunk. She was pronounced dead
at the scene by the DuPage County coroner a few minutes before two A.M. An autopsy later established that
strangulation was the sole cause of death. The marks of
the ligature around her neck were the only sign of vio-

lence on the body, and there were no signs of broken bones or other injuries.

Neighbors and friends of the Knuckles family were stunned by news of her slaying, and by the arrest of her children and their friends. Nancy's friends from the church were aware that she was having trouble with her children, but most assumed that the conflicts were no more serious than most parents have with teenagers nearing the independence of adulthood. In fact, Nancy's boss at the restaurant recalled that the last time he saw her, she told him that she thought her relationship with her children was improving and that she believed her oldest daughter was about to give her life to God.

Law enforcement authorities were more impressed with the ruthless and cold disregard with which the execution had been carried out. A prosecutor told reporters that they acted as if they were unaware they had committed a crime other people would view as especially terrible. They seemed to regret only that they were caught, he said.

Pamela and her boyfriend, Dennis Morris, pleaded guilty to murder, and were each sentenced to thirty-three years in prison.

Barton pleaded innocent, but was convicted of murder and of concealing a homicide, by DuPage Circuit Court judge John J. Bowman in a trial without a jury. Debbie testified at her brother's bench trial that Nancy was murdered because the three children resented her ordering them to clean up the house, telling them what friends to associate with, and establishing other parental rules such as curfews.

Assistant State's Attorney Brian Telander asked for a stiff sentence, pointing out that Barton laughed and smirked throughout the trial and sentencing hearing. Judge Bowman ordered a thirty-three-year prison term on the homicide charge, the same penalty given to Pamela and her boyfriend. The judge added a four-year term for concealing a homicide, with the terms to be ordered served concurrently.

Barton's girlfriend, Cindy Caruso, the mother of the two-year-old who was in the house when Nancy was murdered, was also found guilty of concealment of a homicide, and sentenced to two years in prison. Judge Bowman chastised the sobbing young woman as having "no substance as a human being. . . . You knew what you were doing," he said of her part in attempting to conceal the murder.

Dukes pleaded innocent at a bench trial before Judge Bowman to charges of concealing a homicide. Testifying in his own defense, he claimed that Morris had threatened to kill him or hurt his pregnant girlfriend if he informed police about the murder. But he was found guilty and ordered to serve four years in prison. Telander had argued against probation, pointing out that Dukes was previously sentenced to prison on a theft charge and had other misdemeanor convictions. Wright was given a two-year prison term for concealing a homicide.

Debbie and the fourteen-year-old girl who had stayed overnight at the house were each sentenced in Juvenile Court to two years probation on charges of concealment. The other fourteen-year-old girl who posed in the pyramid photo had arrived at the house after the slaying and did not know that Nancy had been killed. She was not charged in the case. Debbie served her probation under the guardianship of church friends of her mother in Michigan.

Pamela was sent to the Dwight Correctional Center, about forty miles southeast of Ottawa, where the troubled family had once lived, to serve her prison term. Almost immediately she enrolled in community college classes and began taking extension courses from Illinois State University. Less than four years after she helped choke the life out of her mother, Pamela—dressed in graduation cap and gown—was awarded an associate of arts degree. Her father, sister, and grandmother attended the ceremony.

A few months after the graduation ceremonies, Judge Bowman vacated Pamela's conviction and permitted her to withdraw her guilty plea to her mother's murder. The judge based his 1989 ruling on grounds that her lawyer had mistakenly told her she would be eligible for the death penalty if she was convicted after a trial.

According to Illinois state criminal codes at the time, defendants in murder cases had to be at least eighteen years old at the time the crime was committed to be eligible for execution.

But Pamela was only seventeen when her mother was murdered, too young to have faced the grim possibility of receiving the death penalty. In Illinois, execution is carried out by lethal injection. Only one condemned prisoner has been executed there since 1962, and he asked for the death penalty to be carried out.

Pamela was released from prison on bail on August 31, 1990, pending a new trial. Her attorneys revealed shortly after the ruling that she would plead innocent by reason of insanity.

Efforts to schedule her new trial quickly bogged down, however, when State's Attorneys moved to obtain documents and testimony from a psychiatrist who interviewed her at the DuPage County Jail soon after her arrest.

Pamela's attorneys said that although they planned to use an insanity defense, they did not expect to call the psychiatrist, Dr. Lyle Rossiter, to testify at her new trial. Two other psychiatrists, two psychologists, and a social worker who examined Pamela after her guilty plea was vacated, were listed as possible defense witnesses, however.

Contending that when an insanity defense is used, they have a right to examine the entire psychiatric history of the defendant, the state called on Dr. Rossiter to produce all reports, notes, and memoranda stemming from his December 1984 examination of Pamela. A few days later they also advised him that he would be called by the prosecution to testify at the new proceeding.

But Judge Bowman turned down the prosecution request, and the Illinois Appellate Court upheld his decision. In its ruling, the court pointed out that the examination by Dr. Rossiter was conducted at the request of Pamela's defense, and consequently the psychiatrist's knowledge of her mental condition was covered by rules governing attorney-client privilege. At the time of the ruling on March 31, 1992, Judge Bowman was a member of the Appellate Court, although he did not take part in the decision at that level.

Prosecutors responded to the ruling by appealing the decision to the Illinois Supreme Court. The court agreed to hear the appeal, and at this writing early in 1993, action was still pending. Pamela, meanwhile, remained free on bail.

Chapter 2

Mom, Dad, and the Axeman

As they guided their emergency vehicles through the snow-covered streets of Cape St. Claire, paramedics were half expecting the call to be just another nuisance, contrived by a bored loony to keep them busy and create a little excitement on a crisply cold and quiet Tuesday morning.

Even after they got their first hurried look at the handsome, almond-skinned teenager standing at the kitchen door of 1242 Mount Pleasant Drive in the comfortable blue-collar subdivision a few miles outside the northeast edge of Annapolis, it seemed unlikely that the call would be exceptional.

The boy was dressed in an aging pair of blue jeans, a half-buttoned pajama shirt, and was without shoes despite the frigid temperatures that had swept into the Chesapeake Bay area with the new year. He appeared composed, however, and exhibited none of the grief or panic common to many witnesses to serious accidents, sudden injury or death. A pretty little Asian girl, who appeared to be of grammar school age, stood at his side clutching his hand.

Nevertheless, the emergency run on that frigid morning of January 17, 1984, was anything but routine. For law enforcement investigators and court officers, it would hoist the curtain on a grisly double murder and family tragedy that would rank as one of the most distressing crimes in the history of Maryland's Anne Arundel County.

The boy was Larry Swartz, a popular seventeen-year-old wrestler, and cocaptain of the junior varsity soccer team at the nearby Broadneck High School. The girl was his nine-year-old sister, Annie, a third grade student at the Cape St. Claire Elementary School. Asked where his parents were, the boy calmly directed the paramedics inside the house.

One of the paramedics walked down the stairs and saw the feet of a man who appeared to be lying inside a tiny study just off the stairway landing. The emergency technician had to enter the room before he could make out the rest of the body. The husky, balding victim was on his back near an overturned typing stand. He was a gory mess. Huge splotches of blood and tissue stained his shirt, trousers, and necktie. Even his beard, and a pair of glasses lying a few feet away, were smeared with blood. A series of ragged holes pockmarked his shirt. At first glance it appeared they might have been caused by bullets. But there was no sign of a gun.

The paramedic barely had time to feel for a pulse and determine that there was none, when he heard his partner yell that he had found another body. Just outside the house a few feet from an egg-shaped pool in the backyard, a tall, gaunt woman was sprawled on her back. She was naked except for a knee sock bunched around one ankle, and her legs were obscenely splayed in the classic posture of rape victims. The snow around her was dyed a sickly red with blood. Another scarlet patch of snow was closer to the door.

As shocking as the condition of the man's body was, the woman looked worse. Not only was she nude, but her scalp was a bloody mess. It had been torn nearly off her skull. A line of ugly red gashes serrated her neck, the scarlet contrasting sharply with the pale corpse stretched out in the snow. A white patch over the woman's left eye added one more curiously bizarre touch to the already grotesque scene. Disregarding strict police prohibitions against disturbing the bodies of possible murder victims, one of the paramedics gently drapped a green blanket over the undecorously exposed corpse.

The men had returned to the house and were making a cautious inspection of rooms and closets to determine if an intruder might still be inside, when a neighbor telephoned. She was worried because of the ambulance parked in front of the house. Larry told her that he thought his parents had been killed. The neighbor insisted that he bring Annie to her house, and the boy pulled on a windbreaker and carried the girl across the street.

By the time Larry returned, police from the Arundel County Sheriff's Department had begun to filter into the house and were cordoning off the grounds. Larry told investigators that the bodies were those of his parents, fifty-one-year-old Robert Swartz, and forty-three-year-old Kathryn Ann "Kate" Swartz. Bob was a highly skilled electronics expert who repaired computers and had prepared manuals and trained technicians in space communications. Kate taught English and speech at Broadneck High School, the same school Larry attended.

The boy, whose black curly hair was still uncombed and stuck at odd angles from his head in unruly clumps, told officers that he awakened at about seven o'clock, and Annie—who had been up for about fifteen minutes —told him that their parents were missing. Larry said he peered through the kitchen window, saw his mother's body in the snow, and telephoned for help.

Investigators were immediately struck by the handsome teenager's apparent cool detachment. He didn't sob or cry out in anger at the loss of his parents; his complexion showed no sign of pallor; and there was no sweating or other symptoms to indicate that he might be in shock. Instead, he seemed to accept the tragedy that had so suddenly descended on his family with a kind of fatalistically dull resignation.

Uniformed officers accompanied Larry back to the neighbor's house to wait while homicide detectives and crime scene technicians began combing the ranch-style house and snow-covered yard for clues. The entire house was a mess, but it was quickly apparent that the dirty laundry stuffed in closets and dropped helter-skelter on floors, the dirty dishes, unmade beds, and disarranged tabletops, were the result of sloppy home-making, rather than the frenzied handiwork of a burglar. Kate's purse was in plain sight alongside some jewelry and a pile of coins on a dresser in the master bedroom. And there was no indication that any other possessions that are the usual targets of burglars were missing.

The furniture was surprisingly stark for a home headed by two professional people with the salaries they presumably earned. A rough redwood picnic table had been pulled into the kitchen, and the living room was sparsely furnished with a few mismatched odds and ends, including old green armchairs that looked like they had been picked up in a Salvation Army second-hand shop.

The house was also filled with promising bits of evidence. One of the most intriguing was a bloody hand-print on a sliding glass door. Two puzzling sheafs of legal papers concerning a Michael Swartz were found on a table in the living room and on another table in the foyer near the front door. Other documents and books were tossed willy-nilly onto the floor and chairs, as if they were discarded by someone hurriedly looking for something.

The basement held a treasure trove of beguiling clues, as well. Blood splatters were streaked on the walls and floor. A computer, a printer, a television set, and a lamp had been knocked over and shattered. Papers from a toppled typing stand were scattered in the rubble. And blood smears stained the knobs on both sides of the door to the study. It appeared that the husky middle-aged computer whiz had fought gamely for his life.

A cursory inspection of the jagged gore-ringed holes that pockmarked his chest and neck appeared to bear out the initial theory of a shooting. But a closer look led officers to conclude that the wounds were more likely made by a knife. An autopsy would settle the question later. A check of Swartz's trouser pockets turned up his billfold with $150 in cash and a handful of credit cards. A large silver crucifix hung around his neck.

Huge amounts of blood were also found in the main room of the basement. A pool of it had collected on a black, vinyl recliner chair facing a television set, and had seeped onto the carpet. A pair of eyeglasses with only one lens were on the floor next to the chair a few feet from an empty beer can. Blood also streaked the carpeting in front of the glass door to the patio, as if someone had been dragged.

Inspection of a small laundry room disclosed a swirl of wet clothes in a washing machine, including a pair of blue jeans, sweat pants, and a T-shirt with BROADNECK & BRUINS inscribed across the front.

Outside the house, investigators turned to the body of Mrs. Swartz in their efforts to solve the puzzling murder mosaic. They realized immediately that valuable fiber evidence may have been contaminated and lost through the misguided act of sympathy in covering the corpse with the blanket. The simple act could make any such evidence recovered from the body virtually useless in court.

A heavy flannel woman's pajama suit with blood stains on the front and back was recovered a few feet from the body. A single green sock was jammed inside one of the padded footies.

The blanket wasn't the only threat to evidence that

police had to deal with. The snow-covered yard was rapidly filling with footprints, many of them made by police themselves as they spread out in their search for clues. While they were searching, a neighbor showed up and advised that he had discovered blood splatters in the snow in front of his house about a block away.

Uniform officers, along with homicide detectives Gary Barr and Tommy Mock, followed him to his house and found a set of human footprints, as well as some paw prints that appeared to be those of a dog. They followed the prints and blood trail through the neighborhood and into the woods. A few feet down an embankment, Mock, a twenty-year veteran of the department, discovered the print of a bare foot. Then he and his partner found other tracks of what appeared to be one bare foot and one print with a less distinct outline, which could have been a stockinged foot. At some locations the prints were interspersed with another set of footprints made by someone wearing shoes.

As they were beginning to consider the possibilities that an already terribly injured Kate Swartz might have been chased naked, but for one sock, through the snow by her killer, another startling find was reported. A police officer had discovered a log-splitting maul among the trees behind the house. After it was photographed where it was lying in the snow, the maul was picked up to be tagged and studied as evidence. But no laboratory tests were required to reveal the matted blood and hair on the dull end of the tool.

Minutes after Barr and Mock had arrived to spearhead the investigation, they trudged across the icy street to talk to Larry and Annie at the house of the kindhearted neighbor who had temporarily taken them in.

It may have seemed to Larry that he had been telling bits and pieces of the story all morning, but when the detectives asked, he began retracing his account of the events all over again, as calmly and dispassionately as before. Sitting in the privacy of a basement recreation room along with the detectives, Larry said that he had apparently fouled up one of his father's programs while fiddling with the computer, and they quarreled over it early the previous night.

Both his parents were still awake when he went to bed a short time later, and he said he slept soundly until shortly before midnight, when his sister awakened him to tell him she had heard screaming. Larry said he told her she must have been dreaming and to go back to sleep. When he awakened the next morning, he continued, Annie told him that she couldn't find their parents.

Then he looked out the dining room window and saw his mother in the snow. Covering his sister's eyes so she wouldn't see the bloody spectacle outside, he telephoned for help. Larry apparently didn't recall that he had previously said that he peered out the kitchen window when he discovered his mother's body.

The boy volunteered information that he was adopted by the Swartzes when he was six years old. And Annie, who was born in South Korea and abandoned, was adopted when she was four. Larry confided that he had another brother, a few months older than him, who had also been adopted.

But Michael Swartz was no longer living with the family. He was in a psychiatric hospital undergoing court-ordered testing, and had been treated as a family outcast since he was thirteen or fourteen. He simply didn't get along with his adoptive parents, and they wouldn't accept him back into their home, so he had been shuttling back and forth from one juvenile institution to another until landing at the hospital in nearby Crownsville a few weeks earlier.

Larry claimed that Michael had broken into houses. He said that his brother hated their parents, and he added that his mother had confided to him that she was afraid of Michael. Looking down at the floor as if reluctant to cause trouble for his brother, Larry also pointed out that the family's two dogs knew Michael and would

have been unlikely to bark or challenge him if he were
hanging around the house on the night of the murder.

Larry's voluntary information about his brother fit in
neatly with the discovery of the papers relating to Michael's legal troubles arranged so conspicuously in the
death house. Too neatly. Larry seemed too anxious to
throw suspicion on his brother. Nevertheless, Michael's
whereabouts near the time of the double slaying would
have to be carefully checked out. In the meantime, the
detective team turned to questioning Annie.

The girl perched uneasily in her brother's lap as the
detectives gingerly led her through her recollections of
the events of the previous night and the early morning.
Replying in a near whisper, Annie said that she was
awakened by strange noises, and when she glanced
at her wristwatch, it was about eleven-thirty P.M. It
sounded like her father was screaming for help.

Annie said she scrambled out of bed and padded out
to the carport, looking into the backyard, where she saw
a man with long, curly black hair walking away from her.
He had a shovel over his shoulder that was dripping
blood, and was dressed in blue jeans and a gray sweatshirt with the name BROADNECK imprinted on the back.
Asked if he was as tall as Michael, the child agreed that
he was. Michael was a lanky six feet, six inches. Larry
was only five-foot-nine.

As Barr and Mock talked to the brother and sister,
another team of detectives walked the few hundred
yards from the Sheriff's Department's Criminal Investigative Division headquarters to the Crownsville Hospital Center to check out Michael Swartz. Staff members
in his dormitory assured the investigators that Michael
had been securely locked up in the building throughout
the night. When the officers talked to Michael, a spare-
framed youth with shaggy shoulder-length dark brown
hair, a few minutes later, he confirmed the information
from the staff members. He had been locked into the

dorm. The detectives claimed they were investigating a burglary, and didn't tell him about the double murder.

Michael's alibi appeared to be solid, but police had a grisly unsolved double killing on their hands that the press was playing up big, and people were afraid. No one could understand why someone would so ruthlessly murder such a wonderful couple.

Bob was the second son of Joseph Franklin Swartz, Jr. —a sober, no-nonsense high school teacher from Maryland's Eastern Shore—and his wife Gladys, who grew up on Chincoteague Island in Virginia. But Bob was born in a suburb of Pittsburgh, Pennsylvania, after his father had accepted a teaching job there, and grew up in relative privilege during the difficult years of the Great Depression. The family moved a few times while Bob's father served as a U.S. Navy officer during World War II, and by 1950 Bob enrolled as a freshman at Youngstown University in Ohio. His father was an associate professor there, and had his heart set on Bob following his career as an educator. But Bob, like his older brother Joe, decided to become an engineer.

Two years after he enrolled at the university, however, Bob dropped out of classes and joined the Navy as an enlisted man. The Navy sent him to electronics school, then to his first duty station: the U.S. Naval Base at Port Lyautey in French Morocco. When his four-year enlistment expired in 1956, Bob accepted an honorable discharge as an electronicsman first class, after moving up through the ranks as rapidly as possible through normal promotion schedules.

Bob worked at a variety of jobs before being flown to the Arctic Circle to handle radar maintenance for a defense contractor. But eventually, after banking a good portion of the high pay he earned working in the Arctic, Bob returned to Youngstown, reentered the university, and—at his father's continued urging—switched majors and at last earned a bachelor's degree in education. He

had moved again and enrolled at the University of
Maryland, when he met Kate.

Kate was born an Iowa farm girl, the baby in a family
of four children. Her parents were hardscrabble tenant
farmers, Leonard and Teresa Sullivan. Kate was still in
elementary school when her parents moved to the town
of Dunlap in West Central Iowa, about midway between
Sioux City and Council Bluffs, to operate a truck stop
restaurant.

The youngest of the Sullivans' three girls was a natural student. She earned high grades throughout elementary school, junior high, and high school, and graduated
as valedictorian of her class. A devout Catholic, she
chose Marycrest College, a women's teaching school operated by nuns, to continue her education. Marycrest is
in Davenport, across the state from Dunlap, on Iowa's
eastern border with Illinois. When she graduated four
years later with a bachelor's degree in education, she
found a job with a school in Davenport.

During her first two summer breaks from classes,
Kate went to Mexico with other members of a Catholic
order and helped teach poor people about sanitary living. Within two years her command of Spanish was so
improved and her sense of adventure so strong that she
moved to the Denver, Colorado, area. She accepted a
job as a high school Spanish teacher, but a few years
later packed up and headed East, enrolling as a graduate student at the University of Maryland and beginning
work on a master's degree. Bob and Kate met at the
university.

Kate was tall and angular, with a nose that looked too
big for her face, but she had personality plus, and a keen
intelligence and zest for life that knocked Bob Swartz
for a romantic loop.

Stocky and prematurely balding, Bob had never been
a ladies' man, and from his high school, college, and
Navy days on into easy middle age, he had dated inter-
mittently and seldom seriously. Kate had been equally

casual about dating and her relationships with men. She completed her graduate work and returned to teaching, and Bob had dropped out and taken another job in the electronics field before they married. Shortly before the marriage, Bob converted to Catholicism.

Kate couldn't have children, so they decided to adopt. The little boy who was to become Lawrence Joseph Swartz was six years old and had been through a series of foster homes when he was at last adopted. Public documents and court records would later disclose that Larry's birth mother was an unmarried teenage waitress when he was conceived in New Orleans, and his father was reputedly a handsome East Indian pimp.

Michael, about six months older than Larry, was eight when he joined the Swartz family. His mother was Caucasian, his father an American Indian, and he was a pretty little boy who would grow into a handsome young man. Like Larry, Michael had lived in a series of foster homes and was unhappily familiar with rejection. But this time he survived his tryout period, although it was two years before he was formally adopted.

Michael's acceptance into the Swartz family wasn't a match made in heaven. So close in age and background, he and Larry got along fantastically well and quickly became best pals. But Larry got along much better with his parents than his new older brother did.

The relationship between Michael and his adoptive parents was a troubled one from the beginning. The Swartzes were demanding with both boys, and it was especially difficult for Michael to do anything that pleased them. Kay screeched at him, and Bob beat him —sometimes with his fists.

The performance of both boys in school was a source of family dissension. Michael, who had the higher IQ, did better than Larry until the Swartzes insisted that he skip the third grade. Then Michael's grades dropped.

Larry's poor grades were excused to some extent after Bob and Kate had him tested by experts and he was diagnosed as having a learning disability. His grades also improved a bit after he was admitted to the school's special education program.

Michael had a stubborn streak, was sometimes openly rebellious. Larry was more easygoing and seldom created discipline problems. He was clearly the family favorite—until Annie arrived and Michael left.

From the moment Annie was carried off an airplane in New York and into the arms of her adoptive parents, she was the new favorite. The boys were as smitten with the charming four-year-old as their parents were, and spent hours playing with her and teaching her to speak English.

Michael's troubles followed him from home to school, where he sometimes had to stay after class on disciplinary detention. Bob began beating his oldest son with regularity, sometimes marching him downstairs to Michael's bedroom, at other times wherever and whenever his volatile temper erupted. At least once he knocked Michael down and repeatedly kicked him. When he was fourteen, Michael disobeyed his parents' orders to stay home and climbed out a window to join some pals roaming around. When he returned home, he found himself locked out. Kate responded to his pleas to be let inside by peering out a window and advising him that he was outside to stay. The next morning the Swartzes reported to Michael's social worker that he was a runaway. Given a choice of going to a foster home or facing legal action by juvenile court authorities for being a runaway, Michael agreed to move out.

With Michael out of the house, Bob and Kate began to pick at Larry. They punished him for poor grades, criticized his friends, and established rigid curfews and restrictions on his free time. Bob directed his temper outbursts at Larry, and the close relationship the boy had previously enjoyed with his mother began to erode.

Larry briefly regained favor with his parents, especially Bob, when he decided that he wanted to become a

Catholic priest. The fall after completing the eighth grade, the boy entered St. Mary's, a high school seminary in Pennsylvania. Suddenly, Bob was proud of him again, and bragged to friends about his son who was going to be a priest. But the sudden surge of pride was short-lived. Larry just couldn't handle the crushing academic pressure at the seminary. His grades were terrible, especially in the important subjects of Latin, English, and algebra. After Larry completed two semesters at the seminary, a priest wrote his parents and suggested that he shouldn't return after the summer break.

Larry admitted to confidants that his grades had something to do with his change of direction in career goals, but said that another factor was more important. He had decided while isolated from the outside world and left in the austere society of male clerics, that he liked girls too much to become a priest.

Larry's difficulties with his parents resumed as soon as he was home again. By this time he had stepped firmly into the terrible teens, and quarrels over household chores, spending money, curfews, chums, drinking, driving privileges—and eventually, girls—were added to the previous disputes over grades. Some of the most bitter disagreements revolved around his desire to take driver's education at school and obtain a license.

As soon as Larry was sixteen and eligible to sign up for driver's training at school, he began pestering his parents to sign an approval slip for the class. Several of Larry's pals were already signed up, and his parents told him that he could take the course the second semester. His parents had also advised him that they expected him to earn a C average in his classes after leaving the seminary, and his first report card had all C's, except for a single D. By the end of the first semester of his sophomore year, Larry's report card was filled with C's, and two D's. Bob told Larry that he had failed to keep his part of the bargain, and he could forget about taking driver's training the second semester. Kate agreed that Larry could wait awhile to learn to drive.

They finally allowed him to sign up for driver's education at the beginning of his junior year and said he could get a license after completing the course. But the other problems at home continued. At times Michael was grounded and permitted to go out by himself only to school, church, or to wrestling matches, soccer practice and games, since he was cocaptain of the junior varsity. He was chewed out for beer-drinking binges, and once, Kate confiscated some suspicious pills he was carrying in a jacket pocket that appeared to be drugs, although they turned out to be harmless.

Bob and Kate's relationship with Michael wasn't improving either, and in fact had spun further downhill. They had him written out of their will, and told him they wouldn't accept his collect telephone calls from the foster homes and institutions where he lived while awaiting his eighteenth birthday. Larry, however, accepted his brother's calls, and the two troubled boys talked for hours. But their parents didn't visit their eldest son and didn't invite him to visit them. Kate told confidantes that she was afraid of Michael.

Then Bob and Kay advised Larry that they wouldn't let him get a driver's license after all. His grades had plummeted again, and a sprinkling of D's were the best marks that he was bringing home. The C's had evaporated. Larry told his friends that he was looking forward to his eighteenth birthday, when he would be old enough to move out of the house.

Investigators didn't immediately learn all the details of the family's troubled history. But they weren't racing to absolve anyone until they had more information. And Larry, as well as Michael, was one of the people whose activities they were determined to take a closer look at. Both Larry's lack of visible emotion and his curious eagerness to throw suspicion on his older brother made investigators apprehensive and wary of his story.

There were also possibilities that others outside the immediate family might have been responsible. Both Bob and Kate were obsessed with their opposition to legalized abortion. Devoutly religious, their Church and its teachings were integral elements of their daily lives. And they had been horrified by the 1973 U.S. Supreme Court *Roe* v. *Wade* decision, ruling that women had the legal right to abortions during the first trimester of pregnancy.

Bob and Kate were convinced that the court had legalized murder of the helpless unborn. Regardless of whatever the courts had to say about abortion being legal, there was no question in their minds that it was immoral and against the will of God. And they threw themselves wholeheartedly into the fight to somehow get the nation to once again outlaw the practice. The couple joined the newly formed National Right to Life Committee, and became leaders in the activities of the Annapolis chapter, which met in the sacristy of their church, St. Mary's. Every time there was a march on Washington by Right to Lifers, Bob and Kate had gathered up the boys and made sure the family was there, in the forefront.

Bob was a strongly opinionated man who, once he had taken a stand on issues, was known by neighbors and acquaintances for donning emotional and mental blinders. He could be bullheaded and heavy-handed, and he had no time or tolerance for listening to the other side of issues he had already made his mind up about. He became a fanatic about his antiabortion crusading, and on Saturdays paraded in front of a Planned Parenthood clinic in Annapolis, which offered abortions, calling out and insistently attempting to talk with women who were hurrying inside, or shoving flyers into their reluctant hands. Kate did her crusading from home, pounding out vitriolic letters to the editor of local newspapers.

The harassment at the clinic became so intense that

employees sometimes telephoned police. When policemen tried to question the pickets and reason with them,
Bob bristled and challenged them to take him to headquarters so that he could talk to the chief. He was self-
righteous, and always primed for a screaming match
with anyone who dared question his actions. Investigators had to consider the possibility that he might have
stepped over the line during his aggressive antiabortion
tirades and so angered someone that they resorted to
homicide to silence his irksome protests.

Despite Michael's apparently solid alibi, the Crownsville Hospital had a reputation for slipshod security.
And the Detectives Barr and Mock were determined to
double-check his story and confirm beyond all doubt
that he couldn't have slipped out on the night of the
murder.

Michael was away from the dormitory when the
detectives asked a supervisor to lock them in his ward.
The ward was set up much like a military barracks, with
rows of beds. But unlike barracks, windows in the ward
were locked and covered with heavy wire screen. At the
far end of the ward there was a nursing station that was
staffed throughout the night, then the first of a series of
locked doors that anyone attempting to leave would
have to negotiate. The officers couldn't find a way to
break out.

Furthermore, an attendant told the detectives that on
the night of the murder he had said "good night" to
Michael at about eleven-fifteen, as he left at the end of
his shift. The time of the murder had been virtually established as occurring at about eleven-thirty P.M., based
on Annie's recollection of hearing her father's screams,
and the recall of neighbors who said they heard the family dogs barking at about that time. Even if Michael had
somehow managed to slip out of the ward and off the
hospital grounds, there was no way he could have
reached the Swartz home in fifteen minutes.

The inquiry had also failed to turn up any indication

that someone angered by Bob's picketing outside the Planned Parenthood clinic may have committed the murder. It was true enough that his aggressiveness on the picket line was responsible for some serious ruffling of feathers. But detectives hadn't been able to find anyone either on the clinic staff or among the patients who would qualify as a serious suspect in the grisly crime.

Detectives continued to focus on Larry and his account of his activities on the night of the slayings. And they began talking about an arrest if FBI technicians studying the bloody palm print taken from the sliding glass door were able to match the telltale smear with the high schooler's hand. In the meantime, Larry was briefly questioned again and changed his story. He told his interrogators that he had gotten drunk in his room the night his parents were killed. His attorney refused a later police request to permit Larry to take a lie detector test.

Police obtained a search warrant and returned to the death house for another look around. Newspaper journalists and television reporters with cameras were waiting outside the house when the homicide officers arrived. Barely twenty-four hours had elapsed since the initial police search the previous morning.

Among the first items of potential evidence to be collected was Larry's wet laundry in the washer, where he had told them he left it before going to bed the night of the killings. The clothing was eventually sent to FBI laboratories in Washington, D. C., to be tested for bloodstains; which, although invisible to the naked eye, could still be present and detectable after the washing process.

Police were also looking for a knife. They took several pieces of cutlery from the kitchen, and a hunting knife that they found in Larry's bedroom closet. Later tests, however, failed to turn up traces of blood on any of the knives. Additional fingerprints and palm prints, some of them bloodied, were also collected from throughout the house. A couple of blood-smeared bottles of liquid cleaner were picked up as well. The search team even took a sink trap from a bathroom, and tore off a section of a wooden doorjamb. All the material was transported to the FBI laboratories.

Autopsies performed on Bob and Kate at the Maryland State Medical Examiner's offices in Baltimore had already confirmed the intensity of the rage with which the murders were carried out. Bob had been chopped to pieces. He was stabbed seventeen times from his chin and neck to his solar plexus. Any one of several of the injuries were potentially fatal. His right and left carotid arteries, which carry blood to the brain, were punctured. Another plunge of the knife had inflicted a wound so deep that it severed a vein that carried blood to the heart. His lungs and his stomach had been skewered. And his arms and shoulder were freckled with an ugly clutter of stab wounds.

Kate was stabbed in the neck seven times. Two of the injuries, the most serious of the stabbing wounds, punctured her esophagus. But the most serious injury was inflicted with an object much heavier and more blunt than a knife. Her skull was cracked like a walnut, with a single blow from a weapon that crushed bone and brain into a bloody gel. Pathologists found no traces of semen in her vagina, and a blood alcohol test registered a modest .01—about the amount that would show up after consuming one beer.

The stab and slash wounds on the husband and wife appeared to have been inflicted with the same knife. The dimensions and contours of the cuts and punctures suggested that the weapon had a single-edge blade and was most likely a hunting knife, rather than a piece of kitchen cutlery.

Immediately after a viewing at the funeral home, Bob and Kate's wake was held at St. Mary's, the church that had been such an integral part of their lives and which they had so faithfully supported. The next day, their funeral was held at the church. Detectives Barr and

Mott attended all three of the somber events, doing their best to remain inconspicuous as they focused their attention on Larry and his behavior.

The handsome high school junior showed no emotion as he peered into the open caskets at the bodies of his parents during the viewing, and appeared equally unmoved during the wake and funeral. Michael was not allowed to leave the Crownsville Hospital for the viewing or the wake, but was permitted a few minutes of privacy with the bodies of his adoptive parents at the mortuary before they were transported to St. Mary's for the funeral mass.

Minutes before the mass officially began, Right to Life members who had worked closely with Bob and Kate marched solemnly down the aisle and laid single red roses on the cloth-draped coffins of the couple. The red roses symbolized life.

During the funeral itself, the priest spoke of the Resurrection, of Bob and Kate's strong Christian belief, and of the children they left behind. "Michael, Larry, Annie. You are the young, broken ones. Much of what has happened will take time to understand and to heal," he advised. And he pointed out that each of the youngsters was especially chosen by Bob and Kate to be their sons and daughter.

Three days after the Saturday funeral, Larry tearfully confessed to his lawyers that he was the killer.

The agonized confession put Larry's attorneys, Ron Baradel and Joe Murphy, in somewhat of a bind. The confession was privileged information and couldn't be used against the boy in court. And as Larry's attorneys, the lawyers couldn't simply pass on the story to police and the prosecutor. Suddenly, however, instead of merely protecting the rights of an orphan who was a suspect in a murder, the lawyers found themselves representing an admitted parricide, a young man who had savagely slain both parents.

The same day that he broke down in his lawyers' offices and confessed the slayings, Larry submitted to having prints of his fingers and palms taken by police. A few hours later an FBI evidence technician advised Anne Arundel County authorities that he had a match with the bloody palm print taken from the sliding glass door at the house. Warrants were prepared for Larry's arrest on two charges of first-degree murder. His lawyers had no choice but to surrender him to police. That night, Larry was handcuffed and driven to a lockup in the Anne Arundel County Detention Center. The next morning a judge set a $200,000 cash bail for the penniless teenager. Larry remained there more than fifteen months awaiting a trial.

Although Maryland law provides for the death penalty in first-degree murder cases, Anne Arundel County prosecutor Warren Duckett announced soon after the arrest that he would not seek to have the youngster sent to the gas chamber. Nevertheless, conviction on one or both charges of first-degree murder would mean that Larry would spend the rest of his teenage years and young manhood behind bars. His attorneys began planning an insanity defense.

Larry had broken down when he confessed to his lawyers, and wasn't pressed at the time to provide a motive or other details. But in subsequent interviews with psychiatrists and others, he outlined the events of that terrible night.

According to his statements, his father exploded in anger early that evening, and chewed him out for messing with his computer and fouling up a disk with a tax program that had taken hours to prepare. Larry was already nursing a grudge against his mother for using a nasty name to describe a girl he had a date with. And after his father disappeared back into the study, Larry returned to his upstairs bedroom and began drinking some rum he had stashed under clothes in his dresser drawer, while he silently brooded over his troubles. They wouldn't let him drive. They bitched about his grades, his pals, and his girlfriends. Nothing he did seemed to please them.

Larry finished the rum, then went downstairs and put some clothes in the washing machine. His mother, with one eye covered by a patch after a recent operation, was watching television and sipping a beer in the family room. As he passed her on his way back upstairs, she asked him how his exams had gone that day. He said he thought he flunked Spanish but may have done better in another subject.

She told him he would probably flunk all his tests, including some the next day. Larry thought of the driver's license, and he thought of his mother's casual sarcasm over his scholastic troubles. A wood-splitting maul was lying nearby, and he picked it up and slammed it down on the top of her head. Larry said he dropped the maul after hitting her, picked up a steak knife spread on a small table with other silverware in front of the television set, and began stabbing her around the neck.

Bob apparently heard the commotion and came to the door of the computer room to see what was going on, and Larry turned and stabbed him in the chest, near the heart. He said that his father screamed and staggered back into the room, slamming the door. Larry followed him inside and continued plunging the knife into his upper body.

When his rage finally cooled, Larry said, he began desperately trying to figure out a way to cover up his terrible crime. He dragged his mother outside into the snow by one arm and undressed her, reasoning that if he could get rid of her clothes, he could hide his fingerprints. Then, because he wanted to humiliate her, he violated her with his finger. He said he tossed the knife and the maul into the swampy area behind the house.

The teenager insisted he could not remember chasing his mother through the snow, and the story behind the perplexing trail of footprints and blood is still a matter of controversy among people close to the case. Larry said that after the murders, he returned to the house and comforted Annie, assuring her that the screams she reported hearing had existed only in her dreams.

He said he lay down in his room but couldn't sleep, and finally threw up on his pillow. After vomiting, he got up, undressed, and, putting on clean clothes, bundled the pillow along with his bloodstained garments and tossed them into the swampy area as well. They were recovered by his attorneys after Larry pinpointed their location. The clothing found in the washer was placed there before the killings.

Prosecutor Duckett and Larry's attorneys reached a plea bargain agreement the day before his trial was scheduled to begin. Murphy had left the defense team to accept an appointment as a circuit court judge, and been replaced by a prominent criminal attorney, Richard M. Karceski. It was Karceski and Duckett who hammered out the deal.

More than one hundred potential jurors had assembled in the courtroom for beginning of voir dire when a bailiff announced that they were all free to leave. A few minutes later, Larry, pale and gaunt from his fifteen months in the county lockup, was escorted into the courtroom by a sheriff's deputy. Larry took the witness stand, and Judge Bruce C. Williams questioned him to make sure that he understood the agreed-upon plea of guilty to two counts of second degree murder. Larry confirmed that he understood, and after a statement from Duckett, the judge accepted the plea.

Aware of the strong emotions surrounding the high-profile case, the judge selected his words carefully as he prepared to pronounce sentence. He described the case as one of the most tragic ever to occur in Anne Arundel County, perhaps in the entire state of Maryland. He talked of Larry's troubled childhood, and of adoptive parents who may have been overly strict and not as understanding as they could have been.

He said that although Larry appeared to be an average, normal seventeen-year-old boy, psychological evaluation had indicated there was in fact much that was abnormal, "a great deal that needs treatment, and a great deal that perhaps explains what happened." The judge pointed out that the court had the responsibility of protecting society and meting out punishment for Larry's crime, while also doing what was possible to provide for rehabilitation. Judge Williams ordered two concurrent twenty-year sentences, and suspended all but twelve years of each.

Larry is serving his sentence at the Patuxent Correctional Institution, about halfway between Baltimore and Washington, where he receives intensive psychiatric therapy. As of this writing, he has earned his high school equivalency diploma, taken some college courses, and is already eligible for parole.

Chapter 3

A Hollywood Tragedy

It would seem almost to be too much of a cliché to suggest that the strange life and death of actress Susan Cabot mirrored the bizarre B-movies she starred in back in the placid 1950s for Hollywood's king of schlock, Roger Corman.

The fact is, the true story surrounding the shocking death of the onetime B-movie queen is probably too weird and psychologically subtle to qualify for consideration as script material by even the most low-budget and amateurish horror flick.

If the story of the life and death of Susan Cabot is ever made into a movie, it would most appropriately be framed as a Gothic masterpiece. The film would be a chilling but fascinating combination of Gloria Swanson's *Sunset Boulevard* and Bette Davis's *Whatever Happened to Baby Jane?* with a touch of Alfred Hitchcock's *Psycho* sprinkled into the plot for good measure.

The two-person cast of major characters is compelling:

At center stage there is Harriet Roman, who was once the hauntingly beautiful screen actress Susan Cabot. She is long retired from the glittering Hollywood scene, where she put the finishing touches on her career working in such forgettable films as *The Wasp Woman* and *The Saga of the Viking Women and Their Voyage to the*

Land of the Great Sea Serpent. At fifty-nine, her career is behind her for good, with no reason to believe it can ever be resurrected. And her personal life has deteriorated as well as her professional life. She is an emotional cripple, who lives amid the self-made squalor of her house in the fashionable Los Angeles suburb of Encino.

Oblivious to the filth and chaos that surrounds her, she spends her days in bitter reflection of a talent that was never fully exploited and a career never completely realized. Above all, her mind dwells on her beloved, vulnerable only child. She lives only for man-boy son Timothy, who, like his mother, is a pathetic emotional wreck.

Cowed by the incessant carping and nagging of his overprotective, domineering mother, twenty-two-year-old Timothy Scott Roman (according to rumors) may or may not be the half-Jewish, half-Arab bastard son of King Hussein of Jordan.

Born a dwarf and injected for fifteen years with growth hormone from an estimated 400,000 human cadavers, Timothy has grown to five feet, four inches, and weighs 120 pounds. But he looks and behaves like a fourteen-year-old.

Steeped in violent fantasies of lurking Japanese *ninja* assassins and violent karate killers, he is a psychological time bomb waiting to explode.

The explosion which at last exposed the baroque drama, shattered the silence of a balmy Wednesday evening on December 10, 1986. It was one of those typical Southern California nights—warm and dry.

Neighbors first became aware of the trouble when police and paramedics raced to the expensive hillside house at 4501 Charmion Lane, where the troubled mother and son lived. Despite its choice location at the top of a hill overlooking the San Fernando Valley, and the tiny blinking white Christmas lights strung on the six-foot-high metal fence surrounding it, the house had a forbidding appearance. Tucked securely behind palm and pine trees, as well as the fence, the white-brick house had the uncomfortable look of a small fortress.

Inside, the million-dollar property was filthy, cluttered with dirty clothes, bags of garbage, and old newspapers and magazines stacked willy-nilly. It was a mess. But the master bedroom was sheer horror. It looked as if it had been turned into a slaughterhouse.

The woman once known as actress Susan Cabot was sprawled facedown on her bed. Dressed only in a purple negligee, she was dead. Her once-lustrous dark hair had turned to a dirty gray and was matted with blood and pieces of tissue and bone from horrific head injuries. It appeared that she had been brutally clubbed with repeated blows to the back of her head. Splatters of blood stained the bedspread, the pillow, sheets, the floor, and the wall.

When homicide detectives from the Los Angeles Police Department's West Valley Division arrived at the house, uniform officers pointed out a short, dark youth in the living room and explained that he was the son of the victim. Timothy was disheveled, crying, and barely coherent. Between sobs, the young man spluttered out a story about a murderous attack by a mysterious black-clad intruder.

As coroner's officers, police photographers, and evidence technicians went about their grisly business inside the master bedroom, Timothy explained that he had gone to bed about nine-thirty that night, but got up about a half hour later to fix himself a snack. He said he had barely walked into the kitchen, however, when he was confronted by a stranger who was masked and dressed completely in black. The intruder was described as looking like a *ninja*, one of the professional assassins of Japan's feudal period who were known for their stealth, secrecy, and bloodthirsty efficiency in the art of murder.

Timothy said he was taken by surprise, and easily

overpowered when the stranger leaped at him, cutting him on the arm, and hitting him on the head with a blunt object that knocked him out. The young man pointed out a cut on his left arm and a bruise on his head to the detectives. He estimated that he was sprawled on the kitchen floor for about a half hour before regaining consciousness and telephoning for help.

He explained that he didn't immediately go into his mother's bedroom to check on her safety because he was afraid, confused, and in a state of shock after the vicious attack in the kitchen.

Yet, when a paramedic with the Los Angeles Fire Department arrived and began examining him a few seconds after police had rushed to the house, Timothy blurted out that he thought his mother was inside her bedroom, dead.

The paramedic would later testify in court that his examination of Timothy accompanied by the young's man's remarks immediately set off alarm bells in his mind. "He said he was knocked out, but his injuries didn't seem severe enough to knock anybody out," the witness declared. "Things were not adding up in my mind."

The paramedic had found only a minor bruise on his patient's head, which wasn't even serious enough to cause swelling. And the cut on Timothy's left arm was shallow, not at all serious. It wasn't the kind of injury anyone would expect from a vicious and determined *ninja* killer.

The detectives also had doubts about the young man's story. Not only were his injuries of a suspiciously minor nature, but there was no evidence of forced entry to the house, or of a struggle in the kitchen. Nevertheless, Timothy's story had to be checked out. He said that a burglar in black had broken into the house, and he provided a detailed description of the stranger's appearance.

Investigators initiated a door-to-door canvass of

neighbors. No one else reported having seen a mysterious stranger in black skulking through the neighborhood that night or any other night. But neighbors did have other stories to tell.

Police learned that Timothy had a fascination with the unarmed martial arts that developed in the Orient, with its heroes such as the late Bruce Lee—and with *ninjas.* Even his choice of pets demonstrated his fixation on the Orient. He had two huge *Akitas,* handsome, intelligent dogs first bred in Japan, which resemble Siberian huskies and can be vicious and mean.

Investigators also learned that the mother and son frequently quarreled, and had in fact been having a noisy argument earlier that night. It didn't take long after detectives began punching holes in the youth's story before he broke down and admitted he had been lying about the *ninja* intruder. But he wasn't ready to take the blame for the brutal bludgeon murder of his mother.

The baby-faced young man simply stopped cooperating with the police. He refused to answer any more questions, and said he wanted to talk with a lawyer. Timothy was driven to the LAPD West Valley police precinct and booked on suspicion of murder, while investigators continued their search of his home for clues.

Before Timothy balked at further cooperation, he had given police permission to search the house for evidence in his mother's slaying. Investigators wanted the murder weapon, and they suspected that it might be found in the suspect's room. But the *Akitas,* who had the run of the house, wouldn't allow anyone inside the bedroom. Snarling and showing their teeth, they menaced officers attempting to search other areas of the house as well.

Police wisely called for help from animal control experts. But even they had trouble with the vicious dogs that were so loyally guarding the dark secrets hidden inside the cluttered house of horror. The first team of animal control officers who responded to the call tried unsuccessfully to corral the *Akitas* before giving up and announcing that it was too dangerous to continue without safer equipment.

Eventually, as the first rays of the sun were probing the valley sky with tentative streaks of light, animal control reinforcements managed to remove the dogs. The *Akitas* were snagged with nooses draped from the end of long poles and captured without injury to anyone.

Timothy had been driven back to the house from the West Valley headquarters, and was present when detectives at last walked into his bedroom. And they struck paydirt almost immediately. Peering into a large box of laundry detergent they found in a laundry hamper, the officers removed a blood-smeared weight-lifting bar and a scalpel. The heavy metal weight-lifting bar appeared to be just the type of object that might have been used to bludgeon the life from the retired actress.

More muscle-building equipment littered the floor of the room, and the youth's bedroom walls were decorated with more than a dozen posters from martial arts action films. Several of the posters were from films featuring Timothy's hero, Bruce Lee.

The posters and the littered house itself revealed as much about the young man and his mother to investigators as did talks with neighbors. The mother and son had been private people, and no one seemed to know much about them. One woman observed that whenever she had seen her strange neighbors, they were always together. "She never went anywhere without the boy," the woman said. "He seemed to be completely dependent on her."

Nor did the retired actress's sudden, violent death stir up much reaction in Southern California's film community. There was no glittering galaxy of stars, big-time Hollywood producers or processions of grieving fans at the funeral, which was held on the last Sunday before Christmas. Instead, the funeral was a simple Jewish ceremony at the Malinow and Silverman Mortuary Chapel in West Los Angeles, attended by about forty people, including the victim's mother, Muriel Shapiro, of Tarzana, and former husbands Martin Eden Sacker, a Los Angeles businessman, and Michael Roman, of New Orleans, a former actor.

A financial manager in the health care industry and Timothy's stepfather, Roman told the press that he was still having difficulty coming to terms with the tragedy. He said he was having special trouble accepting the accusations against his stepson. He said Timothy was Susan's son from an earlier marriage, and described the relationship between his former wife and his stepson as "very close, very loving."

A weekly tabloid later reported that a British actor had fathered the troubled young man during a brief romantic fling with the film beauty.

While speculation over his parentage was beginning to fuel the gossip columns, Timothy spent the holidays, his first without his mother, held without bail in a Los Angeles County Jail cell, charged with her first degree murder. Dressed in a rumpled prison jumpsuit, the twenty-two-year-old was clearly bewildered and puzzled —sometimes in tears. He looked more like a frightened schoolboy picked up for truancy than someone accused of the brutal bludgeon murder of the one person who loved him most.

Police and the press were busy meanwhile piecing together a mosaic of the tragic actress's star-crossed life. Born in Boston in 1927 as Harriet Shapiro, she was still a schoolgirl when her family moved to the Bronx in New York City. She had a turbulent childhood. But she did well in her lessons at Columbus High School there, and later at Washington Irving High School in Manhattan, where she became involved in the dramatics program.

She was a natural actress, with a fine operatic singing voice, and after graduation from Washington Irving, she joined an independent theater group in East Sebago Lake, Maine, where she made her professional stage debut in the production *Guest in the House.* As a struggling young actress, she continued her work on stage, and began acquiring bit parts in early television dramas.

As Susan Cabot, she made her film debut in 1950 playing the role of a sensual island maiden in the Columbia Pictures film *On the Island of Samoa.* It was the precursor of many exotic movie roles she would play during the next ten years. But her step into films also coincided closely with the end of her life with Martin Sacker, whom she had married in 1944 wartime ceremonies in Washington, D.C. The couple separated in 1951, and divorced a short time later.

The young actress's decade-long screen career provided her with plenty of screen exposure, but few opportunities to move up to major stardom. Her strikingly lovely dark brown hair, brown eyes, and olive complexion obviously played a prominent part in locking her into the stereotyped roles she was destined for—as a Samoan native, Sioux and Apache Indian maidens, and a sensuous Persian beauty.

Although she was part of a star-studded stable of promising young newcomers put together by Universal Studios in the 1950s, most of the choice roles in those heady years went to men: actors such as Tony Curtis, Rock Hudson, Jeff Chandler, Audie Murphy, or Rory Calhoun, who starred in action-adventures, costume dramas, and shoot-'em-up westerns.

Susan Cabot nevertheless managed to snag her share of solid supporting roles in some of the popular films of the day. In 1951 she appeared with Van Heflin, Yvonne De Carlo and Rock Hudson in *Tomahawk.* The same year she appeared with Audie Murphy and Lee Marvin in *Duel at Silver Creek,* and in a bit part as a murder victim with Humphrey Bogart and Zero Mostel in *The Enforcer.*

She continued appearing with popular male and female stars in top films of the day through 1953 and 1954, including *Battle at Apache Pass, Gunsmoke, Son of*

Ali Baba, and *Ride Clear of Diablo.* She even wound up with the handsome heroes in *Gunsmoke,* and *Ride Clear of Diablo.*

Near the end of the decade, however, Susan's career began to take a new, perhaps unexpected twist. Instead of moving up to starring roles in the higher-rated films, she began appearing in Roger Corman's movies. An independent producer who was head of American International, Corman developed something of a cult following for his exploitation movies, most of which capitalized on bizarre storylines and titles.

In addition to her roles in *The Saga of the Viking Women* and *The Wasp Woman,* Susan starred in other Corman productions, including *Sorority Girl; War of the Satellites; Machine Gun Kelly;* and *Surrender? Hell!* In the *Machine Gun Kelly* opus, she appeared opposite Charles Bronson.

Earlier in her career, her off-screen life had taken a predictable route. As a glamorous starlet, fan magazines were continually linking her name with those of male costars and other celebrities. But the conventional daily press didn't take much notice of her until 1959, when she became involved in a titillating international affair with the young and handsome jet-setting King Hussein of Jordan. Suddenly she was headline news.

The Hollywood gossip mill was fired with stories about the improbable romance, after she was seen dating the dashing young monarch around Hollywood and Palm Springs, following their first meeting at a dinner party.

She didn't welcome the sudden flood of attention. The desperately private actress was close-mouthed when the gossip mongers attempted to question her about her relationship with the king. Her affair with Hussein was no casual fling or publicity ploy, and she insisted that it was nobody's business but their own.

Nevertheless, she couldn't shut off the rush of publicity. One news story printed in April 1959 observed that

she had flown to New York the previous evening, sup-
posedly to audition for a part in a Broadway show. The
writer said that her friends, however, had indicated
the trip east was linked closely to her romance with the
young king. The actress was quoted as remarking,
shortly before she checked out of the Beverly Hills Ho-
tel, that King Hussein was the most charming man she
had ever met.

The same story pointed out that the king had can-
celed an official visit to Castle Air Force Base the previous week in order to date the Hollywood beauty. The
writer added that Miss Cabot had previously been married to Sacker, and that the king had been married to
his twenty-six-year-old cousin, Princess Dina Abdul
Hamid.

Although both were divorced at the time, they would
nevertheless have been painfully aware of incredible ob-
stacles that would seem to bar any consideration of a
serious romance—or marriage. The young Arab king
was the leader of millions of Moslems. And Susan
Cabot, the former Harriet Shapiro, was Jewish.

The unlikely romance blossomed, however, until,
when it was apparently at its peak, Susan abruptly and
mysteriously quit Hollywood. She quickly faded from
the public eye, although her exciting interlude with King
Hussein would lead to persistent rumors that the son
she subsequently gave birth to was the illegitimate child
of the short-statured Jordanian ruler. The suspicions
would follow her to the grave.

When Susan Cabot finally resurfaced again in print, it
was 1973. *The Hollywood Reporter,* a trade magazine
that faithfully records movements of movie personalities, caught up with her at her home in Beverly Hills,
where she was living with her second husband, Michael
Roman, and her nine-year-old son Timothy.

The magazine reported that after Susan turned her
back on Hollywood, she lived in Europe and Washington, D.C., for several years. But she had returned to

Hollywood and was anxious to resume her career, preferably in films that would enable her to capitalize on her beautiful singing voice with operatic roles. While waiting to revive her career, she was spending much of her time studying psychology, painting, and singing.

The article also credited what it said was Timothy's difficult and dangerous birth, with helping the actress develop a consuming interest in medicine. According to the account, she underwent a difficult pregnancy and doctors had worried that both mother and son might not survive. The story was concluded, however, with the admonition that both mother and son survived the ordeal and Timothy had developed into "a hale and hearty youngster."

The cheerful conclusion wasn't quite on the mark. Timothy was far from "hale and hearty." And there would be no revival of his mother's acting career. Even her once-happy second marriage crumbled, and the troubled mother and son wound up living in virtual seclusion at their home in Encino.

In fact, some thirteen years after the article appeared, defense attorneys at Timothy's trial and pretrial proceedings for the murder of his mother were painting a gloomy and bizarre portrait of the final years of the faded screen beauty and her troubled son. Much of the courtroom contest over Timothy's future was played out in more than two years of arduous pretrial activities, and defense attorney Chester Leo Smith pulled some startling skeletons from the late actress's closet of closely guarded family secrets.

The attorney revealed in pretrial motions that there was reason to believe the young defendant might be the illegitimate son of King Hussein. Now, stories that had once been circulated as unconfirmed rumors had become a matter of court record.

A longtime friend of Miss Cabot, Smith also disclosed that for fifteen years Timothy was subjected to injections of an experimental growth hormone produced from thousands of dead bodies because he was born a dwarf.

The lawyer cited the possibility of his client's royal parentage in a move to improve safety conditions for Timothy while he was in custody.

Smith claimed that Miss Cabot had received regular $1500 monthly payments from King Hussein, and observed that "it looks like child support." The lawyer said that if it was true that Hussein was indeed the father, his client would be half Jewish and half Arab, as well as a direct descendant of the Prophet Mohammed.

Consequently, he said, the possibility of Timothy's mixed parentage could make it dangerous for him in jail because "religious Arabs would not look favorably upon a descendant that was half Jewish, and might try to kill him."

Citing his longtime personal friendship with the actress, Smith said that he had acquired information indicating that the relationship between the actress and the king was ended because she was Jewish. Van Nuys Superior Court Judge Darlene Schempp agreed to improve security for the defendant, but based her action on his need for frequent medical treatment. She made it plain that the issue of the defendant's parentage was not a factor in the decision.

Smith also used the information about his client's medical history and troubled childhood to win court approval for a comprehensive round of psychiatric and other medical testing for Timothy to determine if the years of prolonged treatment with the growth hormone as part of an experimental program administered by the National Institutes of Health may have contributed to the slaying.

At one point in the interminable proceedings, while commenting on the growth deficiency that had made the defendant dependent on strong medications with severe side effects, Smith declared: "I think Roman [Timothy] is just a statistic that went bad."

According to the petition and other information, efforts to force Timothy's growth with the controversial injections began in his early childhood and weren't discontinued until research disclosed that the hormone could produce serious life-threatening side effects. A short time after the experimental program was ended, the hormone injections were replaced with a new treatment method using newly developed synthetic substances.

Medical records disclosed that Timothy was among 10,000 patients treated with the experimental hormone from 1970 through 1985, when sales were discontinued because certain batches of the substance were found to be infected with a virus that causes Creutzfeldt-Jakob Disease. The deadly viral disease can cause a degeneration of the central nervous system, and produce symptoms including loss of coordination and memory, confusion, and slurred speech. And according to articles from medical journals that Smith submitted to the court, the disease was known to have caused some deaths among patients participating in the experimental program.

Smith pointed out that the parents of patients who received the treatment were aware that some risks were involved, but they proceeded because they didn't want their children to be dwarfs. The lawyer said that medical records tracing the defendant's treatment for dwarfism with hormones later found to cause neurological and other problems in some patients was directly linked to the actress's slaying.

Even as court officers maneuvered and tilted in the pretrial hearings with each other over his fate, Timothy was still taking medication, including steroids. And Smith asserted that the medications periodically caused behavioral changes in his client. Timothy was so concerned about the disturbing side effects of the medications that he had taken it upon himself to attempt to cut down on the dosages.

Smith would also claim in a related U.S. District Court action that Timothy was born with brain damage, which was later aggravated by injection of the growth hormones into his legs twice weekly from 1970 through 1985. The youth had a history of grand mal seizures, a form of epilepsy that causes loss of consciousness, his lawyer said. And Timothy claimed in the federal court civil proceeding that his mother suffered a mental breakdown after learning that some other patients who had received the hormone injections subsequently developed Creutzfeldt-Jakob Disease.

As a dwarf and without treatment, Timothy would have grown only to about four feet tall, the attorney explained. But with the aid of the hormone, steroids, and other drugs to stimulate growth, the youth was artificially stretched to his present five feet, four inches.

"They medically added more than a foot on him," Smith declared. But he added, ominously: "When you force the size of an individual to increase, you also force brain cells to increase. What happens is that doctors are performing a balancing act."

Medical records established that Timothy's growth problem had led to repeated hospitalizations while he was a boy. In 1975, when Timothy was eleven, a pediatrician had diagnosed him as "an emotionally immature, somewhat disturbed child who is having difficulty handling the demands of growing up." A few years earlier a psychologist had blamed some of the boy's troubles on his mother's "theatrics."

Even though the physical evidence showed that doctors had successfully called on their medical skills and new drug and hormone therapy techniques to stretch Timothy to near-normal size, the defense attorney's message was clear: There was reason for serious concern that the years of arduous, frequently painful therapy had left deep emotional and mental scars on the young man's fragile psyche.

A tutor who had helped Timothy with his high school

math recalled that when the youth forgot or otherwise
failed to take his prescribed medications, "he was virtually unable to add two-digit numbers."

Although at the time of his arrest Timothy had recently turned in an adequate performance in art and
biochemistry courses at nearby Pierce College in Wood-
land Hills, he was a frustrated young man with no serious academic achievements. He had proudly confided to
acquaintances that he was a full-time art student, but a
college administrator later disclosed that wasn't exactly
true. The administrator pointed out that the young man
had taken only one art class. "And based on his grade
point average," the school official said, "I wouldn't call
him an outstanding student."

Timothy's off-campus life wasn't any more promising.
He had worked at a collection of odd jobs, but apparently failed to settle in on pursuing any serious vocational goals. And he had few friends. Much of his leisure
time and energies were devoted to his interest in the
unarmed martial arts, weight lifting and body building.

The frustrations of college life, and his obvious inabil-
ity to find early success in the outside world, were aggravated by his equally troubling relationship with his
mother.

According to one of the psychiatric reports prepared
after his arrest, the lives of the mother and son were
inexorably intertwined. They were especially close, and
she hardly ever went anywhere without him. "Much of
the youngster's immature behavior has been inappropri-
ately reinforced by his mother," one of the experts
wrote. He added that as an actress, Miss Cabot tended
to be "somewhat overly dramatic and overly concerned."

Outside the courtroom, reporters were approaching
former friends of the victim for information that provided further insight into the distressing relationship between the mother and son. Former screen siren Mamie
Van Doren, who had known Susan Cabot since the early

1950s when they were both under contract to Universal Studios, confirmed that Timothy was a premature baby. And she was quoted as saying that his mother had described him as a bit slow, and in need of special tutors.

Miss Van Doren said Susan loved Timothy very much, however, and it was difficult to believe that the mother and son had experienced such a tragedy, according to the article.

The courtroom strategy, meanwhile, was becoming obvious long before the case was ready to move to trial. Timothy's early medical problems, aggravated by his years as a human guinea pig in the experimental hormone program, may have played a key role in his mental and emotional state at the time his mother was killed. And by focusing on the victim's fragile mental condition, her unkempt home, and her authorization of experimental and controversial drugs for treatment of her son's dwarfism, she might be cast in the role of unwittingly contributing to her own death.

Smith contended that Timothy's exposure to his overprotective and emotionally disturbed mother, and the severe growth deficiency that had made him dependent on strong medications with severe side effects, had left the youth an emotional wreck.

While using the medical and psychological information to bolster his client's defense, however, Smith sought a court order sealing the data from public inspection. He argued that public disclosure of some of the information could jeopardize the defendant's right to a fair trial. Attorneys for the *Los Angeles Times* opposed the move, however, and the court ruled in the newspaper's favor.

Deputy District Attorney Bradford E. Stone, who headed the prosecution team for Los Angeles County, also quickly moved to block the defense strategy. Even if the defense proved that the victim was eccentric and her son emotionally underdeveloped, it didn't change

the fact that the circumstances of the crime still
amounted to first-degree murder, Stone contended.

At the preliminary hearing in Van Nuys Superior
Court, the prosecutor said there was no question that
the defendant was the sole perpetrator. He pointed out
that the fierce dogs guarding the inside of the house
would not have permitted a stranger to enter Timothy's
bedroom and pick up the barbell, then return it after
using it to bludgeon Miss Cabot to death. Only Timothy,
their owner, could have accomplished that without being attacked, Stone declared.

The prosecutor also pointed to the negligible injuries
Timothy had claimed he suffered at the hands of the
intruder: a little bump on his head and a quarter-inch
cut on one arm. "That's hardly the degree of injury one
would expect from a death-defying battle with a *ninja*
warrior," he scoffed.

In apparent anticipation of a possible manslaughter
defense, Stone dismissed any notion that Timothy may
have killed his mother in a sudden, uncontrollable rage.
Defense attorneys commonly attempt to show that a
killing occurred in a sudden rage, in order to indicate
the crime of manslaughter rather than the more serious
offense of murder. But Stone wasn't buying either a
charge or the possibility of a verdict of manslaughter.

"If he flamed out, how do you explain that the murder weapon got from his bedroom to hers, where she
was beaten to death?" he asked. "That takes some degree of thinking and planning."

The prosecutor also took a quick shot at a possible
plea of diminished mental capacity. He pointed out that
at the time of the slaying, Timothy was a student at
Pierce College. The prosecutor declared that the defendant's ability to pass college courses indicated he had
the mental ability to plan a crime.

Pleas of innocent and of innocent by reason of insanity were initially entered for the defendant on the
murder charges. But the insanity plea was withdrawn a

few weeks later when Smith brought in another attorney, James Barnes, to assist in the case. Barnes had
acquired a local reputation for good solid defense work
in 1986 when he was a Los Angeles County deputy public defender and represented another young man
charged with matricide.

Torran Meir was a sixteen-year-old Canoga Park
straight A student and considered by many neighbors
and school acquaintances to be a model teen when he
was arrested and accused of setting up the strangulation
murder of his nagging mother, Shirley Rizk, with two
pals. Furthermore, investigators said, the boys then tried
to kill his eight-year-old half brother, Rory Rizk, first
with poison, then by putting him in a car with the dead
woman, setting the vehicle on fire, and pushing it over a
cliff. The car exploded and burned, but the young boy
survived. Prosecutors said that Rory walked in on the
murder of his mother, leading to the attempts to eliminate him as a witness.

Meir was subsequently acquitted of murder and attempted murder charges, but convicted of voluntary
manslaughter and attempted voluntary manslaughter
and sentenced to twelve years in the California Youth
Authority system. But according to California law, Meir
could be released anytime the Youth Parole Board decided to let him go. Barnes had presented a spirited
defense that heavily focused on the years of abuse the
teenager had undergone from his mother.

The lawyer's accomplishment in avoiding a murder
conviction for his client appeared especially impressive
after each of Meir's two cohorts were sentenced. Both
youths were sent to prison for terms of fifteen-years-to-
life on the more serious charges of second degree murder.

When Barnes left the public defender's office to move
into private practice, he immediately joined Timothy's
defense team. One of his first acts in the case was to
withdraw his new client's insanity plea and replace it

with a plea of not guilty. Barnes explained his action by pointing out that insanity is a difficult defense to use successfully within the framework of California state criminal statutes.

The insanity plea is used much more sparingly, in fact, than most people who are not closely connected with the criminal justice system seem to believe. And when it is used, its success rate isn't very impressive. Although national surveys have indicated that a majority of Americans questioned believed fifty to sixty percent of defendants charged with major felony crimes plead an insanity defense, it's simply not so. Professional studies show that the rate of insanity pleas is closer to two or three percent. And most of those are unsuccessful.

For one thing, there hasn't been a consensus by the various jurisdictions for many years about an exact definition of legal insanity. Initially, U.S. courts were governed in insanity cases by the M'Naghten Rule, which was the standard used by the British judiciary system. Simply put, it questioned if the defendant could distinguish between right and wrong—whether or not he understood the nature and quality of his act. Eventually, however, various court decisions began to recognize such phenomena as "irresistible impulses" and other such factors. It wasn't long before the issue of insanity had became incredibly confusing and muddled, especially for juries faced with hours of testimony filled with incomprehensible legal and psychiatric gobbledygook.

Proving legal insanity offers no promise of an automatic and easy ticket to freedom for defendants of serious felony crimes. Not even for defendants with such disturbing emotional and medical backgrounds as Timothy Roman's.

Timothy remained behind bars as the pretrial proceedings dragged on. In one action, Smith moved to have evidence gathered from the house ruled inadmissible because detectives had reputedly ignored the youth's

impaired mental state when they arrested him. The lawyer argued before Superior Court judge Richard Kolos-
tian that "a reasonable person observing the living
conditions of the interior of this luxury house would
know its occupants were in a state of mental abnormal-
ity."

And he contended that Timothy wasn't mentally fit to
answer the questions of investigators after his mother's
slaying, because he was an emotional wreck due to his
ordeal while submitted for so many years to the experimental hormone therapy program. Smith repeated earlier claims that the growth hormone caused wide mood
swings, as well as other dangerous side effects.

However, detectives claimed that Timothy was coop-
erative when he was dealing with them and didn't show
any signs of mental instability on the night of the murder. Stone pointed out that officers discovered the scalpel and the barbell after he had voluntarily telephoned
them to report his mother's death. They didn't become
suspicious of him until he began to contradict himself in
his statements, the prosecutor declared.

Dressed in his oversized blue jail uniform with black
sneakers, Timothy stared into the distance and showed
no emotion as the motion was denied.

On May 1, 1989, more than two years after Susan
Cabot, née Harriet Shapiro, was brutally bludgeoned to
death in her bed, her only child went on trial for first
degree murder. His plea had been changed once more,
back to not guilty by reason of insanity.

Prosecutors contended that the defendant was a savage killer who, after murdering his mother, quickly began laying the groundwork for a defense by blaming the
crime on a mysterious *ninja* intruder who never existed.
"Our side is reasonably succinct and fairly straightforward," Stone said in a pre-trial statement. "He knew
what he was doing. He killed a human being, and he
planned it in advance. We don't know why."

As expected, Smith also continued to stress his client's agonizing experience with the ill-fated growth experiment carried out under the auspices of the NIH. He charged that the defendant was "a product of a federal medical experiment by the National Institutes of Health that was well-intentioned, but disastrous. He could not actually have formed the mental state that was an element of the crime." Smith claimed that the youth wasn't responsible for the death of his mother or of other actions that evening, because of medical problems that had left him with "the mind of a child."

Timothy's conflicting statements to police on the night of the murder were the result of a faulty memory caused by "low electrical voltage in his brain," the attorney claimed.

Stone dismissed the defense attorney's claims as "a smokescreen." The prosecutor added that Smith was merely trying to confuse the jury with issues that were not germane to the case.

But the long-awaited trial barely got under way before it skidded to an abrupt halt. Smith developed health problems and was forced to withdraw. A mistrial was declared, and a new trial date was scheduled for early October. Timothy's new defense attorneys, Richard P. Lasting and Michael V. White, would have six months to prepare the case.

By the time the second trial was convened on October 5, several important changes had been made. The defendant not only had a new defense team, but there would be no jury. Judge Darlene Schempp, would preside over the case, decide guilt or innocence and determine a possible sentence. There had been other significant changes as well. The previous charge of first degree murder had been scaled down to second degree murder. There would be no possibility of a death penalty, no chance of Timothy facing execution in the State of California's gas chamber.

And Timothy was no longer pleading innocent by reason of insanity. He had entered a straightforward plea of not guilty. The latest plea change could have a vitally important effect on the defendant's future. By once more dropping the insanity plea, he had removed the possibility of being sent to a mental hospital or psychiatric section of a prison for an indefinite period of treatment.

Despite the change of plea, however, his emotional and mental problems were still keystones of his defense strategy. The defense continued to contend that he had and still did suffer from mental problems that caused agitation, confusion, and made him unaware of his actions prior to, during, and after the slaying of his mother. The testimony of mental health and other medical professionals would play an important role in determining the fate of the defendant.

Dr. Barbara Lippe, a pediatric endocrinologist at the University of California Los Angeles (UCLA) testified that Timothy had brain damage, low blood sugar, difficulty reasoning, and congenital hypopituitaryism. He was born without the pituitary glands that play such a key role in the growth and maturity of children into adults. She had treated him as a patient since 1969. Consequently, although by the time of the second trial he had observed three birthdays behind bars and was twenty-five years old, he still looked like he was fourteen. And he had to take regular injections of the male hormone testosterone.

Other testimony and evidence indicated that the victim had been living in self-enforced seclusion and in constant fear of poverty. "Susan was terrified that one day she and her son would be destitute and on the street," her clinical psychologist, Dr. Carl Farber testified.

Yet, the evidence showed that her obsessive financial worries were not justified. She had a more than adequate steady income from royalties earned by her old movies, some shrewd real estate transactions, and additional funds derived from her hobby of buying classic

cars and having them restored for resale. She and her son could have looked forward to living comfortably, even if she never worked in films again.

But Dr. Farber talked of other, more sinister details of Miss Cabot's background and psyche with his testimony. The witness stated that during the actress's childhood she was sexually and physically abused during a period when she was shuttled among fourteen different foster homes. The experience left her subject to severe fears and bouts of depression, he said. Her therapist also quoted her as saying that she would have committed suicide if it wasn't for her intense love for her son. He compared the relationship between the pair to that of "an injured mama lion and her cub."

Despite the importance of the medical testimony, the most dramatic period of the trial occurred on the second day—when Timothy took the witness stand to personally tell his story of the terrible night his mother was killed. There were glaring differences between the tale he told the court and the story he had originally recounted to homicide investigators at the scene of the slaying.

He said his mother was suffering from asthma and a nervous breakdown, and was bedridden that night when he tried to call paramedics for help. Instead of letting him help her, however, she began yelling at him, asking who he was, he testified. Then, the witness said as his voice dropped to a near whisper, she picked up the barbell and swung it at him.

Tears welled in the young man's eyes and trickled down his cheeks as he continued with his story. "She picked it up and started swinging at me," he said. "I grabbed it . . . the last thing I remember is trying to push her away, just trying to get out of that room."

He told the hushed courtroom that he couldn't remember if he hit his mother with the barbell. But he admitted that he later hid the bloody barbell and a scalpel in his clothes hamper. He said that his mother had snatched up the scalpel, which she used as a gardening tool, and attacked him with it after he wrested the barbell away from her.

When he was asked why he hid the weapons, he replied that he didn't believe anyone would understand that his mother had tried to kill him.

During cross examination, he also admitted that the fanciful yarn about an attack by a black-garbed *ninja* character had been a desperate fabrication. "I made that whole story up," he confessed.

The courtroom was hushed a short time later when the diminutive witness explained that he loved his mother very much, even though she had often yelled at him. He said that she showed two different personalities, one when they were around other people, and another when the two of them were alone.

Dr. Katherine McTaggart-Crosbie, a UCLA therapist who was treating the defendant, provided testimony that seemed to support his claims of important gaps in his memory. She said he had memory problems that left him unable to recall long periods of the past. The therapist explained that he may have forgotten whether or not he killed his mother because the memory would be painful. Consequently, he could have made up the *ninja* story as a way of avoiding painful feelings of guilt.

Dr. McTaggart-Crosbie agreed with previous testimony that Timothy was brain damaged and had other serious medical problems. She said that his medical troubles had left him without the ability to fabricate a more soundproof alibi in the slaying.

After more than two frustrating years of preparation and anticipation, once the trial began, it moved swiftly. A week after the trial began, Judge Schempp announced a verdict of guilty to involuntary manslaughter.

Although the verdict hadn't entirely cleared Timothy of his mother's murder, it was a clearcut victory for the defense. Involuntary manslaughter carried a maximum sentence of four years in prison. Voluntary manslaughter, the next more severe charge, carried a maximum eleven-year sentence; and in California, second degree murder calls for penalties of up to twenty years behind bars.

Timothy had already spent two and a half years in jail awaiting trial before he was at last freed on $24,000 bail, so even the maximum sentence under the conviction would leave him with no more than eighteen months to serve. And few felons in American prisons today serve every day of their sentences.

In addition to less severe sentence provisions, there was another advantage to Timothy in his conviction for involuntary manslaughter, instead of more serious charges. According to California state criminal statutes, conviction on charges of involuntary manslaughter would not stand in the way of his inheriting his mother's estate, which was believed to be worth more than $600,000. Conviction on more serious charges, which would have indicated an intent to kill, would have made him ineligible for the inheritance.

Judge Schempp said in her ruling that she did not believe that the young man planned to kill his mother. She said instead that she believed he struck the fatal blows after the ailing, reclusive woman attacked him in a delirious frenzy.

Just about everyone involved appeared relieved by the trial's conclusion. Even Stone, who prosecuted the case, conceded to the press that he wasn't dissatisfied with the verdict. "Based on evidence presented by the defense, it became real obvious that he did not premeditate the slaying," Stone said. "I still get the gut feeling he snapped from the stress of living with his mother all those years."

Stone pointed out that evidence had shown that on the day of her death, Miss Cabot was experiencing an "extreme psychotic episode," which he said would have contributed to the tension already present in the home. And Timothy's grandmother, Mrs. Elizabeth Roman, told reporters that the family was overjoyed. "It has all been so draining," she said. "Now we will have a chance to start a new life, and help Timothy start over."

At the sentencing two weeks later, there wasn't much surprise, if any, when Judge Schempp ordered probation for the tragic young man. The judge said the probation order would contain a provision requiring that he continue to submit to therapy. Noting that he had already spent nearly three years in custody, she suspended a three-year prison sentence.

In pronouncing the sentence, the jurist stated that Miss Cabot's death was precipitated by her own behavior. "This was a very tragic occurrence . . . brought on by the bizarre and often irrational behavior of the victim," Judge Schempp declared. She described the tragic slaying as an isolated incident, an act that was not the result of criminal intent.

After the sentencing, White disclosed that Timothy would live with his adoptive grandparents, the Romans, and would consider returning to Pierce College and looking for a job. "He just wants to put this behind him," the attorney observed. "He can't be happy after a tragedy like this, but now he'll be able to live a healthy, normal life."

Chapter 4

Daddy's Precious

If there were a contest for the world's most loving and indulgent parent, George Telemachos would be a difficult candidate to beat.

He doted on his darling daughter and gave her everything that it was in his power to give. When she was sick, he spent tens of thousands of dollars for the best medical care available anywhere in the country. When she was a little girl, he filled her room with dolls, stuffed animals, and other toys. When she reached her teens, he gave her fistfuls of money, expensive jewelry, and a new car.

But the hardworking Romanian immigrant's love and generous gifts weren't enough. When Katherine Maria Telemachos was nineteen, she decided that she wanted her father's life.

Ironically, from the time that little girl he called Katy was born in Hollywood, Florida, on May 16, 1971, her father lived in dread for her life.

George Telemachos had barely observed his twenty-first birthday in 1952 when he left his Romanian homeland and emigrated to New Zealand. Through hard work and thrift he opened his own restaurant after a couple of years, and in 1967 was married.

The couple's first child, Tony, was born with a faulty liver. So Telemachos, now with a wife and a chronically

sick baby, emigrated again. This time he headed for the
United States, where he hoped to find better medical
care for Tony, and settled his little family in Broward
County, along the warm southeast coast of Florida.
Their second and last child, Katherine, was born there
—with the same dangerous liver ailment her brother
suffered from.

Katy was four years old when her brother died.
Telemachos and his wife Mary hadn't given up their
firstborn without a fight. They flew the child to New
York, London, and anywhere else they heard there was
a specialist who might be able to preserve his life. When
they failed, they turned their love and attention to pre-
serving the life of their only surviving child, Katy.

The couple spent thousands of dollars on medical
care for their babies, and Telemachos raised the money
with the restaurants he operated in the Fort Lauderdale
area. When his wife filed for a divorce in 1977, income
from the restaurants paid for the legal fees, the alimony,
and child support. And it continued to pay for Katy's
medical bills. The year of the breakup, Katy's father
took her on a summer vacation to the Smoky Moun-
tains.

The marital rift was nasty. Katy's parents fought for
ten years in court and out of court over her custody and
child support payments. At one point after Telemachos
threatened in a letter to a friend to kill his former wife,
the divorce court judge issued a restraining order
against him. In 1978 when the divorce decree was
granted by the courts, Telemachos moved out of the
master bedroom in his house and gave it to his daughter
so she would have plenty of room for her dolls, stuffed
animals, and clothing during her visits. He moved into
one of the three smaller bedrooms in the carefully
tended stucco bungalow.

The decade-long court battle was finally concluded
with the couple agreeing to share custody of their child.
According to records in Broward County Divorce

Court, it was agreed that she would live with her father in his comfortable Cooper City home at the edge of the Everglades.

While Katy's parents were jousting over her custody and care, her liver was failing. She was a few weeks past her tenth birthday when surgeons at Children's Hospital in Pittsburgh, Pennsylvania, replaced her worn-out liver with a new organ from a donor. The new liver lasted less than a year before the child was back in the hospital for another transplant. This time the organ wasn't rejected, and Katy's surgery was lauded in the medical community as one of the first successful liver transplants in the United States. It was 1981.

But the transplants weren't covered by health insurance, and they cost Katy's father nearly $60,000. He considered the staggering medical bills to be little enough to pay for his daughter's life. During Katy's hospitalization, her father stayed at the Ronald McDonald House with the parents of other ill youngsters. And he spent every minute he could at her bedside until she was well enough to bring back to South Florida.

Under the watchful eyes of both her parents, Katy regained her strength and participated in normal activities with her schoolmates. At Cooper High School she performed with the drill team and marched with the honor guard. She was approaching graduation from high school when a new medical emergency occurred, however. The powerful medication she took to fight rejection of her donated liver weakened her kidneys and they began to fail. Katy was so sick and weak toward the end of her final year, that during a senior trip to Disney World in Orlando, she had to be pushed in a wheelchair. Her mother donated one of her own kidneys, and the organ was successfully transplanted into Katy's body at Jackson Memorial Hospital in Miami. She was eighteen.

While she was a patient, her father visited faithfully every night, bringing her favorite foods from local restaurants to replace the less appetizing hospital fare.

When she was released from the hospital, he celebrated the occasion by presenting her with a new car. The teenager didn't like it, so he replaced it with another, a bright red Ford Probe sports car. On May 16, 1990, he gave her a gold necklace worth several hundred dollars for her birthday.

Despite Katy Telemachos's history of illness, and her parents' acrimonious divorce, in many other ways she appeared to be a teenager to be envied. Both her parents were devoted to her, and her father's love bordered on obsession. He showered her with gifts, and all she had to do if she wanted something was to ask for it. She needed only to look at him and say, "Daddy." It was her magic word, and it served her as well as "presto" or "alacazzam" ever served the most skilled stage magician. Money, clothes, and whatever else she desired appeared as if by magic.

When a neighbor girl began taking piano lessons, Katy decided she had to take lessons as well. So her father bought her an expensive piano. After a few weeks she lost interest in the lessons. But whatever Katy wanted, she got.

Telemachos knew he was spoiling his daughter, and attempted to establish rules and pass on some of his own respect for hard work and honesty. He badgered her about hanging around with the wrong crowd, and pushed her to attend college, but found it almost impossible to refuse anything she asked for. He explained to friends that he couldn't help himself. From the time his Katy was a sickly baby, he had lived in constant fear that she might not live to see her next birthday.

He couldn't stop himself from repeatedly telling friends and acquaintances how beautiful his little girl was. He devoted his life to her, and had few hobbies. When he wasn't working or with Katy, he watched soccer games if he could find a match on television. When there was no soccer to watch, he sometimes read *Reader's Digest* or *National Geographic*. Or he worked in his yard. He was especially proud of a mango tree on his property, and shared the tasty tropical fruit with neighbors and other acquaintances. But Katy was his obsession.

He even gave her a part-time job as a clerk at the Baker Street Tobacconist, a tidy little shop he bought at the Hollywood Fashion Mall after retiring from the restaurant business in Hollywood, Florida, and Fort Lauderdale. Officially he paid her $100 for a three-day week, but he actually handed over much more money than that, $200 and $300 at a time. Katy was spoiled and had a taste for life in the fast lane. In South Florida with its sunshine, inviting beaches—and runaway drug trafficking—that can be very, very fast. And the life she wanted for herself couldn't be financed on $100 a week.

Acquaintances began to exchange stories about Katy that would later be translated in the courts into depositions: tales of abortions and of guns. She shaved one side of her head and combed the rest of her hair away from it, punk-rock style. According to at least one later report, she toked on marijuana while she watched over her father's shop. And she talked tough and dirty.

The teenager's adoring father wasn't unaware that the darling little girl he had so solicitously sacrificed for and watched over seemed to have turned into a rebellious teenager whose behavior was deplorable and choice of friends was atrocious. He fussed about her dating, attempted to monitor her other activities as well, and gave her a beeper so he could stay in constant contact with her. He apparently knew about at least one of the abortions; he knew about one of the two guns—a .38-caliber revolver and a smaller caliber pistol she was said to carry in her purse and in her car; he knew about the reputed marijuana smoking; and he suspected that she had been robbing the till at the tobacco shop.

He also knew about Erik J. Delvalle, Katy's husky boyfriend, who traced his ancestry to Puerto Rico and was a high school dropout who worked on low-paying construction jobs. The couple first met at the tobacco shop, when Delvalle stopped there to buy a package of cigarettes. They dated only a few weeks before Delvalle gave Katy a ring and she accepted his proposal of marriage. In his way, he was as obsessed with the girl as her father was.

But Telemachos was outraged at his daughter's choice of a boyfriend, and he made it clear that he wanted nothing to do with the young man. Katy would later claim under oath that her father resented the fact that her boyfriend was a blue-collar worker, and didn't think he was good enough for her. "He didn't like Erik at all," she observed. The Romanian immigrant, who still spoke the fractured English of many of the foreign born, called Delvalle a bum. He pronounced the word perfectly.

His choice of words and pronunciation were also plain enough when his daughter and her boyfriend showed up together at the Baker Street Tobacconist and he loudly ordered them to get out and stay out. Earlier he chased them out of his house when he returned home and found them there. Telemachos had finally had all he could tolerate of his daughter's outrageous behavior, of money missing from the cash register, and of Katy's boyfriend.

Katy and her fiancé reacted by signing a lease for an apartment in nearby Miramar. A couple of days later she rented a van and they began moving in.

At about two A.M., Saturday, July 21, 1990, Officer John Posson of the Cooper City Police Department was on patrol in a squad car when he spotted a yellow rental van stopped behind the Pioneer middle school. A white T-shirt was draped suspiciously over the license plate.

Posson left his patrol car, took a quick look toward the van to confirm his earlier conclusion that it was empty, and began checking out the doors and windows at the school. There was no sign of forced entry there, so the police officer returned to the suspicious van to look around with his flashlight.

Three cool Buds were stashed under the front seat, and a single surgeon's glove was stuffed into the door pocket on the passenger's side. A woman's wallet was lying on the dashboard. Credit cards and a driver's license carried the name Katherine Telemachos.

Posson returned to his squad car and waited silently in the shadows, keeping his eye on the van. A few minutes later, the figures of three people crossed a small footbridge over a canal and climbed into the van. The patrolman notified headquarters that he was following the van and asked for assistance. Supported by a backup unit, he pulled the vehicle over a few blocks from the school.

The occupants identified themselves as nineteen-year-old Katherine Telemachos; twenty-one-year-old Erik J. Delvalle; and their friend, nineteen-year-old Vincent Bernard Magona. The young men and the woman, all visibly nervous but polite, explained that they were visiting a friend across the canal and parked behind the school because it was near the footbridge. It was a plausible story, and there was no reason to hold them, so after the officers recorded names and addresses, the three were told they could leave. The van pulled away slowly. The driver was studiously careful to obey all traffic signs.

Nearly a day and a half later, a merchant who operated a store near the Baker Street Tobacconist decided to check up on Telemachos because he hadn't opened up his shop for two days. She enlisted the help of a neighbor, and together they found his car parked in the garage, and the door leading from the garage into his house ajar. It was nearly noon when they walked cautiously inside.

The interior was in a shambles. Drawers had been ripped out of cabinets and dumped on the floor; pillows slashed open with a knife; and clothing searched and discarded in rumpled piles. Alarmed and reluctant to venture into the bedroom, Telemachos's friends hurried from the house and telephoned police.

Uniformed patrolmen, quickly followed by homicide investigators, hurried to the house. Inside, they found the owner curled up on his right side in a fetal position on his bed. He was dead, his skull shattered by a bullet that appeared to have been fired point-blank into his forehead. A cluster of pinprick spackles that dotted his eyelids indicated he was asleep or at least had his eyes closed when he was killed. The gunpowder spray also provided unmistakable evidence that the weapon was held only inches from the victim, perhaps even pressed flush with his flesh, when it was fired.

The force of the slug smashing into flesh and bone had knocked the dentures from the victim's mouth, and they were lying on the bedclothes a few inches from his body. The bedclothing near his head was drenched in blood.

The experienced police officers realized that it wasn't the kind of killing usually tied to burglars. Professionals rarely kill, and when they do, it's usually because someone has returned home unexpectedly or awakened and surprised the intruder in the house or bedroom. Telemachos's death wasn't the work of a nervous or panicked amateur. It had all the earmarks of a cold-blooded execution.

The homicide investigators quickly began developing leads on a strong suspect, or suspects. It appeared obvious that the killer or killers entered the house through the garage, where Telemachos's pet dog Cocoa slept. Curiously, the feisty little mutt apparently hadn't raised an alarm, although she was known by neighbors to bark whenever strangers were around. And the ransacked house seemed to be almost too littered to be the work of a real burglar after money or valuables.

Even though Telemachos's expensive Movado watch was missing from his right wrist, and his billfold was emptied of cash, the topsy-turvy condition of the house itself was suspicious. It appeared almost as if the intruders had wanted to prove to someone that burglars were there. Another strange aspect about the bizarre burglary, which would quickly begin to make sense, was the deliberate smashing of two pictures that had been mounted on the wall above the bed. They were framed photographs of Telemachos's only surviving child, his daughter Katy.

Detectives also talked with neighbors and other storekeepers or employees who worked near his business at the mall, and quickly learned about some of the troubles Telemachos was having with his headstrong daughter—including the furious row a few days earlier when he ordered her and her boyfriend from the shop. Acquaintances said he was determined to break them up before Katy began attending classes at Broward Community College, as she had promised to do at the beginning of the next term.

And investigators learned from their own colleague's midnight-shift report that the couple, along with another friend of theirs, had been stopped and questioned after their van was found parked near the victim's house at two A.M. on the night of the murder. The Telemachos house is only a short walk across the footbridge spanning the canal from the primary school. The inference was obvious: the trio must have left the murder scene only minutes before they were stopped.

By nightfall on the day Telemachos's body was discovered, Cooper City police had taken his daughter, her fiancé, and their friend in custody as suspects in the shooting. The trio was jailed and held without bail.

Neighbors and acquaintances of the victim, and of the slender young woman who was suddenly being cast in news stories as the architect and mastermind behind his murder, were stunned. Even friends who knew that Katy Telemachos was hardly the fairy-tale princess of her father's dreams, found it difficult to believe that she could have so ruthlessly set up his savage murder.

It was easier for police to believe when they began piecing together statements from her accused coconspirators with other evidence they had been gathering in the first brief forty-eight hours since the slaying. Among the evidence was a box of .38-caliber hollow-point cartridges. Ballistics experts would later identify the slug fired into Telemachos's forehead as a .38-caliber hollow point.

Magona began blurting out his story of the murder almost as soon as he was taken to the Cooper City Police Department headquarters for questioning. He told police that Katy had taken him and his pal to the house on a dry run, to show them the door they would enter and to give her father's dog a chance to get used to them. And he told them about the murder two or three nights later.

"They showed me inside the house with them, went in, went into a person's room," he nervously recounted. "I went over by the window. He went over by the bed, told me to look outside, and then he shot him," Magona said of his buddy. He added that Delvalle fortified himself before the postmidnight murder mission by drinking five beers.

When police asked what Magona expected to get from his friends for his part in the slaying, he replied that he was promised $300. He said that Delvalle went through the dead man's pants pockets after the shooting, took several hundred dollars, and gave him $100.

Continuing his statement, Magona said his friends wore plastic gloves while they were in the house. "Like surgical gloves?" Detective Mike Graham asked. "Yes," he replied. Magona said that Delvalle tossed the gloves out of the van while they were driving away following the murder.

It took police about six hours after Delvalle was taken in custody before he agreed to tape a confession. Katy invoked her constitutional rights and refused to discuss it. But investigators learned that she masterminded the killing.

The boys said as they were fleeing the house, Delvalle tossed the .38-caliber revolver used in the murder off one side of the footbridge into the canal. The extra cartridges were thrown into the water on the other side. Magona said his pal told him the cartridges were hollow points.

Delvalle at first told authorities that he was the triggerman. Then he changed his story and said his girlfriend had done the shooting. Explaining his story switch, he declared, "I'm not going to fry for this."

Delvalle and Magona were a curious pair, neighborhood pals since shortly after the Magona family moved to South Florida from Islip, Long Island, New York, about ten years earlier. They lived across the street from each other, and continued their friendship as they grew into young men.

Magona was timid and tagged along after his more confident friend. At the time of his arrest, the five-foot-seven-inch, brown-eyed teenager was attending commercial art classes at a vocational school and lived in Pembroke Pines, part of the urban sprawl between Fort Lauderdale and Miami. Like Katy, he had never been in trouble before.

As a small child, Magona had Tourette's syndrome, a neurological condition that among other things manifests itself through twitching. But as many people who suffer from the disorder do, he outgrew the twitching condition as he matured.

Nevertheless, he had learning difficulties and for several years attended a private school for children with developmental disorders. Diane P. Blank, a licensed clinical psychologist from nearby Hollywood who later evaluated Magona for the court, reported that he had an IQ of 96, which is in the normal range. But she described him as having a need to impress others and to be accepted and liked.

"His naiveté and childlike manner could very likely have led him to the problems he faces today," she wrote.

Delvalle had experienced a few brushes with the law, but only for minor offenses. While he was in San Francisco in 1985 he got in over his head abusing a variety of drugs, which resulted in frightening hallucinations and talk of suicide. He was treated at the McCauley Institute there and released after about six months.

The young man appeared to be getting his life back on track after returning to South Florida and apparently avoided serious drug abuse, although he indulged a taste for beer. He was alternately tough and tender-hearted, according to reports by people who knew him. He was muscular, with a boxer's face, and had a reputation for a quick temper. But he was also an especially loyal member of the youth group at the Holy Sacrament Episcopal Church, and got his pal Vinnie to begin attending the weekly meetings with him. He didn't curse, and he didn't like it when acquaintances swore in front of him.

He was also infatuated with the pretty, dark-haired, privileged girl he had met at the tobacco shop.

A seventeen-year-old girl who knew Delvalle from the church youth meetings told investigators he had confided to her and others about the planned murder a day or two before the shooting. Delvalle and his girlfriend, whom he and their friends knew as Kathy, or Katherine, believed that Telemachos was worth $4 to $5 million, and that she would inherit the fortune, according to the statement. In his statement to police, Magona also said his friends thought Katy's father was a millionaire.

Ironically, police would later learn, Telemachos was not only worth much less than $1 million, but he proba-

bly wouldn't have lived long even if he wasn't murdered.
He was critically ill with heart and lung ailments.

The girl from church said Delvalle told her Kathy
claimed her father had sexually molested her, so the
murder would be justified. Other teenagers had heard
the same story from Delvalle. Police never uncovered
any corroborating evidence. But the story must have
horrified and outraged Katy's boyfriend.

The girl said that Delvalle, his pal, and girlfriend met
with her the morning after the shooting and bragged
that they had carried out the murder. Asked about her
reaction to her father's death, Katy was quoted as saying
she didn't feel anything. She hated her father. Delvalle
was the one who was upset, the girl told police. One
moment he would be bragging, the next moment crying
and worrying about the electric chair.

As police and prosecutors continued rounding up evidence and witnesses, and Magona was released on bail
to custody of his mother, Katy and her boyfriend remained locked up in the Broward County Jail in Fort
Lauderdale. The troubles the lovebirds had experienced
followed them inside.

Jail guards weren't as tolerant of Katy's sharp tongue
and spoiled ways as her father had been, and she was
barely locked up before she was placed in an isolation
cell. Her health problems also continued, and she underwent surgery on her reproductive system at the
Broward County Medical Center while awaiting trial.

Meanwhile her boyfriend was cranking out one mis-
pelled and ungrammatical love letter after another to
her.

Delvalle and Magona didn't seriously contest the
charges against them. And because they had each made
statements that incriminated Katy, the court approved a
motion by her defense attorney to sever her trial from
theirs. Later a similar decision led to severing the trials
of the two young men, as well.

Magona hung tough for a while, and refused a plea

bargain offer that prosecutors linked to an agreement calling for him to testify against his friends. But a few months later, after Judge Greene rejected defense arguments that the teenager's arrest was illegal, and after psychologists decided he was competent to stand trial, Magona changed his mind.

He agreed to testify against his pal and Katy, and was permitted to plead guilty to second degree murder and conspiracy to commit first degree murder. The plea sidestepped the grim possibility of conviction for first degree murder and a sentence of death in Florida's fearsome electric chair. Under the reduced charge, the most severe penalty he could face would be a term of up to twenty-two years in prison, if he was sentenced as an adult. If the judge decided to sentence him as a juvenile offender, the maximum penalty would be four years in prison followed by two years of house arrest.

Magona's parents and a priest were in court with him when he testified that he had accompanied his friends to the home of Katy's father on the night of the shooting. Asked why they were there, he replied in a voice that could barely be heard: "To kill Mr. Telemachos." As Delvalle watched and listened intently, his friend stated that he was acting as a lookout and was peering out a window, so he didn't actually see the shooting. But it appeared that Delvalle was the person who pulled the trigger, the nervous youth told the court.

At the conclusion of the hearing, Judge Greene announced that he would sentence Magona after the trials of his codefendants. The judge added that he would consider the degree of Magona's involvement and the truthfulness of his testimony at the trials in determining the sentence.

Several months later Magona was sentenced, as a youthful offender, to three years in prison, with the term to be followed by two years of community control. The judge recommended continued education tied to a boot camp program, and also ordered restitution of

$5789.50. Magona was given credit for fifty-two days already spent in jail.

Delvalle pleaded guilty after his girlfriend's trial to charges of first degree murder and of conspiracy to commit first degree murder. Broward Circuit judge Charles M. Greene sentenced him to life in prison, with a minimum of twenty-five years to be served on the murder count, and a twelve-year sentence for conspiracy. The judge ordered the sentences served concurrently, and gave Delvalle credit for 491 days already spent behind bars. The young man, still vowing his love for Katy, was also ordered to pay court costs of $5789.50.

Shortly before Delvalle's sentencing, prosecutor Jeffrey Marcus filed documents expanding on the purported motive for the shooting. He disclosed that about a week before the slaying, the lovers had taken checks from Katy's father, cashed them for $8600, and used some of the money to buy furniture for their new apartment. Telemachos had to be killed before he learned about the checks, the prosecutor said.

Katy was also given an opportunity to plea bargain. She could plead guilty in exchange for a sentence of life imprisonment, or she could go to trial for first degree murder and take a chance on conviction and a possible death sentence. She took the gamble and rejected the plea bargain.

Fifteen months after Telemachos was shot to death in his bed, his daughter went on trial in Broward Circuit Court for his slaying. She was charged with conspiracy to kill and with first degree murder. Marcus said the state would ask for the death penalty.

The defendant's accused coconspirators each appeared as witnesses in the high profile trial, but they provided startlingly different testimony. Delvalle said he carried out the murder on his own, and his girlfriend didn't know about it until after it was over. Magona said she masterminded her father's murder because she wanted his money, and she walked into the bedroom to watch him die.

Magona's account of the murder was chilling. He told the jury that Katy quieted the dog while he and Delvalle creeped into the sleeping man's bedroom. Inside, Magona said, he peered out a window while his companion pressed Katy's revolver to her father's forehead and pressed the trigger once. A hollow-point cartridge smashed through the victim's brain.

Magona said that Katy came into the bedroom after hearing the shot, and watched while her father gagged on his own blood and desperately gasped for air. According to the witness, she didn't show any emotion, but commented on noise her father was making. "She didn't say much, except to discuss that's the way you breathe when you're choking on your blood," he said. Only a few hours earlier, she had eaten dinner with her father.

The victim was still struggling for air as his daughter and her boyfriend began ripping open drawers and dumping things on the floor, the witness continued. "They started to tear things down to make it look like a burglary," Magona said.

Mary Torres, Katy's mother, who was remarried then widowed following her divorce, was sitting behind her daughter during the grisly testimony. Mrs. Torres put her hands to her head and sobbed while the witness described the last moments of her former husband's life and the cold reaction of the young woman they both loved. The defendant meanwhile busied herself leafing through some legal papers spread out on the defense table.

Magona said that he and Katy went shopping at a department store with her father's money the day after the shooting. Katy bought a coffeepot, a can opener, and some other appliances for the apartment she and her boyfriend had just moved into.

Katy schemed her father's murder because she wanted his money and was sick of his nagging her about her boyfriends and not attending college, the witness testified. When the prosecutor asked why he joined in the murder scheme, Magona blamed peer pressure.

Delvalle told the jury he killed his sweetheart's father to stop him from interfering with their love affair. And he insisted that she didn't know of his murder plan. After making statements first that he was the gunman, then accusing his girlfriend of being the shooter, the witness had returned to the early version.

He testified that he dropped his girlfriend off at a club along the Fort Lauderdale beachfront at about eleven P.M., the night of the shooting. He and his pal Vinnie drank a couple of beers and smoked a few joints and decided to kill Katy's father, he said.

Continuing, Delvalle said he and his buddy had sneaked into the house in Cooper City and walked into the bedroom, when Telemachos woke up and said hello.

"I don't know if he was dreaming or if he knew it was me," Delvalle told the jury. He said it startled him. But a moment later he pulled Katy's .38, pressed it to her father's forehead and pulled the trigger. He said he told his girlfriend about her father's murder later that night.

"She reacted pretty badly when I told her," the witness gallantly declared. "I pleaded with her not to say anything and see how things turned out."

But the most dramatic testimony of the trial came from the defendant, who backed up her boyfriend's story that she hadn't known about the murder scheme until her father was already dead. Tears were welling from Katy's eyes and streaming down her cheeks as she told the jury that although she sometimes quarreled with her father, she would never plot his death.

Swiping at her eyes with a tissue, she sobbed, "I always loved my dad. I knew everything he worked for was for me."

The slender, five-foot-ten-inch, dark-haired young woman insisted she didn't know her father was going to be killed. "I couldn't believe he was that much in love with me that he could take my father away," she said of Delvalle.

During cross-examination, Marcus asked her if she had manipulated her boyfriend by telling him that her father was worth $2 million. "No," she softly replied.

Marcus asked if she had told Delvalle that if she continued seeing him, her father would cut off her money. "No," she said again.

The prosecutor accused her of shedding crocodile tears as she held her boyfriend's hand and cried less than a month earlier when Delvalle testified about the murder and pleaded guilty.

She denied it. "Those tears were for my father," she said.

Despite the witness's frequent tears, the jurors were stone-faced. There was no hint either of stern disapproval or of sympathy. Katy Telemachos's pleading histrionics were being played out before a tougher audience than her doting father.

And when Marcus summed up the case for the prosecution, he wasn't depicting the defendant as a sickly little girl, but as a devious master of manipulation and deceit who cold-bloodedly plotted the execution murder of her loving parent. She not only convinced her boyfriend to murder her father, but then got him to lie for her on the witness stand, the prosecutor declared.

"She even lied to Delvalle, telling him she was pregnant in jail with his baby," Marcus told the jury.

He described the twin motivations for the murder as greed and hatred.

"This case was shockingly evil," Marcus asserted. "She forfeited her father's life for money."

The jury deliberated two days before returning verdicts of guilty to both charges, conspiracy to kill, and first degree murder. Dressed in black, Katy accepted the verdict quietly but chewed nervously on her lower lip and looked as if she was struggling to hold back tears as the verdict was read. Her mother, Mary Torres, cried.

Judge Greene instructed the jury to return in three weeks to determine its recommendation of the penalty. Marcus said the prosecution would ask for execution in Florida's electric chair. The only alternative sentence for a first degree murder conviction was life in prison, with no possibility of parole for twenty-five years.

Defense attorney Howard Zeidwig told reporters he didn't believe the law would permit his client to be executed, because the admitted gunman was expected to get off with a life sentence. He said that even if it was true that his client had plotted the murder, her father would not have wanted her to be given the death penalty. And he pointed out that Katy had never previously been convicted of a crime, a factor that could be expected to work in her favor.

On December 4, 1991, the jury voted eight-to-four favoring a recommendation to Judge Greene of death in the electric chair for Katy. The recommendation was a surprise to some court watchers, who had expected more lenient handling because the defendant was female.

Although it's true that females commit far fewer murders than men, they are responsible for approximately ten percent of homicides nationwide. Yet, studies show that only about 1.5 percent of prisoners on the nation's death rows are women. And of more than 160 inmates executed between 1976 when a U. S. Supreme Court ruling permitted reinstatement of the death penalty, and the recommendation from Katy's jury in 1991, only one—serial poisoner Velma Margie Barfield, in North Carolina—was female.

No woman has ever been executed by the State in Florida, although several have been sentenced to die in the electric chair, and at the time of the trial four were on death row. One of those four would be moved off the pink-painted death row for women at the Broward Correctional Institution near Fort Lauderdale when she won a new trial before Katy's sentencing date. More than three hundred men were locked up on death row in the prison at Starke awaiting dates with the killing machine inmates call "Ol' Sparky." If Florida ever electrocutes a female, she will be transferred to a cell at Starke a day or two before the execution.

Judge Greene overruled the recommendation, and ordered a prison sentence of life plus thirty years. Ironically, the experienced jurist said he agreed that the death penalty would have been appropriate punishment.

"This case was one of the coldest, cruelest, sickest, and most offensive homicides I have ever heard," he declared. However, he said that he opted for mercy after considering the young murderess's life experiences and illnesses.

Although overruling a jury's recommendation in a capital case isn't an everyday event, it is not unprecedented. Recently, a trial judge had gone the other way when he overruled a jury recommendation of leniency for a seventeen-year-old gunman who killed three restaurant workers in a robbery, and sentenced him to death. The Florida Supreme Court reversed his order of death, however, ruling that the judge should have taken the defendant's youth and miserable childhood into consideration.

This time, Judge Greene was overruling another jury's recommendation, by ordering leniency for a particularly coldhearted killer. He read from a twenty-nine-page sentencing document, and for the first half hour as he talked about the heinousness of the crime, it appeared that he was going to comply with the jury recommendation and order death. But as the defendant began to realize that he had decided on a more lenient sentence, she softly asked her lawyer, who was standing beside her, "Am I getting life?"

He nodded his head affirmatively.

Katy began to cry. She was still sobbing as Judge Greene pronounced the sentence of life in prison, with no parole possible for twenty-five years. And she was dabbing at tears as she bent her head to kiss her mother on the cheek, while being led out of the courtroom by Broward County Corrections officers.

Her attorneys continued to fight for her freedom, however. And in documents filed with a motion for a new trial, they pointed out that she is still ill, has a limited life expectancy, and will probably need another kidney transplant in the future.

They asserted furthermore that evidence developed during the penalty phase of the trial indicates she "was an excellent daughter to her mother, and a good daughter to her father, and was an excellent friend to her best friend. . . ."

At this writing, Katy Telemachos' appeal from her conviction is pending, and she is in custody at the Broward Correctional Institution.

Chapter 5

The Girl in the Closet

Lovesick Oliver Petrovich kept his black sweetheart in a closet to protect her from his straitlaced and stubborn father. It was a love story as fanciful as any fairy tale.

But when Oliver's father learned of his son's secret love and threatened to kill her, the fairy-tale romance turned sour. And the twenty-three-year-old ne'er-do-well's thoughts turned from love to murder.

Before Oliver met Karlene Francis, his life was a classic study in failure and mind-numbing boredom. He had few friends, and kept to himself most of the time. His only long-term passion was cars; although, for a time, he developed an interest in guns and law enforcement. Even though he managed to produce average grades, he hated school. He wasn't very good at sports, and he was shy around girls. By early 1988, and already out of high school almost five years, Oliver's life seemed to be going nowhere. He was a depressingly lonely young man.

A neighbor would later recall that although Oliver was good-looking, he was a quiet boy who never seemed to have friends around. Another neighbor, who lived across the street from the Petroviches' neatly kept two-story brick and cedar house in Great Neck, Long Island, also observed that he was quiet and was seldom seen with friends, although he was well-behaved.

But a former classmate who knew Oliver in high school was more direct in describing the lonely young man. He recalled Oliver as a bit of a nerd.

Oliver's hardworking, no-nonsense father, Peter, seemed to have a lot to do with the youth's troubles. Peter Petrovich was an autocratic, domineering, and fastidious man who ruled Oliver and his mother, Anna, with an iron hand. The elder Petrovich had no patience with failure or frivolity, and Oliver's less-than-impressive school record and his obsession with cars qualified for almost nonstop criticism.

Peter Petrovich left his native Yugoslavia with his twenty-year-old bride Anna in 1964, when he was thirty-five. His first name then was "Svetozar," but he adopted the Americanized name "Peter" when he emigrated. He was an industrious and ambitious man who chafed under the restrictions imposed on him by the Communist government of his native country, and he saw a chance for a better life in the United States. He had decided that in carving out a better life for himself and his family, he would leave his old name behind, along with the Old World.

Fortune smiled on the Petroviches once they arrived in America. Less than a year after their arrival, Anna gave birth to a healthy son, whom they named Oliver. And less than fifteen years after the Petroviches emigrated from Europe, hard work and thriftiness had earned them a showpiece $500,000 brick and cedar Cape Cod house at 64 Jayson Street in an expensive and ethnically diversified neighborhood in Great Neck, and a twenty-unit apartment building in Flushing, Queens.

Although by 1988, when he was fifty-nine, Petrovich had amassed assets worth several million dollars in cash, real estate, and other holdings, he continued to hang on to his job as a supervisor with a bottling outlet in College Point, Queens. Despite the demands of his full-time job with the bottling company, however, he also personally managed and did almost all the maintenance work on his apartment building. He drove to the building to make minor repairs on weekday evenings after work at the plant. His weekends were also spent at the apartment building, usually with Anna and Oliver in tow, making major repairs and renovations, and collecting rent.

Sustained and honest work was the keystone of Peter Petrovich's life. And after barely more than two decades in the United States, his hard work, thrift, and a single-minded determination to succeed, had made it possible for Peter and Anna Petrovich to achieve the American Dream. Neighbors and other acquaintances respected the hardworking couple. They would eventually talk of Peter's industry with a near sense of awe.

Yet, despite his full-time job and the demands of managing and maintaining the apartment building, Peter still found time to work on the family's comfortable Cape Cod. If he wasn't at the bottling plant, or in Flushing, he was at home in Great Neck, working on the house, caring for the lawn, or busy with some other domestic project. He was an excellent woodcarver, and when he had time, he fashioned some beautiful pieces of work. "He was always busy with his woodcarving or fixing something," said an admiring neighbor. "Pete wasn't the type to lounge around in a hammock in the backyard, or to park himself in front of the TV and spend the day watching football or drinking beer."

Anna also made a good impression. Neighbors and friends who were fortunate enough to be invited to the Petroviches' for one of Anna's delicious home-cooked meals, always marveled at the neatness of the house. She was a fastidious housekeeper and devoted homemaker. She was also an avid gardener who loved flowers, especially impatiens. During the spring and summer seasons, strangers sometimes stopped their cars in the quiet street to admire the colorful arrangements of her front yard garden. Anna regularly delivered gifts of flowers or vegetables from her garden to neighbors.

And every morning, she was outside bright and early, sweeping the sidewalk and the street in front of her house.

During the Christmas holiday period, the Petroviches decorated their house inside and out with sparkling lights and bright ornaments. They always exchanged cards with neighbors. The frugal Anna would save the cost of stamps by slipping the cards under the front doors. The senior Petroviches enjoyed the fine house they worked so hard to acquire and maintain.

But to a lonely, unexceptional youngster like Oliver, Peter Petrovich and, to a lesser extent, Anna, were at best constant naggers. At worst, they were intolerable tyrants determined to force him to live under the same antiquated and socially constricting rules they lived by in the "Old Country."

In efforts to discourage Oliver's obsession with cars and to encourage him to earn his keep, Petrovich found his son a job as a truck driver and mechanic with a Pepsi-Cola bottling company in Mount Vernon. Although Oliver did well on the job, the encouraging performance didn't change what his parents considered to be his wasteful fascination for cars. The expense of indulging his obsession, in fact, continued to eat up most of his weekly paychecks.

Oliver had his heart set on becoming a policeman, and talked often about leaving Pepsi-Cola to go into law enforcement. He even bought an old police squad car that he tinkered with and drove. He enjoyed working with guns nearly as much as he liked cars, however, and it seemed to him that police work would permit him to indulge his passion for both. But somehow, even though Oliver once took a written test to join a local police department, he never got around to changing professions.

As winter eased into the spring of 1988, life seemed to hold little joy for the twenty-two-year-old sad sack. Then fate stepped in, and in mid-April he met Karlene in a Mount Vernon shopping mall. She wasn't a "girl next door" type. Instead, she was a tattered and forlorn Cinderella—a pathetic and hungry lost kitten.

When the skinny black girl approached him in the mall's parking lot and asked for money to buy something to eat, his heart went out to her. The appearance of the desperate, sad-eyed teenager tugged at him. It might be true that he himself was unhappy, he realized, but at least he had a warm place to sleep; clean, comfortable clothes; and all he wanted to eat. She had none of those comforts, however. Oliver offered to buy her a meal, and took her into a nearby restaurant.

As the eighteen-year-old girl dug hungrily into her food, she told her sympathetic young benefactor that she was living on her own. She supported herself as best she could with work at fast-food restaurants, but had never managed to settle down into a permanent job. It wasn't easy for a teenager on her own, with few job skills and no outside help.

Oliver was fascinated and touched by her story. Although he hadn't struck out on his own, he found it was easy to relate to what he believed were striking similarities in their lives. It appeared that they were two lonely souls in an uncaring world, misunderstood and unloved. Their stories, it seemed, were much alike.

Despite Karlene's bleak circumstances, she was bright. And Oliver could see that the girl with the unhappy eyes and turned-down mouth was pretty. And when she told him that almost no one called her "Karlene," but instead used her nickname, "Angel," he thought it was perfect. "Angel" fit the charming teenager just right, he decided.

There must have been something about Oliver, as well, that touched the young girl. It wasn't just that he was handsome; he was also kind. He hadn't hesitated to help and befriend her, when many other whites simply looked through her, as though she were not there. Some had been deliberately cruel and insulting.

Although Oliver may have appeared to others to be an unlikely Prince Charming, Angel could tell that he was genuinely nice. She liked him. And there was no question that he was attracted to her. So after finishing her meal, she agreed without question to his suggestion that they ride around for a while in his white Oldsmobile station wagon and talk.

In later remarks, she would recall her first impression of Oliver. She said that he was one of the nicest boys she had ever met.

While the unlikely couple drove around Mount Vernon, daylight faded and temperatures dropped as early evening darkness cloaked the city. Oliver thought of Angel sleeping huddled in a doorway or wrapped in cardboard to keep warm. He simply couldn't bring himself to dump her out of the car into the chill April night. More importantly, he was afraid he might never see her again if he allowed her to leave.

So he asked if she wanted to go home with him. He told her that she could sleep in his station wagon after he parked it in the garage. His parents were usually in bed by ten P.M., and there was no chance that his father would see her when he left for work in the morning, because he left his car outside.

The prospect of striking out on her own in search of a safe, warm place to sleep at such a late hour wasn't very attractive to Angel either, and Oliver's offer was tempting. Besides, she was also reluctant to end the new friendship so soon. She had enjoyed one of the most pleasant evenings she could remember. So she accepted her newfound friend's gallant offer.

By the end of the week, Oliver was slipping Angel into the house and up to his room, where she would stay all night. In the morning he would sneak her outside again on his way to work. While he worked, she hung around the mall where they had first met. Most days she would window-shop for a while, then go to a movie until he picked her up again in late afternoon.

One day during the second week after the unlikely lovers had undertaken their bizarre living arrangement, they were surprised by Anna as they walked into the living room on their way out of the house. Fortunately, Oliver's father had already left for work. Anna was understandably surprised when she learned about the family's secret house guest. But Oliver explained to his mother how they had first met, and pleaded with her to allow the homeless teenager to remain at the house during the day. He said he worried about her roaming the mall while he was working.

Reluctantly, Anna agreed to let Angel stay at the house. But she cautioned that their secret guest had to stay out of sight while Peter was home. If Oliver's father learned what was going on, the worried woman warned, they would all be in serious trouble.

For a while the arrangement worked out well enough. In the mornings after Peter left for work, Angel would come downstairs. She kept Anna company and helped her with the household chores while Oliver and Peter were away. Most days, when it was close to the time for Peter to return home, she would scurry up to Oliver's room to wait for him. But sometimes she and Oliver would arrange for her to leave the house early and meet him nearby. On those evenings, they would have dinner out, sometimes watch a movie, or simply drive around talking and enjoying each other's company.

After their nights out, however, they had to wait until the elder Petrovich went to bed before quietly slipping back inside the house together. Oliver's car, with its souped-up engine and exhaust system, was noisy, so on those nights he would park it a block away, then walk Angel the rest of the way to the house. Sometimes Oliver would sneak his girlfriend in through a window; at other times, he would simply let her in the front door. Then he would go back to get his car and drive it into the garage.

The queer subterfuge continued for several weeks.

But something was eventually bound to go wrong. Although the young sweethearts appeared to be oblivious to the danger, Anna was growing increasingly nervous. She still clung to the old-fashioned concepts of wifely loyalty, and she was tormented by guilt feelings for keeping such an explosive secret from her autocratic husband. Yet, she seemed to genuinely like Angel, and was grateful for her company. And she was pleased to see her son happy. It was as obvious as it could be that despite the young couple's weird living arrangement, Oliver and Angel were experiencing some of the happiest times they had ever known.

The happy couple's luck began to unravel during the second weekend in May. They were leaving the house when they unexpectedly ran into Oliver's father working in the yard. Peter had planned earlier to go to his apartment building, but had changed his mind at the last minute and decided to catch up on his yard work.

The moment he saw his son walk out of the front door with the girl, he began to yell. Peter was furious. But Oliver had inherited some of his angry parent's explosive temper and stubbornness. He stood his ground and screamed back at his father.

The elder Petrovich's angry accusations made Oliver quickly realize that his father thought he had picked the girl up somewhere and brought her to his room for a one-night stand. As straitlaced as he was about many things, the hardworking immigrant wasn't a puritan. He didn't seem to be all that upset because Oliver had brought a girl home and kept her in his room overnight. His outrage was focused on the fact that she was black.

As Angel stood by, helplessly watching the father and son screaming at each other, Peter turned his attention to her. He heaped racial and other insults on her, ranting and threatening. "You come back here again and I'll shoot you," he warned. At last the elder Petrovich ended the ugly confrontation by yelling at his son that if he ever saw the girl around the house again, he would kill both of them.

"My father was a racist," Oliver remarked much later. "He hated blacks, Puerto Ricans, Chinese, Japanese . . . anyone whose skin was not white. He was afraid Angel would bring black people to rob and kill us." Despite, or perhaps because of his father's racial attitudes, the only girl Oliver dated before Angel was also black.

Angel cried while she and Oliver drove away from the house. She wasn't crying so much because of the names she had been called. It wasn't the first time she had been on the receiving end of cruel racial slurs. She was more afraid of losing Oliver.

But while Angel was hurt and fearful, Oliver was furious. He was as incensed over his father's crude name-calling as he was about the hotheaded threats to kill them. And in his anger, his thoughts also turned to murder. As he raced his car along the quiet streets, he began to consider ways to free himself and his girlfriend from what he considered to be his father's stifling tyranny. It seemed that the simplest and most obvious way to free himself from the elder Petrovich was to kill him.

Oliver shared his thoughts with Angel. She was horrified and tried to talk him out of any further thoughts of committing such a terrible act. There were other more acceptable solutions. She suggested that they could run away together. But Oliver vetoed her suggestion. Where could they go? They had no money. How would they live?

Despite Angel's fears, during the next few weeks Oliver continued to toy with the idea of killing his father. In July he asked a fellow employee at the bottling plant to get him a gun. His acquaintance agreed but never followed through.

In the meantime, the brooding young man continued to sneak his girlfriend into the house. But the lovers had been caught once by Peter Petrovich, and he was already suspicious. So Oliver had to be more careful than ever before. It was more difficult to sneak Angel inside, and harder for her to leave the house unseen by her boyfriend's father.

Occasionally Peter would climb the stairs to the second floor at night while Angel was there and pound with his big fists on his son's closed bedroom door. When that happened, the startled sweethearts would jump up and Oliver would help Angel hide in his narrow walk-in closet. She would scurry inside and huddle in the cramped hiding place until Peter satisfied himself that his son was alone and leave.

Oliver would later explain that, "Angel was so skinny she could sit in a chair in the closet and not be seen." Sometimes she would sit silently on the chair, covered by a wall of books and clothing for hours until her boyfriend felt it was safe enough to tell her that everything was all clear. The narrow closet was only about six feet wide and four feet deep, and it was stiflingly hot in the summer.

While leaving the house early one morning near the middle of August, Oliver and Angel nearly got themselves into trouble a second time. Peter was again busy working on his front lawn, and Oliver spotted him barely in time to push Angel back inside the door before they were seen. Breathing sighs of relief, the shaken lovers slipped out the rear of the house.

But the constant intrigue and danger was taking its toll. The pressure was becoming unbearable. Oliver decided that he simply had to go through with his plan to kill his father. But he couldn't figure out a way to carry out the murder and get away with it. He considered one plan after another, none of them very well thought-out. He considered staging a phony hit-and-run accident with his car; an accident at his parents' apartment building in Queens; and finally, strangulation. But although Oliver was a strong young man who was a husky five feet, ten inches tall, and 190 pounds, his father was even more powerful and stockily built. Even at the age of fifty-nine, he was not a man to lightly challenge to a one-on-one life-and-death contest. Like the earlier schemes abandoned because of their impracticality or extreme risk, the plan to strangle Peter Petrovich was reluctantly discarded.

At last Oliver decided he would have to shoot his father. He selected Peter's .12-gauge Browning shotgun, which was kept in a corner of the master bedroom downstairs, as the murder weapon. The poorly thought-out plan called for covering up the slaying by staging a fake burglary at the house. But once Oliver decided to blame the killing on a burglar, he failed to follow through with any detailed planning to make the break-in look convincing. He behaved as if he expected those details to take care of themselves.

He had other concerns. Angel was still dead set against violence as a solution to their problems. And there was his mother to contend with, as well. Oliver realized that even though she had reluctantly joined in the conspiracy to hoodwink her husband in order to protect the two young sweethearts, it was impossible to believe that she would condone Peter's murder. The slaying would have to be carried out while she was away from the house. And luring her away would be difficult because she seldom went far without her husband.

The weeks drifted into September. Then, late in the month, Anna began to threaten to betray the young couple's secret to Peter. She had been growing increasingly nervous and conscience-stricken about keeping such an explosive secret from her husband, and she insisted that Oliver find some other place for Angel to stay.

Although Anna was only twenty when she left the "Old Country," she was still devoted to the traditional roles of men and women which are so much a part of the ancient cultures of the Balkans and many other areas of the world. She believed strongly that a wife should honor and, especially, obey her husband. As time went on, she had finally been faced with the painful conclusion that the happiness of her son was not worth the betrayal of her husband.

On Saturday, September 25, 1988, the string ran out on the weird charade the Petrovich family and Karlene "Angel" Francis had been living.

The last tragic hours of Peter and Anna Petrovich were later re-created by their son in statements to police. According to Oliver, his parents had invited a friend and the woman's pretty nineteen-year-old daughter for dinner that evening. "They were trying to set me up with her," Oliver explained. He pointed out that his parents' friend and her daughter were white.

Oliver didn't want Angel staying in the closet all day, so he drove her to Flushing and told her to return at seven P.M. The mother and daughter invited for dinner still hadn't arrived by the time Angel returned, so Oliver helped her scramble through the front window while his parents were in the kitchen. He saw to it that she was safely in his closet, then returned downstairs and walked into the kitchen.

By ten P.M. it was obvious that the invited guests weren't going to show up. Peter was already upset about the broken dinner engagement when Anna confessed to him that Angel had continued to hide at the house even after the ugly confrontation in the front yard that summer. And she admitted her own guilty part in the subterfuge.

Predictably, Peter greeted the tearful confession with a roar of outrage. He screamed at Oliver and he screamed at his wife. Anna's guilty apologies and attempts to explain her motives for collaborating in the deception were useless. Oliver refused to apologize, and didn't try to explain. Peter had been storming around the kitchen, ranting and threatening for almost an hour and was still bawling out Anna when Oliver stalked out.

The young man's face was flushed and he was shaking with anger. He was almost as angry with his mother for

Nancy Knuckles surrounded by her children, Debbie *(left)*, Bart and Pamela.
(© Chicago Tribune)

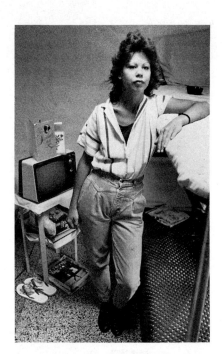

Pamela Knuckles, at the Dwight Correctional Center, after sentencing for the slaying of her mother.
(© Chicago Tribune)

Susan Cabot, in the 1958 film, *War of the Satellites*.
(The Kobal Collection)

Timothy Scott Roman with his attorney during a hearing in Van Nuys, California, prior to Roman's first trial for the slaying of his actress mother, Susan Cabot.
(Scott Garrity/*Los Angeles Daily News*)

Teresa Bickerstaff during her trial for the murder of her mother and two brothers. (Courtesy of *Medina County Gazette*)

Richard Jahnke with Sharon Lee Tilly *(left)*, a child abuse worker, as they leave the Laramie County Courthouse after the jury began deliberations to determine if Jahnke was guilty of the shooting death of his father. (AP/Wide World Photos)

Deborah Jahnke *(right)* and her mother Maria talk about their family's experiences. (AP/Wide World Photos)

Cheryl Pierson and fiancé Rob Cuccio, with the engagement ring he gave her on the day she completed serving her jail term. (*Newsday* photo, courtesy of the Los Angeles Times Syndicate International)

Sean Pica, six months after beginning his prison sentence for the contract murder of James Pierson. (*Newsday* photo, courtesy of the Los Angeles Times Syndicate International)

Ross Carlson *(left)* with attorney David Savitz at a hearing in Littleton, Colorado, to determine if Carlson was mentally capable of helping in his own defense on charges that he murdered his parents. (AP/Wide World Photos)

Patty Columbo being led from the Criminal Courts Building in Chicago to the women's lockup after sentencing for the murders of her parents and little brother.
(Ray Gora, © *Chicago Tribune*)

Frank DeLuca, Patty Columbo's boyfriend, being led from the court after having been found guilty of murder.
(© *Chicago Tribune*)

betraying his secret as he was with his father for reacting with such an outburst of rage. Oliver walked into his parents' bedroom, picked up the shotgun, and loaded three shells into the weapon.

Much later, Nassau police detective Brian Parpan would quote Oliver as telling homicide investigators that one shell was for his mother and the other two were for his father. "He knew he would need two for Peter Petrovich because he was a tough man and would be hard to kill," the detective explained.

After loading the shotgun, Oliver returned downstairs and hid the weapon under a sofa before walking into the kitchen. His mother and father were seated at the kitchen table waiting for him. But nothing had changed, and Peter greeted him with a renewed spasm of accusations and threats.

Peter demanded to know how his son dared to disobey him by bringing Angel into the house again. Oliver responded that he loved Angel.

"How can you love something like that?" his father spat back at him. "It's unnatural—like loving an animal." Peter continued to berate Oliver and Angel with a string of curses and insults. At last he ordered his son to get Angel out of his house or be thrown out with her. Then Peter stormed out of the kitchen.

When Oliver walked out of the kitchen a few moments later, he ignored his mother, who was crying. He believed that she had betrayed him, and was unmoved by her tears. He had made up his mind that she too had to die, along with his father. Retrieving the shotgun from behind the dining room sofa, Oliver carried it into the dining room on his way to the kitchen. Then he had second thoughts. If he shot his mother, the blast of the shotgun would surely alert his father. And the elder Petrovich was no one to trifle with, even if the burly man was facing a shotgun. Consequently, Oliver set the gun down, propping it against the wall near the dining room doorway. In the kitchen a few feet away Anna was standing at the sink, her shoulders slumped, miserable, as she washed dishes. She continued to cry as she scrubbed mechanically at the food stains on bowls and plates. She didn't hear the soft steps of her son as he moved stealthily into the room.

Padding softly up behind his mother, Oliver snaked out a muscular arm, trapping her neck in the crook of his elbow, and squeezed. He was trying to strangle her with a chokehold. But Anna Petrovich had long ago lost the girlish figure she had when she arrived in the United States, and her body had swelled to a solid 200 pounds. She was a formidable opponent for her homicidal son, especially when she was fighting for her life.

The mother and son thrashed furiously about the kitchen, Oliver desperately trying to maintain his chokehold while his mother wildly flailed her arms and legs, trying to escape. Finally they crashed to the floor and rolled toward the doorway. Oliver realized with a sick shock of revelation that he wasn't strong enough to strangle his mother.

But the shotgun was only a few feet away in the dining room, and the husky youth slowly began to drag the furiously struggling woman through the doorway. At last he was close enough. Releasing his hold on his mother, he grabbed for the weapon. Gasping for air, Anna rolled to her knees and groped for the kitchen table so that she could pull herself to her feet.

She was too late. Oliver was already cradling the shotgun in his arms, and he shoved the barrel against the base of his mother's skull. Then he pressed the trigger.

The results were ghastly. Blood, flesh, and brains sprayed all over the kitchen, speckling sink, walls, refrigerator, and the stove with gore. The point-blank blast with the powerful weapon literally blew half of Anna Petrovich's head away. Forensic technicians would eventually find her tongue at the far end of the kitchen table.

"It was absolute carnage. It was like a slaughterhouse," Detective Parpan would later recall. "The lower half of her face, from the upper lip to the jaw, were totally gone."

Alarmed by the commotion in the kitchen and the roar of the shotgun, Peter Petrovich slammed out of the bedroom, running toward the front of the house. His son was also in a hurry, and didn't waste time staring at the horror in the kitchen or grieving over his mother. He pumped another shell into position and headed for the bedroom with the shotgun.

Peter was in the middle of the living room and Oliver was in the dining room when they saw each other. Peter's startled eyes focused only a moment on his son's distorted face before he whirled about in mid-stride and began running back toward the master bedroom. Oliver raised the shotgun and fired.

The shot from the .12-gauge caught Peter a glancing blow on the side of his chest, the pellets chewing away bloody chunks of flesh and the impact causing him to stumble and drop to one knee. But the murderous load of shot wasn't enough to permanently stop the rugged, hardworking immigrant. Driven by fear and desperation, he staggered and crawled into the bedroom, leaving a ghastly trail of glistening red blood and flesh behind him.

Oliver watched impassively from the bedroom door as his father, now on both knees, groped desperately in the corner, apparently looking for the same shotgun that his son was holding in his hands. Calmly, without a word, Oliver strode across the floor and stopped, looming over the injured man. Then he raised the gun once again, placed the barrel against Peter's head and fired. This time it was the bedroom walls, the bed, and dresser that were sprayed and mottled with gore.

Angel was upstairs in the closet while Oliver shot his parents. When Oliver emerged from the bedroom, still clutching the shotgun, she was near hysteria. Oliver took the trembling girl in his arms and tried to calm her. He reminded her that they couldn't afford to panic. They had to control their fear and emotions. They had to think logically, he soothed. He promised her that the horror would soon be over and the money and the house would be his.

Oliver dropped the shotgun out a side window onto the lawn, in order to eliminate any chance of someone observing them carrying the weapon from the house. Then the couple went outside and Oliver turned on his Oldsmobile. As it was warming up, he retrieved the shotgun, wrapped it in a coat, and put it in the backseat of the vehicle.

With Angel at his side, he drove to the Bronx side of the Throgs Neck Bridge, at the western tip of Long Island Sound, and pulled over to the side of the road. Climbing out, he popped the hood so it would appear they were having car trouble in case police or anyone else noticed the vehicle stopped there. Then he scurried out over an outcropping of land that jutted out into the water and tossed the shotgun away. It was a plan he had devised several weeks earlier to dispose of the murder weapon.

They drove around for a while, as Oliver rehearsed to himself the story he had concocted for the police. He would tell investigators that they had been on a late date and, when they arrived home, found his parents murdered, apparently by burglars.

It was approximately four A.M. when Oliver pounded on the door of Richard Gerhardt, a neighbor.

"He rang the doorbell and said his house door was open, and there might be someone inside the house, and would I call the police," Gerhardt later recalled. "The kid was very serious. He was very scared. He was in a panic."

Within a few minutes police had surrounded the house, unsure whether or not burglars might still be inside. At about four-thirty A.M. a squad of officers charged through the front door. There were no burglars

—only the grisly, near headless corpses of Anna and Peter Petrovich.

Oliver staged an impressive act. When police officers gently advised him that his parents were inside and they were dead, he screamed and moaned, behaving as if he were insane with grief. He had to be forcibly restrained to stop him from fighting his way inside to see their bloody bodies for himself.

But Oliver wasn't dealing with amateur detectives. The investigators, working under the direction of Lieutenant John Nolan, commander of the Nassau County Police homicide squad, soon began suspecting that all was not exactly as it appeared to be.

Parpan, a sixteen-year veteran of the department, including twelve as a detective, later explained some of the reasons for the initial suspicion. There was no indication that anything had been stolen from the house, or even disturbed. "The place was as neat as a pin," he pointed out.

Police immediately separated Oliver and Angel and began to question them in detail. A female police officer told Angel they knew that Oliver had shot his parents. Oliver was "a murderer, a sick man," she said the officer claimed. "I was told I was the only person who could help him, and if I told them exactly what happened, they promised he wouldn't go to jail."

Unsure of herself and fearful about what might happen to Oliver, Angel told the investigator what she wanted to know.

She asked Angel to convince Oliver to confess. According to Angel's account, the officer told her that when she was taken to see Oliver, she should tell him that she knew he killed his parents. She was reportedly advised to assure him, however, that he didn't have to worry because he would be sent to a hospital for a while, then return home and live with her.

Angel was led into his room, and she sat down beside him. She was crying and afraid for him. But Oliver still wasn't completely convinced that he should tell the investigators what had really happened. He suspected that they may have tricked his girlfriend, and in turn were trying to trick him by telling him she had told the truth.

Then Parpan sprung a stunning surprise on the stubborn youth. "Oliver, I'm going to say only one thing to you: 'Throgs Neck Bridge!' " the detective remarked. Oliver reacted as if he was a balloon someone had just stuck with a pin. The air seemed to escape from him all at once.

"All right. You know," he sighed.

It had been an uneven contest to begin with: the naive and foolish young lovers pitted against the experienced law enforcement officers. Mercifully, with Parpan's reference to the bridge where the murder weapon was disposed of, the mental and emotional tug-of-war was over. Oliver made a lengthy videotaped confession. When the shocking statement was transferred to paper, it was seventeen pages long.

His description of how and where he had disposed of the shotgun was so precise that divers were in the water only fifteen minutes before they brought the murder weapon to the surface of the Sound.

Oliver was locked up in the Nassau County Jail on Sunday afternoon, only a few hours after the double slaying of his parents, and was formally charged with two counts of second degree murder. He remained behind bars, held without bail, while a grand jury returned an indictment on the charges. He was arraigned a few days later.

Nicholas A. Marino, a former district attorney in the Bronx who had gone into private law practice with a firm in Wantagh, was appointed by the court to defend Oliver. Faced with a written confession, it was a tough enough job, even for a seasoned veteran of the criminal courts. But Marino's task was made even more difficult by the fact that he was going up against one of the toughest, most skilled prosecutors in the state, Assistant District Attorney Dan Cotter.

One of Marino's first steps was to file a challenge to Oliver's confession, asking that it be barred from the trial. The lawyer charged that police had failed to inform his client of his constitutional rights to remain silent or to have an attorney present during questioning.

Nassau County judge John S. Thorn, Jr., denied the motion, ruling in a Mineola courtroom that Oliver "knowingly, intelligently, and voluntarily waived his rights before making . . . statements to police." Marino then raised the issue of Oliver's ability to understand the meanings of the so-called Miranda warning, advising criminal suspects of their constitutional rights against self-incrimination. Marino contended that Oliver was of abnormally low intelligence, with an IQ of only 89.

Noting that the defendant had obtained grades in the seventies and eighties while in high school, Judge Thorpe dismissed that argument, too. Oliver was "not a person of abnormal intelligence," the judge declared.

But Marino responded by attacking the confession from a new angle. He filed a new motion contending that police had unfairly used psychological coercion to break Oliver down. Marino complained that they took advantage of the strong emotional bond between Oliver and Angel to get his client to talk.

As part of the latest move to have the confession suppressed, Marino also attempted to win a grant of immunity from prosecution for Angel so that she could testify in the pretrial hearing without endangering her own freedom. The young woman risked the possibility of facing criminal charges in connection with the murders if she testified. Cotter had warned that if she took the witness stand, she would open herself up to cross-examination that might incriminate her.

While the motion for immunity was debated in the judge's chambers by the prosecution and the defense,

Oliver and Angel waited out the decision in the Mineola courtroom. Oliver was seated at the defense table, and Angel sat a few feet away in the front row of the spectator's section. The lovesick defendant blew kisses at Angel and scribbled notes on a yellow legal pad, which he held up to show to her.

In one note he groused that he hadn't received any letters from her. In others, he wanted to know how she had traveled to the courthouse, where she was staying, and asked her to visit him later that day.

Oliver relied on reading her lips for replies. Mouthing her answers, Angel said she had been looking at engagement rings. But she also said she feared visiting him at the jail because three guards had tried to pick her up the last time she showed up there.

Although Oliver appeared to be disappointed, he perked up and rewarded Angel with a contented smile when she mouthed the message: "I love you."

A newspaper story published the next day in *Newsday* disclosed that Angel had told a reporter she loved Oliver and planned to marry him soon. Oliver's attorney was also quoted as saying in an interview that his client was obsessed with the teenager. "He'd do anything for her. She was his life and still is," Marino was quoted.

Although the motion for immunity was denied after four hours of argument inside the judge's chambers, Angel elected to testify anyway. She made the decision against the advice of her attorney, Michael Burger.

Angel showed up for her court appearance looking far different than she had when she had depended solely on Oliver for her survival. "You wouldn't have recognized the first Karlene and the second Karlene as the same person," Parpan later remarked. "She was skinny and scruffy-looking when we first saw her, but in the courtroom, in the white jumpsuit, with her long hair fixed and down to her shoulders, she was quite pretty."

She did her best on the stand for her sweetheart. As Oliver looked on admiringly from the defense table, she said that while she was being questioned in the early morning hours just after the double murder, a female detective had assumed the role of her friend. She said the policewoman held her hands and told her to look in her face. Angel said the detective assured her that she was her friend. "She wouldn't lie to me, I could believe her."

Angel appeared to be struggling to hold back tears as she recounted the stressful encounter with the skilled interrogator. Oliver also seemed to be almost in tears while he watched the woman he loved reliving those difficult hours at the police precinct station house.

Responding to gentle questioning from Marino, Angel said the officer advised her that when they took her to see her sweetheart, she should tell him: "Oliver, I know you killed your parents, but you don't have to worry. You're going to go to a hospital and then you'll be able to go home and live with [Karlene]." She said that a few minutes later she was led into his room, where she sat down beside him, looked into his eyes as she had been instructed, and repeated what the investigator had told her to say.

"Based on your relationship with Oliver Petrovich, would he do what you asked him to do?," Marino asked her.

"Yes, to make me happy," she responded.

Cotter's questions weren't as gentle as those of the defense lawyer, when he approached the witness for cross-examination. The prosecutor asked Angel if she had participated in Oliver's scheme to murder his parents. Citing the U.S. Constitution's Fifth Amendment protections against self-incrimination, she refused to answer.

Despite Angel's efforts to help her sweetheart, the legal challenge to the confession was rejected. The decision wasn't surprising. Since the fairly recent introduction by law enforcement agencies of videotape to record confessions, courts have increasingly ruled against calls for suppression based on challenges that contend defendants were involuntarily or unfairly coerced.

Judges and juries can now see for themselves how a defendant has behaved while making a confession. They can see if he or she appears to be excessively frightened, exhausted or suffering from a beating. And they can listen to speech patterns. It is no longer merely a question of weighing the word of a defendant against that of the interrogators or other law enforcement officers. When the decision was made that Oliver's confession could be introduced at the trial, the prosecution was handed what was expected to become its most important single item of evidence.

During other pretrial proceedings, Cotter made a move that at least in part seemed to defuse the romantic slant that Oliver and Angel were being painted with. Although police investigators initially indicated to the press that they believed Peter Petrovich's rabid objections to his son's biracial love affair with Angel was behind the double killing, the assistant D.A. injected another element into the legal equation as a possible motive. He revealed that he believed simple greed may have been responsible for the tragedy—that Oliver wanted the family's half-million-dollar house in Great Neck, and the income-producing apartment building in Flushing.

"If Oliver had killed his parents just so he and Karlene wouldn't be separated," the prosecutor said, "he had other alternatives. They could have run away . . . they could have gone to Las Vegas and gotten married.

"He didn't have to kill them to get away from them. He killed them because he knew the house and the apartment building were worth several million dollars, and he wanted that money."

At the end of September 1989, barely a year after Peter and Anna Petrovich were shot to death in their home, their son went on trial for their brutal murder before acting Nassau County Supreme Court justice Thorp.

Dressed neatly in a new suit, Oliver sometimes sat with tears streaming down his cheeks, or slumped forward over the defense table, burying his face in his arms as Marino and Cotter squared off in the dramatic courtroom contest to determine his fate. A jury of seven men and five women had been selected to make the final decision.

In his opening statement, Cotter told the jury about the bizarre subterfuge undertaken by the young lovers; about the stern disapproval of the relationship by Peter Petrovich; and—citing Oliver's damning seventeen-page confession—about the ghastly final bloody confrontation between the hardworking parents and their only child. And he repeated his contention that the motive for the double act of parricide was a desire by Oliver to inherit his parent's properties.

"This was something that was planned and thought about for a long time, so he could inherit the house," Cotter declared. The prosecutor pointed out that there were other solutions far less drastic than double murder to Peter's opposition to the curious love match. "Why didn't he [Oliver] go to Las Vegas and get married and start a life with her [Angel]?" he asked.

Marino talked of how Oliver had found a destitute teenager, then "befriended, sheltered, and clothed her. He became her lifeline," the lawyer said. Marino told the jury that the relationship had become obsessive. He described his client as "a seriously disturbed young man" who had taken what he came to believe was the only way out of his terrible dilemma.

The lawyer also reminded the jury of his client's low IQ, which he claimed left him with defective reasoning ability. Oliver's attorney contended that his client might have been legally insane when the slayings occurred, or that he had been forced to live under such emotional stress that he was guilty only of the lesser charges of manslaughter.

The jury wasn't faced with the problem of deciding if Oliver had killed his parents. There was no question that he had. The panel instead was expected to determine why the slayings occurred and to weigh the defendant's mental abilities and emotional state at the time.

Some of the most telling moments of the trial occurred when the jury was permitted to watch and listen to the defendant's videotaped confession. The confession tape accounted for the only words the panel heard from Oliver at the trial. He declined to testify. Exercising their right not to take the witness stand is a common move by defendants in murder trials, who are thereby able to avoid damaging their own cases during cross-examination by prosecutors.

Marino did his best to convince the jury that his client had been so mentally crippled that he wasn't responsible for his actions in the double slaying. And individual jurors would later concede that the determined defense lawyer had succeeded during the near three-week trial in planting doubt in their minds about Oliver's mental competency.

But before they had an opportunity to begin debating the degree of his guilt or innocence, Oliver stepped in and made a terrible blunder. Since being jailed nearly thirteen months earlier, he had been listening to jailhouse lawyers. And he had decided to listen to the dubious counsel of his jailed cronies instead of taking his lawyer's advice.

Ignoring Marino's strong objections to the move, Oliver asked Judge Thorp at the conclusion of the trial to rule out manslaughter as a possible verdict. He requested that the court advise the jury to make an all-or-nothing decision: guilty of second degree murder or innocent by reason of insanity. The judge consented to the request.

It was a calculated risk. According to New York inheritance laws, Oliver could still become heir to his dead parents' property if he was found to be innocent— even innocent by reason of insanity. But convictions for manslaughter, although carrying a considerably reduced penalty than murder, would still make him ineligible to inherit their property.

The jury deliberated for nine hours over two days before returning twin guilty verdicts. Some jurors later told news reporters that early in the deliberations they were evenly divided over the defendant's mental competence. And if given the opportunity to return verdicts of manslaughter, they probably would have taken that option based on Marino's argument of "extreme emotional disturbance."

New York state criminal statutes at that time provided a penalty of up to sixteen and two-thirds years in prison on a conviction for manslaughter. Consequently, manslaughter, which would provide for some jail time, could have been an attractive compromise decision. But faced with an either-or decision, the jurors had decided they couldn't simply give him a free ride. Oliver had taken another foolish gamble, and fallen on his face.

Cotter said that he would ask for the maximum penalty at the sentencing. Consistent vetoes by Governor Mario Cuomo have frustrated legislative efforts to restore the death penalty in New York state's criminal code. Consequently, the most severe punishment that Oliver could face would be two concurrent terms of fifty-years-to-life in prison.

On November 13, 1989, approximately four weeks after the jury announced its verdicts of guilty to two counts of second degree murder in the shotgun slaying of Oliver's parents, Judge Thorp pronounced the maximum penalty. The two-time killer was ordered to serve twin sentences of fifty-years-to-life in the New York State prison system. Judge Thorp described the double murder as a "chilling and calculating execution," and he directed that the terms be served consecutively. Consequently, Oliver will not become eligible for parole until the year 2039, when he is seventy-three years old.

Although it appeared that Oliver's greed had done him in while playing out his dangerous gamble with the jury decision, he claimed a different motivation altogether. In a meeting with Parpan sometime later, Oliver told the police detective that he played out his dangerous gamble with the verdict because of his desire to be with Angel. He said that he didn't want to be separated from her for even a few years.

The Nassau County detective developed an odd relationship with the double murderer, as law enforcement officers sometimes do with suspects and criminals they help bring to justice and convict. He accepted collect calls from Oliver for months after the conviction and sentencing.

Angel was never charged with any wrongdoing in the case. Parpan said that Oliver eventually revealed that he hadn't heard from Angel in months. "I don't know if it's her choice or if someone has influenced her," the lawman observed. "I think they really had something going with each other, but I don't think it would have lasted very long, even if the murders had not happened.

"She is much smarter than him!"

Chapter 6

A Family Tragedy

When the Medina County Sheriff's Department initiated a nationwide search for seventeen-year-old Teresa Bickerstaff, many of her neighbors didn't expect her to be found alive.

Despite an All Points Bulletin issued to police agencies throughout Ohio to be on the lookout for the petite teenager, it seemed to be a good bet that if she was found, it would be under a pile of leaves or in a shallow grave. It appeared she had been kidnapped.

The search for the missing teen began after an early morning fire raced through the two-story property of the Fred Bickerstaff family on August 28, 1980, in rural Harrisville Township. A neighbor who telephoned the alarm reported that she heard a loud explosion about seven A.M., and when she peered out her window, saw a heavy cloud of smoke billowing from an upstairs bedroom of the house. By the time firemen from the crossroads community of Lodi arrived at the neatly kept wood-frame house on Kenner Road, quickly followed by a crowd of neighbors and curiosity seekers, it was already too late. The house was enveloped in flames.

Thirty-eight-year-old Donna K. Bickerstaff and her sons, fourteen-year-old Fred J. Bickerstaff, Jr., and thirteen-year-old Kenneth Bickerstaff were already dead. Their pitifully charred bodies were found inside the fire-gutted, year-old ranch-style house by firemen poking through the burned-out shell. The bodies of the boys were in upstairs bedrooms. Their mother's horribly charred corpse had plunged onto the first floor when the upstairs collapsed.

A maze of firetrucks from Lodi and from the Lafayette Township Fire Department, squad cars from the Medina County Sheriff's Department, rescue vehicles and ambulances, and a huge crowd of people were still gathered at the smoldering house at about nine-thirty A.M. when Fred Bickerstaff, Sr., returned home from his job at the Alcoa Aluminum Company plant in Cleveland, some forty miles north. Sheriff's officers informed the distraught family man that his wife and sons were dead.

A muscular man with thick black hair and a heavy, drooping mustache, Bickerstaff told Medina County sheriff John Ribar that he had left for his midnight shift at the foundry at about nine-thirty the previous night. The thirty-seven-year-old man said his wife and sons, and his daughter Teresa, were in the house when he left. He explained that the girl had recently returned home from California, where she was staying with an uncle.

A frantic search by firemen and sheriff's deputies through the still-smoldering debris inside the burned-out building failed to turn up any trace of the girl. Deputies who fanned out through the neighborhood to question residents of nearby houses had no better luck locating her.

The neighbor who reported the fire told investigators she had heard four or five popping noises coming from the Bickerstaff house at about two A.M., and when she peered out the window she noticed that lights were on all over the house. Another neighbor who lived about a half mile away said she telephoned the Sheriff's Department at about five A.M. and told them she smelled smoke. However, a sheriff's deputy who checked out the area around the neighbor's house notified his superiors at about five-thirty that he hadn't found anything suspicious. That was less than two hours before the house was discovered in flames.

But no one reported seeing anything of Teresa that morning, or the family's second car, a two-year-old yellow Datsun. Sheriff Ribar and other investigators began a statewide search for the missing five-foot, ninety-pound girl and the Datsun. The search was quickly expanded to a nationwide effort. Based on descriptions provided by her father and neighbors, Teresa was pretty, with shoulder-length dark hair, full lips, and the tiny build of a pixie.

The sheriff had good reason to be concerned. During a preliminary examination of the bodies at the scene, where he pronounced the victims dead, Medina County coroner Andrew Karson observed injuries that appeared to have been inflicted with a gun and knife. Consequently, he ordered the bodies transported to the Cuyahoga County Morgue in Cleveland, where more sophisticated facilities were available for autopsy.

After talking with Bickerstaff, investigators also publicly disclosed that six or eight guns were missing from a collection the foundry worker had kept in the house. One of the guns was a .357 revolver produced by Ruger, a popular German arms manufacturer.

A few days later a report from the state fire marshal's department was released, with a formal finding in the case of arson. Gasoline had been used to set the fire.

A week after the blaze, Dr. Karson confirmed what Sheriff Ribar already knew. The mother and sons were not the unfortunate victims of an accidental fire. Sheriff Ribar and his investigators had a case of multiple murder and arson on their hands.

According to the autopsies, the victims were shot with a .357-caliber magnum shell, possibly from a Smith & Wesson, Taurus—or a Ruger. Several other scorched and blackened guns were found in the rubble of the house, but it couldn't be immediately determined if any of them was the murder weapon.

Both Dr. Marilyn Cebelin, who performed the autopsies, and Dr. Karson, had yet more chilling information to share with law enforcement authorities and the press. "The gunshot wounds may have been serious enough to be fatal, but the victims were alive following the shootings, and may have died as a result of smoke inhalation," Dr. Karson disclosed. Carbon monoxide was found in Fred, Jr.'s blood, indicating he was still alive while the house was burning.

Metal fragments were found in Mrs. Bickerstaff's neck, and she also had a bullet wound in one foot. Fred, Jr., was shot in the head, chest, and shoulder and had suffered a groin injury that may have been inflicted with a knife. His brother Kenneth was shot once in the head, and stabbed ten times in the chest. Some of the stab wounds punctured his lungs. One rib was fractured, and several others showed signs of injury. The teenager's left forearm and left ring finger were also slashed, injuries that Dr. Cebelin said were probably defensive wounds.

The coroner's official finding stipulated that Mrs. Bickerstaff and Kenneth died of head injuries inflicted by gunshots. Fred died of a gunshot wound and carbon monoxide poisoning. He outlived his mother and sibling, surviving long enough to die of smoke inhalation during the fire.

The mother and sons had died horribly, at the hands of a killer acting in a frenzy of violence and hate. The slayings were an outrageous example of overkill, which can be an important tip-off to experienced homicide investigators that the killer probably wasn't a stranger to the victims. Such unbridled ruthlessness is usually an indication of a strong emotional link between the victim and the perpetrator—or the grisly work of a madman. When burglars, home invaders, or professional hit men kill, they seldom kill with such savagery.

The idea of a slight teenager like Teresa falling into

the hands of such a killer, or killers, was chilling. But investigators quickly determined abduction wasn't the only possible explanation for the girl's ominous disappearance. They learned from her father, other relatives, and acquaintances, that she was a severely troubled teenager.

Her attendance at Cloverleaf High School in Medina had been sporadic during the past couple of years. School authorities said she was twice expelled for skipping school during the 1978–79 terms, and attended only the first few weeks in 1980. She simply wouldn't show up for classes, a school spokesman explained.

During the early stages of the investigation, detectives also considered the possibility that the girl might have been involved with some sort of destructive occult practices or black magic cult. Although investigators had heard of occult ceremonies held at nearby Lake Chippewa, there was no indication that either Teresa or any other member of her family had any dealings with the cultists.

Of more concern, police quickly learned that Teresa was a streetwise nomad who had become entangled in the twin morass of drug abuse and prostitution before she was old enough to drive. She had been in almost constant trouble ever since she moved to Medina County with her family two years earlier from the blue-collar Cleveland suburb of Parma Heights.

She was already hooked on drugs at thirteen, and when she was fourteen, she ran away from home. According to the stories told to investigators, she hitchhiked cross-country to California, swapping sex to truck drivers for rides and meals. Shortly after she returned to Ohio in 1979, she entered a Cleveland hospital for treatment in its drug rehabilitation program.

While she was undergoing treatment, she met Eric J. "Scooter" Davis, a twenty-one-year-old black high school dropout from Cleveland. Almost immediately they began hanging around together. And on at least one occasion she took her new boyfriend home to meet her family in Medina County. Teresa's parents weren't pleased with the budding romance, and, Teresa would later claim, a few days before the murders and fire, her father angrily chased Davis off the property.

Several days after the arson murders occurred, Mrs. Bickerstaff and her sons were buried at Woodlawn Cemetery in Lodi. Her husband was comforted at the services by other family members and friends. His daughter was still missing.

Three classmates of the brothers in the Cloverleaf school district's eighth and ninth grades started a memorial fund to be turned over to the father of their friends. The brothers were athletic and played football for the school district.

Meanwhile, Sheriff Ribar's immediate concerns were the search for the missing girl and the Datsun. After the first few days of the nationwide search failed to produce results, the sheriff had Teresa charged in juvenile court with unauthorized use of a motor vehicle. Spokesmen pointed out to reporters that the charge was a formality, a means for law officers to legally detain the driver and vehicle if they were spotted.

As the investigation continued, the Ohio State Fire Marshal announced a $10,000 reward for arrests in connection with the arson murders. Investigators were hopeful that the reward would help, but at that point the key to solving the perplexing case appeared to be tied to finding the missing girl and the car.

On October 3, 1980, U.S. Customs officials alerted by the All Points Bulletin stopped the yellow Datsun as it was being driven across a border checkpoint at Detroit from Windsor, Canada. The car was being driven by a young black man, with a young white woman as a passenger. Several guns and a switchblade knife were found inside the vehicle. The knife was bloodstained, although laboratory technicians were unable to determine in later tests if the blood was human.

After lengthy questioning, the pair identified themselves as Teresa Bickerstaff and Eric Davis. Sheriff Ribar sent Detective James Williams to Detroit, where he was joined by Pat Berarducci, a U.S. Bureau of Alcohol, Tobacco, and Firearms special agent from the agency's Cleveland office. Together, they interrogated the two fugitives.

Within an hour the runaway lovers were tape recording detailed statements, pinpointing their roles in the ruthless arson-slayings. Teresa confessed that she killed her mother and brothers while her boyfriend started the fire to cover up the murders. Davis made a second tape-recorded statement two days later.

According to Teresa's account, she was planning to leave home, and her boyfriend arrived at the house some time after two A.M. to pick her up. He loaded her father's .357 Ruger, which she had taken from a dresser drawer, and gave it to her. Long before the couple was apprehended, investigators had already recovered a box of .357 magnum cartridges from the recreation room of the fire-gutted house. Crime technicians turned up three of Teresa's fingerprints on the inside flap.

Continuing her story, the girl said she carried the revolver with her when she walked upstairs to pack some clothes. Then her mother awakened and called to her from the master bedroom.

"I don't know what happened. She just went off, and I went off, and the gun went off," Teresa explained. The teenager said she was frightened.

Kenneth began yelling when he heard the gunshot, and she went into his room and shot him, she said. Then Fred, Jr., rushed at her.

"Freddy came running at me with a pillow, calling me a bitch and a whore because he saw my mother drop. He saw her die," she related. She said she shot him, then, without even stopping to think, she shot each of the boys a second time.

"Freddy was just moaning and stuff and making me

crazier than I already was," she stated. "I kept scream-ing, and they weren't dying, and it was tripping me out."

The teenager said that as she returned downstairs with her clothes, "Freddy was still moaning, and Scooter was saying, 'He'll die! He'll die!' " Curiously, despite the knife wounds found on the bodies, Teresa said nothing at all about stabbing any of the victims.

Davis also claimed the murders weren't planned. He said he had agreed to meet his girlfriend at the house, and they intended only to leave together and take the car. But he admitted loading the revolver and giving it to her while they were in the downstairs living room. Then they walked upstairs together.

Davis didn't describe the attack on the boys, but he later told officers, "Teresa was running around hollering that her brother wasn't dead. She shot him again."

The situation became so confusing that he couldn't remember everything in its proper sequence, the Cleve-land youth told his interrogators. "I just tried to get her out of there as fast as I could," he said. "I went back into the house and just threw a gas can and lit a match. I did it on the spur of the moment. I was scared, just scared."

In his initial statement, Davis said he tossed the gun out the window of the car on the way to Detroit. When he was questioned again two days later, however, he changed his story and claimed he gave the murder weapon to a friend in Cleveland he identified only as "Rick."

Teresa's life at home was so unbearable that she de-cided to leave and asked him to come pick her up, Davis continued. He claimed her father beat and verbally mis-treated her. Davis said that when he arrived at the house to pick her up on August 26, her face and arms were bruised. He also quoted Teresa as telling him that earlier that day her brother, Fred, Jr., offered her to a buddy of his for sex. When she broke away from the boys and ran to her room, her mother laughed, according to the story.

The sweethearts explained that they crossed into Canada at Niagara Falls the day after the murders. Davis, who had studied welding, worked for a while in an auto body shop, and also tended cattle for a time while they were in Canada. But after he lost both jobs, they decided to return to the United States and head for Mexico.

Two days after their apprehension at the border, Teresa and her boyfriend were returned to Ohio and locked in separate cells at the old red-brick Medina County Jail behind the courthouse in Medina.

Teresa was charged in Medina County Juvenile Court with three counts of aggravated murder, and grand theft auto. Davis was held on temporary charges of auto theft and possession of a stolen credit card.

When Teresa was escorted from the county jail to juvenile court for a hearing to establish just cause for holding her in temporary custody, she was accompanied by law enforcement officers and a clergyman. The Reverend John Hood, pastor of the Lodi United Church of Christ, told reporters he had talked and prayed with her at the request of her father.

One week after the couple's apprehension, a Medina County grand jury indicted Davis on three counts of aggravated murder, four counts of aggravated robbery, and two counts of receiving stolen property. Bail was set at $100,000. At his arraignment, he pleaded not guilty to all charges. Four counts of aggravated arson would later be added.

Possible grand jury action against Teresa was temporarily delayed until Medina County Juvenile Court Judge H. Dennis Dannley determined if she should stand trial as a juvenile or as an adult. A few weeks later he ruled that she would be treated as an adult, and the grand jury indicted her on three counts of aggravated murder.

Attorney James R. McIlvaine of the nearby town of
Wadsworth was appointed by the court to represent the
girl, and he requested a delay of arraignment until she
could be psychiatrically evaluated. The lawyer told
Common Pleas Court judge Phillip Baird that there
were strong suggestions she suffered severe mental
problems and was not mentally capable of assisting in
her own defense. Over the protests of the prosecution,
Judge Baird granted the continuance, and established
bail at $100,000, the same amount her boyfriend was
being held on.

Several weeks later, Teresa entered pleas of not guilty
on all charges. McIlvaine explained to reporters that
results of his client's psychiatric testing weren't yet complete, and her not guilty plea didn't preclude the possibility of a later change of plea to not guilty by reason of
insanity.

Davis meanwhile busied himself in his cell composing
a series of nineteen handwritten letters to his girlfriend.
The notes eventually wound up in the hands of Teresa's
defense lawyer.

Early in the new year, as Teresa and her boyfriend
remained in jail unable to raise bail, Medina County's
newly elected prosecutor, Gregory Happ, filed additional charges against Davis. Davis, who was represented by Cleveland attorney James Willis, was named
on three new counts of aggravated murder by reason of
aggravated robbery, and on three counts of aggravated
robbery. He entered pleas of not guilty to the new
charges.

Happ, who had defeated a two-term incumbent, told
reporters he decided the additional charges should be
filed after reevaluating the evidence against the couple.

On April 22, 1981, almost seven full months after the
murders, Davis's trial began in the old courthouse that
dominates the Medina town square. The shocking slayings of Mrs. Bickerstaff and her sons, and the arrest of
her daughter and Teresa's boyfriend, was already the

most sensational murder case in the history of the county. A crowd of curiosity seekers was waiting on the blustery mid-spring morning when the courthouse doors opened. And the trial promised to add even more titillation, and horror, to what was already known by area residents about the family tragedy.

Happ rejected a last-minute plea bargain offer by Davis's defense lawyer shortly before the trial began. The prosecutor confirmed to the press after the conclusion of the trial that Willis had offered to have his client plead guilty to three charges of manslaughter. But Happ was determined to seek convictions against Davis on the more serious felony murder charges which would carry much longer jail terms.

Although police and prosecutors had been unable to locate the Ruger .357 believed to be the main murder weapon, they had collected a dazzling array of other evidence for presentation in the trial. And they had rounded up dozens of potential witnesses.

Attorneys took two days to select a jury of eight men and four women. The fireworks began two days later, with accusations during opening statements by the defense that incest allegedly committed by Teresa's father was at the heart of the case. According to Willis's impassioned opening, Davis was an innocent bystander who was struck by the fallout when the girl's long-festering anger and hatred exploded into violence. The lawyer painted a word picture of his client as a black man who fell in love with a troubled girl and became a victim of forces set in motion by someone else when he tried to help her. The lawyer claimed the evidence would show how a family could be destroyed "by sex, incest, and bigotry."

Willis claimed the girl was sexually abused since she was an eleven-year-old sixth-grade student, and that the behavior continued until she was fourteen. At the age of fourteen she was already a drug addict, and ran away to

Cleveland, where she became involved with a pimp and worked as a prostitute, he said.

The defense lawyer said the girl continued her prostitution, including stints at truck stops in Chicago and Wisconsin, before returning to Cleveland and entering the drug treatment program at a psychiatric hospital. It was there she met Davis, who was visiting the hospital, Willis said.

"Eric Davis broke her of her drug addiction and prostitution and took her back to her family," he declared. According to Willis, the efforts of the young miracle worker who rescued the troubled girl from the streets weren't appreciated, however, and when she returned home, she was greeted with brutality. So the couple planned to run away together, and never planned to kill anyone. But the innocent scheme went terribly wrong when Mrs. Bickerstaff awakened as her daughter was preparing to pack her clothes.

"Teresa lost it and shot her. And then she shot her brothers," Willis declared.

"The evidence will show that Eric Davis started a fire, and that dead people burned," he told the jury. The lawyer conceded only that his client set the fire, and firmly denied that Davis committed murder.

Happ, who was joined at the trial by Assistant Prosecutor John Porter, used his opening statement to portray Davis as the puppet master who set up the crime. "Eric Davis instructed Teresa Bickerstaff to carry out his plans with him," Happ declared.

The prosecutor told the jury that Davis confessed telephoning the girl earlier that evening and instructing her to gather up guns that were in the house, "just in case"; that he admitted loading the murder weapon; admitted standing next to Teresa when she shot her family members; and confessed pouring the gasoline.

Teresa's father was the first witness called by the prosecution, and he identified as his property the missing .357 Ruger and several other pistols and rifles, ammunition, and the switchblade knife found in the Datsun when the couple was taken into custody.

During cross-examination, however, Judge Baird sustained objections from Porter and forbid Willis to pursue questions about the allegations of incest.

When Bickerstaff was asked if he objected to his daughter's relationship with the defendant because Davis was black, he replied: "I felt the same way you would feel if your daughter was marrying a white man. I don't believe in mixed marriages," he told the black defense attorney.

Prosecutors scored points for their case against the defense allegation that Bickerstaff had physically abused his daughter, when a teenage pal of the brothers testified he often saw Teresa around her home and never noticed bruises or other signs that she had been beaten. The testimony seemed to contradict both Willis's opening statements that the girl's father physically abused her and Davis's claims that he and Teresa planned to run away together because she was fed up with being beaten.

Peter Petrokis, an Ohio State Fire Marshal's investigator, testified that he found evidence of three different fires in the Bickerstaff house. Traces of gasoline were found in an upstairs hallway, the stairway, on the main floor, and on Mrs. Bickerstaff's clothing, he said. The witness explained that the fire smoldered for several hours in the enclosed house until all the oxygen was exhausted, and the pressure caused an explosion that shattered the windows.

"The fire was not accidental. It was caused by a person or persons," he testified.

Dr. Lester Adelson, a deputy Cuyahoga County coroner, disclosed during testimony that both Kenneth and Fred, Jr., may have been alive when the fire roared through the house. Expanding on the autopsy report which showed Fred was alive, because the level of carbon monoxide found in his bloodstream revealed he'd been breathing smoke, Dr. Adelson said that blisters found on Kenneth's thigh indicated he was still living when the fire occurred.

"A person must be alive to form water blisters. Dead people don't blister," he explained. As Dr. Adelson identified gunshot and stab wounds on the bodies, blow-ups of color photographs taken of the brothers shortly before the autopsies begun were projected on a screen for the jurors. Repeated efforts by Willis to block their use were turned down by the judge.

During cross-examination, Willis attempted to get the pathologist to pinpoint a single cause of death for Fred, Jr., but Dr. Adelson refused to refute the autopsy report. "How much did the carbon monoxide contribute to Fred's death, is the question you're asking," he responded at one point. "The answer is both were causes —the gunshot and the carbon monoxide."

The witness indicated, however, that it wasn't known if the teenager could have survived the shooting if there had been no fire and carbon monoxide in his lungs. The autopsy had shown there was soot in the boy's throat. "Fred was alive in the fire and breathing smoke. Breathing is living," the pathologist said.

The point Willis was attempting to make was an important one. Teresa had admitted during her interrogation in Detroit that she shot her mother and brothers. Davis admitted setting the fire. Consequently, if the victims died from gunshot wounds, it would indicate that Teresa was the actual killer. If carbon monoxide or burns resulting from the fire caused the deaths, then direct blame could be placed on the defendant.

At the conclusion of the defense's case, Judge Baird directed acquittals for Davis on two charges of aggravated murder by arson in the deaths of Mrs. Bickerstaff and her son Kenneth. The jurist ruled that there was insufficient evidence to support the charges.

The two witnesses whom spectators were most anxious to hear from, however, were the defendant and the pretty young woman who reputedly joined with him in the slaughter of three members of her family. Both were called as witnesses by the defense. But Teresa's appearance on the witness stand was brief and disappointing. Citing the advice of her attorney, she exercised her constitutional rights under the Fifth Amendment to refuse to answer questions on grounds her statements might be self-incriminating.

The testimony of Davis, who was the last witness called in the trial, was longer and more revealing. He repeated his claim that the slayings were unplanned, and that he and his girlfriend were merely preparing to run away together. And he continued to blame the shooting and stabbing on Teresa.

When Porter asked during cross-examination if the defendant had seen Teresa's brothers after they were shot, he replied, "Just in passing. I didn't stop to look."

Porter asked if Teresa had told him after the shootings that the boys were still alive. "Yes, something to that effect," he responded.

Davis explained that he was walking down the stairway from the second-floor bedrooms carrying two bags of his girlfriend's clothing when he heard another shot. "But you said five or six times that you heard no other shots," the prosecutor reminded him. Porter demanded to know whom he had lied to, the law enforcement officer he had made the earlier statement to, or to the jury.

"I sort of twisted it a little bit in the statement," Davis said of his confession.

Continuing his account under the sharp questioning of the assistant prosecutor, Davis said that after hearing the last shot, he took the weapon from his girlfriend and walked into Mrs. Bickerstaff's bedroom to collect additional guns kept there. He said he draped a sheet over the dead woman's body.

"Did you look at her?" Porter asked. "I didn't stare," the defendant answered. Continuing to reply to questions, Davis said she wasn't moaning, and he didn't check to see if she was dead or alive. And he didn't call for an ambulance.

Davis told the court he reloaded the empty gun, took a set of car keys from Mrs. Bickerstaff's purse, and went downstairs with Teresa and into the garage where the Datsun was kept. Before taking the car, however, he picked up a five-gallon can of gasoline from the garage, hurled it into the hallway, and tossed a lighted match after it.

A look of astonishment crossed the assistant prosecutor's face at the testimony about the gas can and the match. "Are you telling the jury you didn't pour any gas?" he asked. "Yes sir," Davis responded.

It was a perplexing statement that seemed to conflict with the arson investigator's earlier testimony about finding traces of gasoline at several locations in the house. But it wasn't the only bit of Davis's testimony that conflicted with the statements of earlier witnesses. He claimed neither he nor his girlfriend stabbed her brothers. The coroner had testified, however, that Kenneth was stabbed more than a dozen times, and Fred, Jr., was stabbed once.

Turning to the subject of Teresa's illicit substances abuse, Porter asked the defendant if he had given her any drugs. "No more than reefer," Davis said, using a street name for marijuana.

Porter asked if he had ever given her PCP, a powerful animal tranquilizer that street users refer to as Angel Dust.

"Probably on some occasions, yes sir," Davis conceded.

Porter asked if she got very high when she was using the drugs. "Nothing she couldn't handle," the defendant replied.

On a sunlit Friday morning and afternoon eight days after the trial opened, the defense attorney and the prosecuting team delivered their summations to the jury.

Willis continued to point his finger at racism for a share of the blame in the tragedy by recalling his exchange with Bickerstaff over the question of interracial marriage.

"Deep are the roots of prejudice and bigotry," he intoned to the all-white jury. "And they must be deep in the hearts of the Fred Bickerstaffs of this world."

The defense attorney also attacked his client's confessions, claiming that Davis was hoodwinked by a slick-talking BATF agent. "He signed away his rights so many times it was unbelievable. They were trying to dig a hole for him," he complained.

When it was the prosecution's turn, Porter scoffed at the idea that Davis was motivated to go to the Bickerstaff house on the night of the murder by a desire to protect Teresa.

"Is he a protector? Does a protector give his lady friend Angel Dust? Does a protector plan to rob his girlfriend's house?" the assistant prosecutor demanded. "He's not a protector. He's a manipulator. All he had to do was pull the strings on that puppet."

Porter observed that several members of the defendant's family had attended every day of the trial. "But consider the fact that the Bickerstaff family could not be here," he said. The deputy prosecutor also defended Teresa's father against the accusations by the defendant and defense attorney that Bickerstaff had sexually and physically abused her. "Mr. Fred Bickerstaff only came in here to identify property, and Mr. Willis subjected him to uncorroborated innuendo," Porter complained.

The jury deliberated more than eleven hours over parts of two days before informing the court at about seven o'clock on a Saturday night that they had reached a decision. The panel returned verdicts of guilty to three counts of aggravated murder, three counts of aggravated robbery, and four lesser charges. The jury re-

turned not guilty verdicts on three charges of
aggravated arson. Flanked by his attorney, Davis
showed no emotion as Judge Baird read the verdicts.
The judge scheduled sentencing for eight weeks later, at
the end of June, in order to give authorities with the
Medina Adult Probation Department time to make an
evaluation and recommendation.

Each of the six controversial new felony charges filed
against Davis after Happ assumed the office of prosecutor were included in the convictions.

Davis was permitted to confer briefly with his attorney, and to hug his mother and other members of his
family before he was led from the courtroom by sheriff's
deputies.

According to the Ohio state criminal code at the time,
a life sentence was mandatory for an aggravated murder
conviction. The judge, however, would have consider-
able leeway in determining whether Davis's various sentences should be served concurrently or consecutively.
Depending on the judge's decisions, the convicted man
could eventually be released from prison while he was
still relatively young or he could remain behind bars
until old age or death.

When Davis reappeared in court on Monday morning, June 29, his attorney asked the judge to order all
the prison terms served concurrently with the life sentences. Willis pointed out that his client was from a
good family and had no previous criminal record. "Mr.
Davis was caught up in something bigger than he is. I
ask the court to be merciful," the Cleveland attorney
pleaded.

Davis declined an opportunity to make a presentencing statement.

A few minutes later Judge Baird ordered him to serve
three life terms in prison for the murder convictions,
and three terms of from five to twenty-five years in
prison on the robbery counts. Davis was also ordered to
serve separate five- to twenty-five-year terms for invol-

untary manslaughter and for aggravated arson, and
terms of from two to five years each for grand theft and
for receiving stolen property. The judge stipulated all
the sentences to be served concurrently, except for the
last two counts, which were to be served after the life
terms. And he ordered that Davis be given credit for
269 days already served in jail.

Despite what appeared to be a staggering number of
years extending more than three lifetimes, the sentencing order was framed so that Davis would become eligible for parole in about fifteen years.

A few days after sentencing, Davis was transferred
from the county jail behind the courthouse to the Columbus Correctional Facility, where his permanent assignment to a state prison would be determined.

Teresa wasn't as easy to bring to trial as her convicted
sweetheart. The court was buried under a barrage of
motions and a maze of mind-boggling delays that resulted in five postponements of trial dates.

Her trial was about to begin on May 19, less than
three weeks after Davis's conviction, when she pleaded
guilty on the scheduled opening day to the single charge
against her of grand theft for stealing the family Datsun
and the guns. It appeared that the surprise move was a
brilliant maneuver by the defense, because McIlvaine
followed up the court's acceptance of the plea by asking
that six other counts linked to the theft charge be dismissed. The defense lawyer argued that since those
charges stemmed from a single theft she had already
pleaded guilty to, trying her for those reputed offenses
would violate her constitutional rights by placing her in
double jeopardy.

Judge Baird agreed with the argument and, over prosecution objections, dismissed three counts of aggravated
murder and three counts of aggravated robbery. The
prosecution appealed the judge's decision, and was subsequently upheld in the higher courts. The Ninth Ohio
District Court of Appeals in nearby Akron ordered re-

instatement of the charges. After Ohio's Supreme Court refused to hear a defense appeal of the reinstatement, Teresa's trial finally got under way on January 20, 1982. Her mother and brothers had been dead nearly a year and a half.

Despite the bitter cold of the midwinter day, men and women began lining up as early as seven A.M. to get seats in Judge Baird's courtroom for the trial that experts were predicting would last as long as three weeks. This time, not only Davis, but Teresa as well, were expected to tell their stories. The Ruger .357 was still missing.

Despite some early concern that the pervasive publicity surrounding the case might make it impossible to pick an impartial jury from Medina County, three days later a panel of nine women and three men was sworn in.

During jury selection, McIlvaine had cautioned prospective members of the panel that some of the evidence would be "ugly, gruesome, and shocking to our senses of decency and our moral codes." Prospective jurors were closely questioned about their attitudes toward interracial couples and a defendant who had been a runaway and prostitute, abused drugs and skipped school. One man was dismissed by McIlvaine after admitting he disapproved of interracial couples.

When opening arguments began the next day, the courtroom was packed with print and electronic media reporters from throughout northern Ohio, as well as other spectators, anxious to hear the most notorious murder trial in the history of rural Medina County. People who couldn't squeeze into Courtroom Number 2 waited in the hallway.

McIlvaine had barely begun his statements when he told the jury that the gunman who shot the Bickerstaffs was Davis, not the eighteen-year-old girl the prosecution claimed was the shooter. Teresa let her boyfriend in the house, but Davis pulled the trigger, the lawyer claimed.

The defense attorney said Teresa was on the main floor when Davis walked upstairs with the revolver and she suddenly heard gunshots. Tracing her new account of the events, McIlvaine said: "She has no knowledge of who has been shot. Her brothers have weapons. She runs upstairs and sees her mother lying there. She dropped to her knees and cradled her mother in her arms." Jurors listened quietly, their faces immobile as he outlined the touching scenario.

McIlvaine said his client lied in her earlier statements to police in an effort to protect the man she loved. But she decided she couldn't continue the charade after Davis wrote to her in jail asking her to provide further cover-up for him by claiming her mother and brothers had already been shot before she even let him into the house, the defense lawyer continued.

As Willis had done, McIlvaine also accused Teresa's father of initiating an incestuous relationship with her when she was in the sixth grade, and continuing the reputed sexual abuse for almost three years. The lawyer blamed what he said was Teresa's sexual abuse for her behavior change and troubles with truancy, running away, drugs, and prostitution.

The prosecution hadn't changed its contention that Teresa herself had wielded the gun and the knife against her mother and brothers, however. In Happ's opening statement, he pointed to the taped confession she made to investigators in Detroit, and assured the jury that the statement would be placed into evidence to show she had admitted the shootings. He said testimony would also be introduced to back up the statement.

"We will prove beyond a reasonable doubt that Teresa Bickerstaff murdered her mother and her two brothers," the prosecutor promised.

Teresa's father got his chance to deny the outrageous accusations against him when he was called to testify as the first prosecution witness. During direct questioning by Porter, then during cross-examination from McIlvaine, the sturdy widower denied that he had ever had sexual relations with his daughter.

"I never had sexual intercourse with Teresa," he told the prosecutor. When Porter asked him to face the jury and answer the question, he turned to look at the panel and, speaking in a strong, audible voice, firmly repeated his denial. Prosecutors would later support Teresa's father's strong denial, telling reporters that the incest allegation was never established.

As he had done in the earlier trial, the Cleveland factory worker identified guns found in the house by investigators, and the switchblade knife taken from the Datsun after his daughter and her boyfriend were apprehended in Detroit. He testified that he had owned a Ruger .357. And he explained the floor plan of his house.

At the prosecutor's request, Bickerstaff read the jury two letters his daughter wrote to him shortly after she was locked up in the county jail. The letters, which the witness identified as being in Teresa's handwriting, contained an explanation of the events that occurred in their house on the night of the murders. It was similar to the statement she had given to investigators when she was questioned in Detroit.

In the notes, she said she loved her mother and brothers, but didn't want her father to blame her boyfriend, whom she referred to as "Scooter." Without him, she said, she might have committed suicide. His race was not important to her. That's just the way he was born.

Later, when the prosecution showed pictures of the family to jurors, Teresa broke into tears. Her sobbing increased as the panel was shown a photo of her brothers in their baseball uniforms. And she turned her head away when the prosecutor produced gruesome color slides for the panel of the horrendously charred bodies of her mother and brothers. Even some of the jurors had trouble dealing with the unpleasant images, and their faces paled while they grimaced in revulsion.

Several other witnesses were called by the prosecution during the first day of testimony, including neighbors who stated that they had seen the defendant at various times before the fire but never noticed any bruises on her face or body. One of the neighbors described her as a little shy.

In later testimony, Dr. Cebelin described the injuries to the victims which she noted during the autopsy. The former Cuyahoga County pathologist said Mrs. Bickerstaff was so badly burned that it wasn't possible to determine how many times she was shot in the head. She testified that Kenneth was stabbed before he was shot. And she indicated that Fred's groin injury may not have been a stab wound, but damage inflicted by the fire. The body was in such poor condition that it wasn't possible to make an exact determination.

An uncle of Teresa's from Toledo told the jury that he and his family stayed overnight at the Bickerstaff house earlier on the week of the murders and he overheard his niece in a telephone conversation at about two A.M. She mentioned that her aunt and uncle were there, then appeared to reply to a question. He quoted her as saying, "Thursday? I'll think about it." Earlier testimony had already established that the murders occurred in the predawn hours of Friday morning.

The uncle told the jury Teresa was treated like a queen at home, and spent most of her time watching television. He also recalled, however, that one of the boys confided to him that he hated his sister. While he was talking with Teresa once, she told him a story about a pimp who was shot to death in front of her by a woman in Cleveland. She didn't appear upset while she was recounting the incident, the witness said.

Just before resting their case, prosecutors played the tape of Teresa's confession in Detroit. In the confession she admitted shooting her mother and brothers, gathering up her clothes, and climbing into the car in the garage. Her boyfriend asked if there was any gasoline around, then disappeared back inside the house. He returned a few minutes later and they drove away, according to the account.

McIlvaine called the defendant to testify on the sixth day of the trial, and she told the jury she lied in her confession to police to protect her boyfriend. Davis murdered her mother and brothers, she said.

Responding in a voice that was soft but audible to questions from her attorney, she claimed she hatched the idea of taking the blame for the shootings while she and Davis were still in Canada. "Well, I had decided it would be better for me to take the case because I was a juvenile and had been put away three times," she explained to the silent jury. "Scooter was older and black. It would be harder on him."

She said she changed her mind after Davis wrote her in jail asking her to say he wasn't even in the house when the slayings occurred. Teresa's lawyer read two of Davis's letters for the jury, suggesting that she take the blame and plead insanity.

Teresa said she had already done so much for her sweetheart that it hurt her feelings when he asked for still more. The teenager continued to claim, however, that she and Davis never planned to kill anyone, but were merely preparing to run away. She said they decided she should leave home after her father chased her boyfriend down the driveway, then beat her.

The faces of the jurors were set and grim as she continued her chilling account, testifying that after her boyfriend arrived at the house, he loaded the gun she had stolen from her father's dresser and they talked until her mother called from upstairs. Teresa said she started upstairs, but Davis stopped her and said he would talk to her mother instead.

"He went upstairs, and the next thing I heard was a gunshot," she related. Teresa said she ran upstairs, found her mother on the floor, and bent over to hold the stricken woman in her arms. She claimed that her memory of events immediately after that were hazy or nonexistent. "I heard other gunshots," she said, allowing her voice to trail off slightly. "I don't know if that was in my mind. I wasn't all together." Full awareness didn't return to her until her boyfriend had taken her to the garage and helped her into the car, according to the account.

As Teresa testified, she was dwarfed by the witness chair and appeared much younger than eighteen, her age at that time. But the story she was telling was no little girl's fairy tale. It was the stuff of nightmares, of real-life ogres and bloodthirsty trolls. She told the jury about her life as a prostitute, how she ran away from home when she was fourteen and swapped sex for rides with truck drivers, about her drug abuse, and about the abortion she had when she was sixteen. And she accused her father of sexually abusing her when she was in the sixth grade, and continuing to bother her almost every night until she was fourteen.

When Porter asked during cross-examination if she saw her brothers after they were shot, she replied that she didn't. "When I went upstairs, I didn't even see Scooter. I only remember seeing my mother."

Porter asked if she knew who shot the boys. "It's obvious, I think, who shot them, but I didn't see it," she responded. When Porter continued to press for a name, she replied, "It had to have been Scooter." Throughout her testimony, she referred to Davis by his nickname.

Turning to a new area of inquiry, Porter asked her if she had once threatened a woman she was living with in Cleveland with a gun. The witness denied that she had.

But the prosecution called a rebuttal witness, whose testimony indicated the teenager was lying. The Cleveland woman said Teresa pulled a gun on her during a quarrel and complained that she was fed up with being given orders and with her friend's efforts to run her life.

She quoted Teresa as saying she didn't want to hurt her but was being forced to. The girl once fired the gun out a window of the house at a parked pickup truck, and was proud that she knew how to operate the weapon, the witness said. She explained that Teresa and Davis lived with her and her husband for three months. Teresa was in tears when the testimony was concluded.

The only other witness called by McIlvaine was a young woman who testified that she and the defendant were pals when they were in the sixth grade and Teresa had told her about the reputed sexual abuse.

Defense attorney McIlvaine didn't ask for an acquittal during his summation. He told the jury that his client was guilty of manslaughter, but that she was telling the truth when she testified, repudiating her earlier confession and blaming Davis for the murders. Her confessions didn't match the physical evidence, he said. "Had they looked further, had they not closed the case, they would have seen that."

According to the scenario the defense attorney outlined for the jury, Davis shot Teresa's mother and brother Fred, and when he ran out of bullets, stabbed Kenneth. Once Kenneth was injured and unable to defend himself, Davis then reloaded the gun and fired the fatal shot into the thirteen-year-old's head.

McIlvaine also pounced on the absence in his client's early confessions of any mention of stabbing the victims. "The only reason you wouldn't tell the truth if you are, as they say, confessing to everything, is because you didn't do it. Why not tell?" he asked. "It's no more heinous than anything else you're telling."

Finally turning to the allegations of incest, the defense attorney told the jury that when his client was twelve years old, her father had planted "the seeds of destruction" that culminated in the tragedy of the murders.

The prosecution team painted a different picture for the jurors than the scenario outlined by McIlvaine, insisting that the defendant shot her mother and brothers and was guilty of premeditated murder. In his closing argument prior to the defense summation, Happ told the jury the defendant lied when she testified her boyfriend did the shooting.

The prosecutor also pointed to her statements to police that she shot her brothers a second time because she wanted to end their suffering, as evidence of premeditation. "She had to take the time to think that she wanted to put them out of their misery," he declared.

Asserting she committed the "ultimate theft," he declared: "She stole Fred Bickerstaff's wife and his two sons. They are guilty of loving her, and for that they paid the ultimate price."

Speaking in rebuttal after the defense's closing, Potter cautioned the jury not to make their determination on the basis of a side issue in the case, such as the allegations of incest. "If you allow Teresa Bickerstaff to walk out of here on manslaughter, it cannot be based on the evidence heard," he declared. "It could only be because you decided on a collateral issue that has nothing to do with this case."

The jury deliberated twelve hours over portions of two days before returning with a package of Saturday afternoon verdicts. Teresa remained seated quietly beside her attorney as Judge Baird read the findings of guilty to six charges of murder, including three by reason of aggravated robbery and three charges of aggravated robbery. She was found not guilty of aggravated murder by premeditation. The verdicts represented almost a total victory for the prosecution. The three murder convictions linked to robbery carried mandatory life prison sentences.

As Teresa was led from the courtroom back to the jail to await sentencing, she showed little emotion. She was composed, as she had been throughout most of the grueling seven-day trial. As the defendant in the grisly and lurid murder trial, she behaved like a near perfect ice-maiden, except for the two brief occasions when she broke into tears as the grisly slides of her murdered brothers were shown and her former friend testified against her.

Seven days after the jury's decisions were reported, she was led back into the courtroom, where Judge Baird sentenced her to multiple prison terms designed to keep her behind bars for more than thirteen years before she would become eligible for parole in 1995.

The sentences included a life term for the murder of her mother; twin fifteen-years-to-life terms for the murder of her brothers; five-to-twenty-five-year terms on each of the aggravated robbery convictions; and two-to-five years on the grand theft she had pleaded guilty to for stealing the car and guns. Judge Baird ordered all the terms to be served concurrently, except for the two fifteen-year-to-life sentences in her brothers' slayings. And he gave her credit for the 491 days already spent in jail.

A few days later Teresa was driven to the Marysville Reformatory for Women a few miles northwest of Columbus, to begin serving her sentence.

For more than two years McIlvaine carried his client's case through the state's appeals system all the way to the Ohio Supreme Court. In November 1982 the Ninth District Court of Appeals set aside her sentences on one count of aggravated robbery and on the grand theft conviction. The other convictions were upheld, and the actual minimum time to be served before becoming eligible for parole was unchanged.

A few months earlier the high court had upheld Davis's convictions.

Early in 1984 the Ohio Supreme Court voted in a unanimous seven-to-nothing decision, upholding Teresa's remaining convictions.

More than five years later the lurid case was recalled once more when the long-missing murder weapon was at last recovered by police in Ohio's capital city. In July

1989, when a woman attempted to hock a .357-caliber revolver in Columbus, the pawn shop operater asked for a police check of the serial number to determine if it was listed as stolen. The National Law Enforcement Computer matched the weapon with the number on the gun used in the nine-year-old triple murder.

Medina County's new prosecutor told the press he planned to obtain a court order to have the gun destroyed.

Chapter 7

Hell House

Sixteen-year-old Richard John Jahnke finally reached the breaking point. Years of being cursed and beaten, and of watching his sister and mother brutalized, led to his decision. He had to kill his father.

The slightly built 135-pound, five-foot-six-inch teenager, whose family members called "Richie," changed his clothes to dark blue to help him blend into the shadows of the frosty November night. Then he lined up a .38-caliber pistol, a Marine knife, an Army belt, and a .12-gauge shotgun. Dumping the birdshot, buckshot, and slugs, which his father called "candy cane mix," he reloaded the pump-action Smith & Wesson with three-quarter-inch deer slugs.

And he put the family pets in the basement, where they would be out of the way and safe, then securely shut the door.

As Richie moved purposefully about the house arranging the implements of murder, his seventeen-year-old sister, Deborah Ann, watched and chattered nervously. Richie selected an M-1 carbine from among dozens of weapons in their father's collection. Then he instructed Deborah to wait in the living room with the gun. The children's father loved firearms and almost never left the house without one. Richie wanted his sister to have a weapon for protection in case he missed or was shot by their father and the elder Jahnke went after her. Deborah asked for something without much of a kick.

At last, Richie walked into the garage to wait for his parents to return from dinner. They had eaten out to celebrate the twentieth anniversary of their first meeting in Puerto Rico, when Richard Chester Jahnke was a young soldier from Chicago, and Maria de Lourdes Rodriguez was a twenty-year-old beauty in suburban San Juan.

While Richie waited in ambush, he fingered a command sergeant major's whistle he kept as part of his high school ROTC equipment, then put it to his mouth and blew. The piercing sound was somehow comforting, and helped keep his courage up. Much later he would state under oath, "At the last second I became a battalion command sergeant major."

Finally, a few minutes after six P.M., he heard the putt-putt of a Volkswagen engine, and tensed. Through the blinds covering the glass window on the garage door, he watched the blue VW bug pull into the driveway and stop. The bulky silhouette of a husky man emerged from the driver's side. Both vehicle and man were framed in extremes of black and white by the blinding driveway searchlight. Richie waited until his father, already cursing, was only a few feet away, preparing to open the garage door. Then the teenager pressed the trigger.

Maria Jahnke heard the first roar of the shotgun and turned toward the noise. She was just in time to see the five succeeding shots tear jagged holes through the glass-and-wood-paneled door. Four slugs smashed into her husband's chest, back, and hip, driving him backward and slamming him against the side of the Volkswagen. She was screaming as he crumpled to the concrete driveway.

Moments later she was wailing and bending over the bloody body of her thirty-eight-year-old husband. Much later she would say that she was sure he was gunned

down by one of the many enemies he seemed to go out
of his way to make.

Dashing from the garage and racing into the living
room, Richie yelled at Deborah, "It's done! Let's get
out of here!"

Deborah stared at her brother for a moment, as if she
couldn't fully comprehend what she had just heard.
Then she asked, "What about Mom? Are you going to
shoot her, too?"

Richie was already grabbing his sister's hand and pulling her toward a window in their mother's bedroom as
he replied. He ripped the window open and climbed
through, then helped Deborah. Their mother's life
would be spared. There would be no more shooting.

The brother and sister were barely outside the house
before Richie lost track of Deborah. She was somewhere behind him in the darkness near the single-story
ranch-style brick house on Cowpoke Road. Shivering
from the cold, or the excitement, the boy headed across
the chill Wyoming prairie toward the lights of Cheyenne.

But Deborah was also making her way toward Cheyenne. Behind them, inside the house, their mother was
dialing 911 and blurting into the telephone that her husband had been shot. Then the woman raced back outside to the driveway, where he was sprawled on his back
in a pool of blood, shattered glass and wood, and
shoved a couple of pillows under his head. She hovered
over him while she waited for police and an ambulance.

Robert Bomar, a deputy with the Laramie County
Sheriff's Department, was one of the first officers to
arrive at the shooting scene. Peering at the body as
paramedics frantically tried to revive the shooting victim
with cardiopulmonary resuscitation, Bomar recognized
him and the woman as a couple he had come in contact
with about six months earlier while investigating a case
of reported child abuse involving their teenage son. Locating the boy immediately became a high-priority task.

But even before turning to that problem, Bomar and other deputies had to check out the house in case the killer, whoever he might be, was still inside. Bomar and another deputy cautiously made their way into the house, gripping their weapons at the ready in front of them. The quiet house was full of guns and other weapons. A Ruger .223-caliber mini-14 rifle was propped against a wall by the fireplace. An automatic .30-caliber M-1 carbine was lying on the front-room couch. A .357 magnum revolver was on the floor of the master bedroom near one of the twin beds, and other pistols and rifles were under the beds. Two loaded pistols were in the closet. A loaded Colt .45 automatic and an air pistol were under the bed in Richie's room.

When the officers cautiously pulled open the basement door, they found three dogs, a cat, and more guns. And after retracing their steps and returning upstairs to check out the garage, they found a pump-action .12-gauge Smith & Wesson shotgun on the hood of the station wagon. Several empty shotgun shell casings were on the concrete floor next to and underneath the vehicle. Guns were everywhere. But the pump-action .12-gauge lying on the car hood seemed to be the most likely murder weapon.

Investigators eventually carried thirty-three rifles, shotguns, and handguns out of the house, many of them loaded. Several hunting and skinning knives were also found. But there was no mystery killer lurking inside.

Returning outside, Bomar talked with Maria Jahnke and asked if her husband and son had quarreled that night. She replied that they had. And in response to a question asking if her son could be involved in the shooting, she hesitantly replied that it might be possible. Less than an hour later, in the emergency room at Memorial Hospital in Cheyenne, her husband was officially pronounced dead. Mrs. Jahnke spent the rest of the evening in the home of sympathetic neighbors, whom she hadn't even met before.

It was freezing cold on the prairie, and snow was already piled up knee high. Richie hadn't given any thought to a getaway plan before the shooting, and he eventually trudged off to the comforting warmth of an indoor shopping mall. But he couldn't stay there, so he began walking to the house of a girl he knew from his ROTC class. When a policeman spotted him, he fled and hid for a while under a camper in a trailer park, while officers searched for him with flashlights, a helicopter, and dogs. Finally he knocked at the door of the girl's house and was admitted inside to warm up.

Responding to questions from her stepfather, he confessed that he had shot his father. The girl's family notified police, and a few minutes later lawmen knocked at the door, called out, then walked inside with their guns drawn. Seconds later, Richie was being led out of the house in handcuffs by officers with the Cheyenne Police Department.

Before daybreak on Wednesday, November 17, 1982, morning newspapers were being distributed in Cheyenne with shocking headlines about a local criminal investigator for the Internal Revenue Service who had been murdered in cold blood. As the story developed later that day, the chief suspect in the slaying was identified as the victim's son.

The image of a son ambushing his father was shocking enough. But there was more! News stories and town gossip would quickly be portraying his sister as a suspected co-conspirator who was armed and left waiting in the wings to finish off the unsuspecting parent in case the initial attack failed.

Deborah was one of the most rapt readers of the Wednesday morning headlines about the murder and the capture of the victim's son. Copies of the morning newspapers were already being tossed onto ice-slicked front porches when someone reported seeing a teenage girl answering her description entering Lion's Park near the airport on the city's north side at about daybreak. A few minutes later Deborah was taken into custody at the park and told a sheriff's deputy about picking up one of the newspapers and reading the story.

Richie had exercised his constitutional right to refuse to submit to questioning until he had an attorney present, and after being booked and undergoing some forensics tests, he was locked up in the Laramie County Jail. The next day he was formally charged in the First District Court of Cheyenne with first degree murder.

Deborah agreed to talk with investigators, and related that her mother and brother had begun quarreling the previous evening as soon as Richie returned home from school. When their father returned, the family fuss broadened. Maria complained that Richie had been sassing her. Infuriated, their father began punching Richie, cursing him, and threatening to throw him out of the house. Deborah said she joined in and told her father that if Richie had to leave, she was going as well.

Speaking with an affected English accent she sometimes used, the high school girl told the detectives about other beatings Richie had suffered at the hands of their evil-tempered father. She said their father had special places he preferred to strike his son: on the back of the head, between the shoulder blades, and on the lower back.

In fact, her father beat both his children and his wife, Deborah stated. And she said he had sexually abused her. She described him as a humorless, violent man, with an obsession for guns, who was mean to everyone around him.

Patiently, homicide detectives led the high school girl back to the night of the shooting. Responding to the questions of the investigators, she said that when the quarrel was at last broken off, the parents left the house for their anniversary dinner. That was when Richie told her that he couldn't stand any more abuse, and said that if she wished, she could leave so that she wouldn't be involved in what he was going to do. But then he asked

if she would help. She told the detectives that she
agreed. Deborah said she stayed around as her brother's
backup, in case something went wrong.

Yet, she never really thought he would go through
with the shooting, she said. She stated that she believed
he would simply scare their parents, or lose his nerve.
She also claimed that neither of them ever planned to
hurt their mother. She explained that she fled after the
shooting because she didn't want to be questioned and
forced to tell police that Richie shot their father.

When detectives concluded their initial questioning,
they informed the girl that she was being charged with
aiding and abetting first degree murder. She was locked
in the county jail.

A few days later Richie also began to talk about the
years of abuse he and his sister had endured at the
hands of their father, and the news media and the public
in Wyoming started to reassess their early suspicions
and conclusions about who was responsible for the family tragedy.

Richie didn't attend his father's funeral. His mother
sat with his paternal grandmother and his uncle, who
had flown in from Chicago for the services at the
Church of the Holy Trinity. A minute or two before
the mass began, Deborah was accompanied inside by
the Laramie County sheriff and a deputy. The girl didn't
sit with her mother or speak to her.

Drawing on statements from family members, some
of the few people who had come into contact with the
secretive family over the years, and eventually from
court testimony, authorities developed a bizarre portrait
of a violent, hot-tempered man who seemed to hate and
mistrust nearly everyone. He loved to tell people that as
an IRS investigator, he could make big tax trouble for
anyone foolish enough to become his enemy.

Richard Chester Jahnke behaved as if he fancied
himself to be a real-life "Rambo." A former career
Army sergeant who was not permitted to reenlist after

tours of duty in the Republic of Korea and in West Germany, he was obsessed with guns. Frequently he would get up in the middle of the night, grab a pistol or rifle, and patrol the house and grounds. He talked enthusiastically about how he hoped sometime to come across a prowler so that he could blow his head off. It was curious behavior, since the exclusive subdivision the family lived in was probably as safe as almost any neighborhood in the United States.

He never stumbled onto a prowler, so he picked on his family members. He beat his wife and children for such petty offenses as leaving tub faucets running, chewing food with an open mouth, scraping silverware on dinner plates, breaking toys, or coughing. When Richie was little, he was troubled by severe asthma, and when he coughed, it infuriated his father. So when the little boy felt an asthma attack coming on, he would dash for his room and muffle his coughs with a pillow.

While the family ate at the table, the elder Jahnke would sit ten feet away in the living room, watching closely for violations of his eating rules. Eventually the children began using plastic forks to avoid making scraping noises on their plates.

One time when Richie was ten years old, he climbed out of bed late at night, padded to the kitchen and walked in the dark to the refrigerator to get a snack. He was sitting in the dark, eating, when he heard a click. His father was holding a cocked and loaded gun eight inches from his face.

When Richie would go into the bathroom, his father would pound on the door and yell, "You've got one minute!" Then he would begin to count.

The family moved often, especially when the mean-tempered head of the household was in the Army. The moves were less frequent after he became an investigator for the IRS. But when they did move, the decisions were often made on the spur of the moment. Jahnke would suddenly announce that the people he was work-

ing with were "assholes," and he wasn't going to move
up in his profession unless he transferred to a new office
in another area.

After leaving the Army, Jahnke first settled his little
family in Chicago, then Washington, D. C., then Phoenix. While he was with the Phoenix office, he was once
assigned as one of the bodyguards for the nation's First
Lady when President Gerald Ford visited the city. The
family bought its first house in Arizona and lived there
for seven years, before Jahnke announced one day in
February 1981 that they were moving to Cheyenne.
There were simply "too many assholes" in the Phoenix
office, he complained.

The children weren't enthusiastic about being up-
rooted again and moving to cowboy country. But they
weren't consulted. Their father had made a decision,
and the family moved to the capital city of some 53,000
people in the Equality State. Professionally, the decision
appeared to be a solid one. Jahnke did well in Cheyenne, and as chief investigator in the local office at the
time of his death, was earning an impressive annual salary of $38,500. But he had some expensive tastes, in-
cluding his obsessive purchases of guns, and it was
barely enough for the family to get by on.

He bought the $125,000 eight-room house, which
some newspapers would later refer to as "the house of
Hell," in an expensive northeastern subdivision known
as Cowboy Country. Half his monthly salary was eaten
up by house payments, and during the two years the
family lived there, it was a struggle to keep up financially. Jahnke defended the purchase, however, by
pointing out that lots in the subdivision were large and
fenced in, and neighbors minded their own business.

He liked it that way, and was quick to discourage
friendly overtures from unsuspecting neighbors. The
family had lived on Cowpoke Lane for about a year
when neighbor George Hain walked across the street
one day and knocked on their front door to introduce

himself. Jahnke responded with a scowl on his face, and slammed the door as Hain started to say hello.

A couple who lived nearby had a son about Richie's age. Deborah complained that he was pestering her, and one day Jahnke confronted the boy's father as he returned home from work. Jahnke warned his neighbor to keep the youngster away from the girl. Then he pointedly remarked that he had an arsenal of guns and knew how to use them.

Both the Jahnke children were teased at school. They dressed differently than the other students; older than their years. Richie wore a suit and tie, and both brother and sister carried briefcases. Although Richie was smaller than many of the boys his age, he stuck up for his sister and got into fights with school bullies when they picked on Deborah. He usually lost.

The Jahnkes lived an isolated existence. The children were expected to be home most of the time. Neither they nor their mother were permitted to hold jobs. Jahnke didn't trust outsiders. He had no personal friends, and didn't want visitors. He avoided attending his children's birthday parties, graduations, and award ceremonies because he didn't like crowds.

Richie shared a few good times with his father, however. But even then, the good times frequently involved guns, violence or bullying. When the family lived in Arizona, Jahnke would occasionally take his son to the desert to hunt or to target-shoot at bottles and tin cans. On those days they would get up early and eat a solid breakfast prepared by Maria. Then Richie would help his father load the guns into their Scout, and while Jahnke puffed on a cigar, father and son would drive away to look for jackrabbits and rattlesnakes.

Richie was a good marksman, and killed his first rabbit when he was seven. The boy's marksmanship was one of the few things about him that pleased his father. But the elder Jahnke's most pleasurable times seemed to occur when he was doing something mean.

The father and son were climbing along a ridge one time when they spotted two hunters on the desert below them. Jahnke quickly dropped to his belly and instructed his son to get down beside him. Then the IRS man fired his rifle into the dirt between the two unsuspecting hunters. The men hit the ground, yelling, "Don't shoot."

As Jahnke drove away from the area, he laughed about the dangerous prank. The hunters were a couple of "assholes," he told his son. It seemed that practically everybody but the truculent tax investigator qualified for that description. Sometimes when he was driving with Richie, he would see someone else in an expensive car and jot down the license number for future reference. Anyone rich enough to own a car like that was probably cheating on their income tax, he would explain.

Deborah didn't even share those good times with her father. She would eventually reveal that when she was six or seven, he began lying down for "naps." Then he would fondle her. When she was older, he would sometimes kiss her on the mouth, feel her breasts, and walk into the bathroom on the pretext of checking the pipes as she was taking a shower. Sometimes he stuck his hand down her pants in front of her mother, or Richie, or both. She wrote in her diary about how much she hated that kind of attention.

There were other times, however, when Jahnke submitted his daughter to violent physical abuse. He slapped her and screamed at her, calling her a "bitch," "slut" or a "whore." Sometimes he would complain that she wasn't brushing her teeth properly. Then he would put her in a hammerlock, drag her into the bathroom and roughly brush her teeth until her gums bled. When she broke out with acne, he pulled her into the bathroom and scrubbed her face so red and raw with a washcloth that the pimples bled.

It didn't take much to set the hot-tempered IRS man off. Four days before the shooting, Deborah was making herself some early morning tea when her father walked into the kitchen and ordered her to pour the hot water out of the cup. She wasn't good enough to use the good china, he growled. After she changed cups, he accused her of being poorly groomed. When she protested, he said she was sassing him and began punching her with his fists, pulling her hair, and slapping her. Richie pulled his father off, and while the males were struggling, Deborah punched her father in the face with her fist. Maria finally ended the confrontation by stepping between her children and her husband.

Maria didn't escape the beatings and verbal abuse either. One time when her husband was giving Richie a particularly vicious beating with a belt, she tried to take the leather strap away. In moments, Jahnke had his screaming wife pinned against the bathtub with her face scraping against the floor tiles while he lashed her across the shoulders, spine, and buttocks.

Jahnke would often fly into such a rage during the family beatings that his own nose would began to bleed. He had high blood pressure.

Maria Jahnke soon confirmed the accusations and described her husband as a sick man who became increasingly worse over the years. And she would eventually say that her son had freed her, in fact freed them all. She accused her husband of making the lives of his family pure hell.

Laramie County district attorney Tom Carroll wasn't swayed by the tales of abuse. He described the attack on the elder Jahnke as "a cold-blooded murder, and an execution." The D.A. described the IRS investigator's murder as a classic case of premeditated homicide. He told the press that the shooting was deliberately and carefully thought out, a classic case of premeditation. "Homicides, I take seriously," he said. "No one but the state itself has a right to take a human life."

Why hadn't the children or their mother sought help from authorities if the abuse was as vicious and extensive as they claimed? Carroll asked. They had sought help, in fact. And someone among the agencies and individuals responsible for helping people like him, his sister, and their mother, had fumbled the ball.

Deborah had mentioned family troubles to various people. But talk of abuse was almost offhand, with few specifics. None of the adults she talked to really knew how troubled the family was until it was too late. Richie was more specific.

On May 2, 1982, about six months before the shooting, Richie had fled out the back door of the house barefoot, seeking help after a vicious beating.

The trouble began at about noon that Sunday, when the bearish 210-pound parent stomped into his son's room in a rage because Richie hadn't completed an assigned family chore to clean the basement. The furious IRS man grabbed his son by the hair and dragged him into the basement. Downstairs, Jahnke pounded Richie in the face, on the head, in the ribs, and on the back with his fists while screaming that he was a "bastard," before the boy managed to break free and escape.

Richie went to his high school ROTC instructor, Major Robert Vegvary, for help. Major Vegvary telephoned the Laramie County Sheriff's Department, and Deputy Bomar responded with Pat Sandoval of the Laramie County office of the State of Wyoming's Division of Public Assistance and Social Services. They drove the boy to the emergency room at DePaul Hospital, where doctors examined him and concluded that the massive bruises on his back were the result of a beating. The doctors reported that the teenager was struck with an open and closed hand with an excessive amount of force.

It seemed that the boy's plight had been brought to the attention of the right people. But despite the best intentions of legislators, the courts, police, and social agencies, there are flaws in the system that can sometimes work against the very children and adults whom laws dealing with family violence and abuse are designed to protect.

Bomar, like most law enforcement officers, had seen children who were subjected to terrible abuse by parents or other caretakers. Every day in America, children of all ages from infants to teenagers are raped, cut, burned, scalded, kicked, and beaten. Instances of child abuse that appeared to be far worse than the Jahnke case had been investigated by authorities in Laramie County, and it was decided that there wasn't enough evidence to justify prosecution.

Instead, Ms. Sandoval checked out the possibilities of placing Richie in a foster home for a while. But all the homes available to her were full. Richie was confronted with a choice of staying in Attention Home, a group foster center, or bunking at the jail over the weekend. He decided against either option, and asked to be allowed to return to his family because he didn't want to leave his mother and sister alone with his father.

Richie's parents picked him up, and Ms. Sandoval formally recommended follow-up counseling. A social worker subsequently met with Richie's father at the Jahnkes' house about three weeks after the beating, and warned that if the behavior was repeated, Jahnke would be charged with child abuse. Vegvary also made some follow-up inquiries, and advised Richie to contact authorities again if there was another beating or other serious abuse.

But Richie never again asked for help. And life didn't get any better in the seriously troubled Jahnke home.

Now the same system that sympathetic supporters throughout Wyoming, then around the country, would soon be accusing of failing the teenager, was preparing to put him and his sister on trial in their father's slaying.

Even though Wyoming state criminal statutes provided for death by lethal injection for first degree murder, Carroll said he would not seek the maximum penalty against the teenager. And it had been more than fifteen years since the last execution in the state. But both the brother and sister would be put on trial as adults, he said. Carroll would be supported at the trial by Assistant D.A. Jon Forward.

Mrs. Jahnke used a portion of the $250,000 inherited from her husband's estate to hire James Barrett, a prominent Cheyenne attorney, to represent her children. Barrett, who had extensive experience with child abuse cases, would be assisted by a member of his law firm, Louis Epps.

After spending a week in jail, Richie and Deborah were released on bail of $50,000 each, but attorneys and the court decided against permitting them to return to their home. Richie moved in with his lawyer's family, and later lived with the Central High School psychologist and his family. Deborah went to live with her art teacher's family for a while, then quietly moved to the home of the superintendent of schools. Both youngsters continued attending their high school classes.

When Barrett managed to win separate trials for the teenagers, which he believed would be to their advantage, he decided against representing both of them because of conflict of interest. Terrence Mackey, a respected local lawyer, was selected to defend Deborah.

Barrett attempted to strike a deal, offering to allow his client to plead guilty if the case was transferred to the juvenile system where Richie could not be sentenced to any term extending beyond his twenty-first birthday. The proposal was rejected. So Barrett suggested a guilty plea to manslaughter, if the prosecutor would ask the judge for probation. The request for leniency would be off the record. Carroll turned thumbs down on making a request for leniency. But the prosecution indicated the state would go along with a plea bargain without conditions. That wasn't acceptable at the time to the defense.

Both teenagers had made formal statements to police admitting their roles in the mid-November tragedy. And homicide investigators had collected a vast amount of physical evidence, ranging from fingerprints to paraffin tests, that supported the statements. The D.A. was determined to take the cases to trial.

State District Court judge Paul Liamos, a by-the-book jurist and ex-Marine from the small cow town of Newcastle in the northeastern area of the state, was selected to preside over Richie's case. Pretrial proceedings were rapidly disposed of. Richie's first degree murder trial began on Valentine's Day, Monday, February 14, 1983, less than ninety days after his father's slaying. By that time the family tragedy had become an international story, and newspaper and television reporters from across the country were waiting at the Laramie County Courthouse when the doors opened in the morning.

A jury of seven women and five men, including eleven parents, was selected the first day. Several potential jurors were passed over after stating they had been victims of child abuse or knew people who were.

In opening statements, the D.A. described the IRS agent's shooting as the result of a plot, and said it was carried out like a "military-type operation." The victim was so torn up by the destructive slugs loaded into the shotgun that he suffocated in his own blood, Carroll told the jury.

Barrett had opted to seek acquittal for his client by convincing the panel that when Richie shot his father he was acting in self-defense. Recounting the years of intimidation and abuse, the attorney said that Richie was waiting in the garage to confront his father the night of the shooting. But Richie knew that his father was always armed, so he armed himself with the shotgun, a pistol, and a knife, as well as placing other weapons around the house.

The lawyer contended that when Richie heard his father stomping toward the garage door that night, he fired in fright. It wasn't the first shots fired through the window that struck and killed the victim, Barrett said,

but the last four that crashed through the door panel
while Richie was backing up in fear.

"The evidence will show that Richard Jahnke had a
reasonable apprehension of harm both to himself and to
others, that he acted out of that and out of fear," the
defense attorney declared. And he promised that the
jury would be shown "the evidence of a lifetime and not
one day."

Barrett was as good as his word. But he had to wait
his turn, until after the prosecution outlined the state's
case. For the most part, it was a rather dry recitation of
facts already known or assumed by members of the
press and by the public who packed the courtroom.
Paramedics, sheriff's officers, city police, laboratory
technicians, pathologists, and ballistics experts testified
about the scene of the shooting, the condition of the
body, cause of death, and about guns. Two officers said
Richie confessed to them that he shot his father as revenge for past wrongs.

Some of the most dramatic prosecution testimony was
provided by a captain in Richie's ROTC unit, Michael
Brinkman. Recounting a conversation he had with
Richie at Barrett's office several days after the shooting,
Brinkman said his friend told him that he was afraid if
he was still home when his parents returned, it would
cost him his life. Responding to questions, Brinkman
said Richie told him that "they put weapons at every
window and door in the house."

Asked to explain who he was talking about when he
used the word, "they," Brinkman replied: "Himself
[Richie] and Deborah."

Brinkman said that Richie recounted putting the pets
in the basement, of leaving Deborah in the living room
with the rifle, then moving to the garage. The witness
added that Richie claimed he thought he saw a shadow,
and began to fire.

Barrett used cross-examination to focus on the question of child abuse and of his contention that Richie was

afraid and believed his life was in danger. Richie told him that during the predinner quarrel, his father tried to hit Deborah, the witness said. The defendant was quoted as saying that when he tried to defend his sister, his father threw him down and warned, "You two better not be in the house when I return."

Maria Jahnke also underwent spirited cross-examination when she was called as a defense witness. Referring to her statements about the abuse her husband subjected his family to, D.A. Carroll asked why, if the victim was such a monster, she stood by and watched him do such terrible things?

"I was afraid for the children and myself," she replied in a barely audible voice.

Hadn't she, herself, contributed to the abuse? the prosecutor asked.

"I'm no angel. When you live under such terrible fear, you do things you are ashamed of," she responded. She said she once threatened to leave her husband, and he warned, "No other man will have you. I'll find you and kill you."

Whispering so softly that some of the jurors leaned forward in their seats to hear, she added: "I knew he meant it."

She said her husband wanted her to devote herself completely to him, and to share his resentment of the children. "I wanted to love and do right for all of my family, but I was caught in the middle," she testified. "The children hated me for being his ally; he hated me for being their protector . . . I would lash out at all of them."

Maria's account was potent, but the most devastatingly forceful testimony was that of the defendant. During three hours on the stand, Richie recounted a history of cruelty and violence in his home that had the hushed courtroom entranced. At times his account had the eerie feel of a series of shock television bytes, as he recalled one sadistic act or incident after another.

"He hurt me inside. He hated me so much, he just wanted me to be miserable. He hit me with his fists or a leather belt until his nose started to bleed . . ."

Once when he was six years old, Richie said, his father filled his plate with too much food and forced him to eat it until he vomited.

"My parents were always arguing," he said. "They slept in different rooms; it was a relationship without love. We lived without love, without compassion—it made me feel so inhuman . . . we were all trapped."

Richie testified that he remembered his mother praying aloud that his father would be struck by a car. "She wanted to leave him, but she was scared."

He said his sister thought she would escape from their hellish life when she graduated from high school and went to college. But their father said he wouldn't send her to college. "He'd spent all his money on guns and a house he couldn't afford."

Richie was a loving brother, protective of his sister. "Deborah was going crazy—she was being hurt so much," he said. "She needed to be free. I had to free myself, and my mother, too . . . free us all from the pain and misery my father had caused us, and would always cause us."

Richie said that when he was a little boy, he would go to his room, turn off the lights, and hide in the closet or under his bed when his father was beating his mother. But by the time he was ten or eleven years old, he became disgusted with himself and stood up to his father to protect Maria. His father finally slacked off on Maria's beatings and turned on him, he said. So then he tried to stop what he described as the "games" his father played with Deborah.

"He pushed my sister against a wall, and to discipline her, he grabbed her breasts," he said.

One time after his father put his hand down Deborah's pants in the kitchen, Richie testified, he complained to his mother about it. He said she responded by blaming Deborah for wearing shorts. His mother told Deborah to tell her father not to touch her. "And my sister did," he said.

During cross-examination Richie testified that his sister asked him on the night of the shooting to kill their mother, as well as their father. It was an accusation that seemed certain to resurface at her trial.

Tears glistened in the eyes of some jurors, and of many of the spectators, as they listened to the emotion-wracked testimony.

During summations, Barrett played to the emotion by telling the jury that Jahnke had "murdered his son by inches, took bits and pieces of him away, tried day after day, week after week, to destroy Richie." The defense attorney described the victim's behavior as, "Cruel. Heartless. Premeditated. Willful. Malicious."

Both prosecuting attorneys took a turn at summation, with Forward leading off. In arguing to the jury that the shooting was premeditated, Forward recounted Richie's actions replacing the "candy cane mix" in the shotgun with slugs, positioning weapons at various locations around the house, changing to dark clothes, and locking up the pets.

Holding the shotgun as he spoke, Forward then asked the jury to consider the shooting. "He sees the head and shoulders." The assistant D.A. pumped the empty .12-gauge as he continued. "One shot. But to fire you have to eject and do it again." He pumped the gun again. "Shot him again." There was another dramatic pump of the gun. "We're not through. We've got four more times."

The claim of self-defense was a sham, Forward declared.

Speaking after Barrett's summation, which seemed to put the victim on trial instead of the accused killer, Carroll disagreed that the system had failed Richie. He charged that the boy had every opportunity to speak out so that he could obtain help if he was being abused. And neither the system nor the victim were on trial in the court that day, the D.A. pointed out.

The issue to be considered was whether or not Richie Jahnke murdered his father. "The evidence is not contradicted that he went into that garage with the full intent to kill his father," the prosecutor said. "And he got the job done. And then he tells why he did it. Revenge!

"Well, he's not entitled to revenge!"

Before sending the jury off to begin deliberations, Judge Liamos instructed that in order for Richie to be found not guilty on grounds of self-defense, they must conclude that the defendant had "reasonable grounds to believe he was in imminent danger of serious bodily harm for which he could save himself only by using deadly force against his assailant."

The jury deliberated six hours before returning a late Saturday night verdict of guilty to voluntary manslaughter. Richie was found not guilty on the second and lesser charge of conspiracy to commit first degree murder. Neither side had scored a total victory or suffered a total defeat. Richie no longer faced a possible life prison term for first degree murder, or a sentence of twenty-years-to-life for second degree murder. But he could still wind up facing many years behind bars. Sentencing options available to Judge Liamos ranged from probation to a term at the Wyoming Industrial Institute for juveniles, or twenty years in an adult prison. The jurist withheld his decision, pending a presentence investigation. And he revoked Richie's bond.

As deputies led the teenager from the courtroom to a cell at the county jail next door, he paused to give his mother a hug and whisper, "Stay strong."

Maria was shattered by the verdict. As friends attempted to comfort her, she uttered a futile curse at the dead man. "May he roast in Hell forever," she moaned. "That man always won out against us. He won this time, too."

Public response to the youth's conviction and im-

pending sentence was startling. More than 1500 letters
were mailed to the judge, almost all of them pleading
for leniency. A citizen's group, the Committee to Help
Richard Jahnke, circulated petitions and obtained thousands of signatures asking that Richie be released on
probation.

But when the judge announced sentence on March
18, the decision was a disappointment to the youngster's
supporters. "This is a serious crime, a homicide, the
taking of a human life. That life was taken without anyone speaking on behalf of the victim," Judge Liamos
remarked from the bench.

He said he had decided against probation because of
a desire to "satisfy trust in public justice, as opposed to
private justice." Continuing, he explained that he believed authorities with the state penitentiary handled inmates "of tender years" with appropriate care.

He ordered a five-to-fifteen-year term at the Wyoming State Penitentiary in Rawlins. Gasps of shock and
disbelief filled the courtroom. Richie's mother
screamed. His sister cried. But Richie was dry-eyed and
stoic as sheriff's deputies led him back to a cell.

Even some of the jurors who had wound up voting for
the manslaughter conviction were surprised and angered. One juror described the sentence as "the cruelest
thing they could ever do to him." Others telephoned
Barrett and said they had never expected such a harsh
sentence to be imposed.

Predictably, the prosecutor was less sympathetic. "I
don't feel good. I don't go have victory celebrations
when I leave the courtroom," he told reporters. "But I
do feel satisfied that justice has been served."

Carroll, along with Judge Liamos, were members of
an obvious minority. Both men came under vicious attack from the press and from many private citizens who
believed that Richie was treated too harshly by the justice system. The judge's description was criticized as

heartless. And newspaper editorials talked about a system that had failed.

The Department of Public Assistance and Social Services also came in for a share of the brickbats. Callers on radio talk shows, and coffee klatch gossips, complained that the murder might have been prevented if the social agency had done a better job when Richie was taken there for help. The chief of Wyoming's social service agency responded by ordering an administrative review of the bureau's regulations and procedures.

Barrett took a more practical approach to the setback. He filed an appeal with the Wyoming Supreme Court. After less than a week behind bars, Richie was again freed on $50,000 bond for the remainder of the appeals process.

Deborah's trial on charges of aiding and abetting manslaughter began on March 7, while her brother was still awaiting sentencing. The trial before First District Court of Wyoming judge Joseph Maier continued as the furor over her brother's conviction continued to rage among the public and in the local and national press.

Most of the first day was taken up selecting a jury of nine women and three men, almost all of them parents.

As expected by court officers and the press, Caroll didn't waste any time in his opening statement bringing up the allegation that Deborah asked Richie to kill their mother. He also told the jury of her statement to homicide investigators that she had asked her brother for the gun that kicked the least.

Mackey, who was assisted by paralegal Jeff Brinkerhoff, reserved his opening statement for the beginning of the defense case, after the prosecution had presented its witnesses.

For the most part, the first few prosecution witnesses were the same people the D.A. had called at the earlier trial of the defendant's brother. And there were few surprises in their testimony. Then Richie was called to the stand and questioned as a hostile witness.

Richie was still his sister's protector, and he stubbornly rebuffed the prosecutor's efforts to get him to say, or to agree, that his sister had asked him to shoot their mother. Richie insisted that, as he recalled the conversation with his sister, she asked him "if" he was going to shoot their mother. Mackey and Carroll tangled angrily over the prosecutor's presentation and wording of the questioning as well as the witness's replies.

Producing a transcript of the teenager's testimony at the murder trial, Carroll finally demanded: ". . . is this what your sister said: She asked you to kill your mother, and you answered yes. Is that what your sister said?"

"That isn't exactly what she said, but it is close," the witness replied. And "close" was all that the prosecutor was going to wring out of the teenager.

Mackey opened cross-examination by asking if Richie's father had threatened him on the night of the slaying. Richie said his father told him that he was going to get rid of him somehow.

"And what did you take that to mean?" the lawyer asked.

"I thought he was going to kill me," the boy replied.

Responding to the defense attorney's questions, Richie conceded that he killed his father. But the only thing his sister had to do with it was that she was in the house, he insisted. And he said that he gave her a gun so she could protect herself in case he was killed.

Sheriff's detective Tim Greene was also quizzed about his knowledge of the siblings' discussion of their mother's fate on the night of the shooting. One of the officers who took Deborah's statement after her apprehension at Lions Park, Greene said she told him that after the weapons were spread throughout the house she asked her brother, "What about Mom?" Greene quoted her as saying Richie told her that he wasn't going to harm their mother.

Greene said that later in Deborah's statement she

told the investigators that when her brother rushed into the house after the shooting, she again asked, "What about Mom?" Richie told her that their mother was safe, the detective quoted the girl as saying.

The sheriff's detective was the state's final witness, and when the trial adjourned for the lunch break, there was intense speculation among legal professionals and courtroom wags about the possibility of Mackey calling Deborah to testify in her own defense. In criminal trials, defendants may testify if they wish, or they may refuse on constitutional grounds of avoiding possible self-incrimination. It is usually a risky move when defense lawyers call their clients to testify. Richie had handled himself well on the stand, but it was difficult for courtroom professionals to gauge just how his sister might stand up against vigorous cross-examination from the experienced prosecutor.

Mackey had a surprise in store when the trial resumed an hour later, however. The attorney shocked nearly everyone present in the courtroom by announcing that the defense was resting its case. Neither Deborah nor anyone else would be called as a defense witness. Mackey had chosen to rely on the counterpunching he had directed at prosecution witnesses during cross-examination, and the closing statement that was still to come. It was a calculated gamble, but one that was not without precedent in criminal trials.

Summations would be handled as they had been at Richie's trial, with Forward addressing the jury first; followed by the defense; and finally wrapping up with Carroll presenting the final argument for the prosecution.

Referring to the storm of protest across the country over Richie's conviction and sentence, Forward charged that the youth thought of himself as a national hero, and had tried to personally take all the blame for the shooting. The assistant D.A. charged, however, that Richie had stated under oath his sister told him to kill their mother. Deborah was "as clearly involved in the blood hunt, the death hunt, as her brother," he declared.

"Are we going to put the commandment 'Thou shalt not kill' in the gutter where they put that other commandment, 'Honor thy father and thy mother'?" Forward asked.

Mackey's summation was fervently emotional. He talked about the violence and anger in the household, about the frustration and fear. He repeatedly referred to the defendant as a "little girl." And he asked the jury to see to it during their deliberations that the state didn't replace Deborah's father as her abuser by heaping yet more misery on his client.

When it was Carroll's turn, he reminded the jury that the defense attorney hadn't said much about the fate of the elder Jahnke. "He is dead, dead, dead in the cemetery!" the prosecutor boomed.

Carroll repeated the contention that Deborah urged her brother to kill their mother. He scoffed at any idea that she would select a gun because it "kicked the least" if she had no intention of using it. And again referring to Mackey's closing statement, he said he was "tired of this 'little girl' business. She's eighteen years old this month," he said of the defendant. "She knows better."

The jury deliberated six hours, not including breaks for lunch and dinner, before notifying the judge that a verdict had been reached. They found Deborah guilty of aiding and abetting manslaughter. As the earlier jury had done at the conclusion of her brother's trial, the panel returned a not guilty verdict to the charge of conspiracy.

Deborah cried. Her mother managed to wobble unsteadily out of the courthouse. Then she fainted.

Judge Maier continued Deborah's bond and released her to the custody of the school superintendent, whose family she was staying with, pending sentencing.

Deborah's conviction and impending sentencing had the effect of throwing gasoline on an already roaring

fire, so far as the groundswell of public outrage that
erupted over the judicial system's handling of the cases
was concerned. The storm of editorials criticizing the
prosecutor, the judge, and social agencies continued.
Martin A. Larson, a columnist in the *Spotlight*, a popu-
list newspaper published in Washington, D. C., aimed
much of his criticism at the victim's employer. He wrote
that he was convinced sadists were attracted to jobs with
the IRS because it offered opportunities to inflict suffering on taxpayers.

George Hain, the man who had a door slammed in
his face by the elder Jahnke for his attempt at good
neighborliness, had taken a leading role in the effort to
win lenient treatment of the teenagers. He and his wife
had also taken Maria under their wing, and were doing
their best to help the troubled woman who had become
a near-forgotten victim of the family tragedy.

Hain personally called on Wyoming governor Ed
Herschler, who had the authority to commute Richie's
sentence or grant a pardon, as well as to do the same for
Deborah after her sentencing. Several other people also
added their personal appeals for the governor to intercede. But for the time being, the popular three-term
Democrat made no commitments.

In the meantime, at the urging of his advisors, Richie
began giving interviews to the local and national press.
The teenager described the shooting of his father as the
wrong solution, but said he believed it was also wrong of
the judge to make an example of him by sending him to
prison. And he continued to defend his sister. He said
that on the night of the murder she was a basket case
and had nothing to do with the shooting.

Regardless of whether or not the prosecutor approved, the boy whose father used to humiliate him by
calling him "Leather Lips" had become a national figure—a hero in the eyes of at least some sympathizers.
The press was almost unanimously on his side.

Deborah was sentenced on April 27. Before announcing the sentence, however, Judge Maier chewed out the press for its coverage of the case, which he lambasted as "incomplete, incorrect, and slanted." Reading from a fifteen-page statement, the stern jurist hit out at news reports indicating the victim was guilty of incest and rape. He observed that Deborah had told a psychiatrist "only of 'touching' or 'fondling' " and of her father's lying down on her one time while they were clothed. "More importantly," the judge added in comments that some observers considered exceedingly curious, those incidents occurred before the girl was twelve years old, and never after that.

Once he had finished with the press, Judge Maier ordered the eighteen-year-old girl to serve from three to eight years at the Wyoming Center for Women. And he approved her release on bond of $25,000, during her expected appeal. Deborah was in tears as she was led from the courtroom. Her mother put the family house up as surety for the bail money.

Shaken by the severity of the sentence, Mackey talked to the press in the hallway of the courthouse. "Now children know there is no relief," he said to sympathetic reporters in a voice that was shaking with emotion. "The system won't help."

He pointed out that parents who kill their children often get lighter sentences.

Within a few days Deborah had given her first press interviews. Then she and Richie were interviewed together for ABC television's *Good Morning America.* *CBS Morning News* ran an interview with Deborah, then the network interviewed Richie for a segment on their popular show, *60 Minutes.* Almost every major newspaper in the country ran stories about the case. Their story appeared in *Newsweek, Rolling Stone, People,* and in supermarket tabloids.

Deborah's participation in press conferences ended when she was sent to Excelsior, a facility for girls in the Denver suburb of Aurora, where she could receive regular counseling and presumably benefit from the structured environment. Richie remained in Cheyenne and transferred to East High School for his final year of classes.

On June 6, 1984, the Wyoming Supreme Court announced its ruling on Richie's appeal. By a narrow three-to-two vote, they upheld the conviction. One of the judges, a Mormon, wrote of Richie in his opinion: "He is an all-American boy, except that he has a predilection toward patricide. This is a textbook case of first degree murder." Richie had just graduated from high school, and the ruling was revealed exactly three weeks before his eighteenth birthday.

Barely a week after the ruling, and before the youngster could be shipped off in chains to Rawlins, Governor Herschler stepped in. At a press conference he called at the state capitol, he announced that he was issuing a commutation order. The sentence imposed by Judge Liamos, and affirmed by the split vote of the Wyoming State Supreme Court, was too harsh, he said.

The governor explained that he didn't grant a full pardon because he wasn't convinced that "such a decision would amount to justice in this case. As the Supreme Court recognized, no person is justified in taking the law into his own hands and killing his perceived tormentor."

But he also pointed out that Wyoming's constitution directs that the state penal code should be framed on humane principles of reformation and prevention. And he recalled evidence noted in the State Supreme Court's opinion that described Richie's father as a "cruel, sadistic, and abusive man."

The governor's order provided for Richie to be sent to Bethesda Hospital in Denver for two to four months for evaluation, then moved to the Wyoming Industrial Institute for juvenile offenders near the little town of Worland in the middle of the state's beet country. According to the order, Richie would be released on his twenty-first birthday, June 27, 1987.

On December 12, 1984, the Wyoming State Supreme Court issued a ruling upholding Deborah's conviction, again by a split vote of three-to-two. And again Governor Herschler intervened. A week before Christmas the governor announced that he was commuting her sentence to one year of probation. The probation was to be preceded by a month of intensive psychiatric evaluation at the Excelsior Youth Center, he ordered.

Early in 1985, ABC television broadcast a two-hour docudrama based on the case titled *Right to Kill.* Typically of television docudramas, only facts were changed.

There were still some pleasant surprises in store for the Jahnkes after the commutation orders. Deborah went to college and moved out of Wyoming. And on September 9, 1985, Governor Herschler ordered Richie's release from the boys school on parole. A few days later, he and his sister attended their mother's wedding. Maria had trimmed her weight and married a Cheyenne man who was in the auto repair business.

Chapter 8

Hit Man for a Cheerleader

James Pierson never knew what hit him!

The burly forty-two-year-old widowed father of three was about to climb into his truck to drive to work on a chill early Tuesday morning when the sharp crack of a gunshot exploded and a rifle bullet slammed into his back.

The force of the blow knocked him against the vehicle and sent him tumbling to the pavement. Blood gushed from the wound, rapidly soaking through his heavy winter jacket and shirt.

Pierson's body had barely slumped onto the driveway before the skinny form of a young man, his unkempt hair sticking up in clumps on his bare head, scampered toward him gripping a rifle in one hand. Standing over the prostrate form, the youth coolly pumped four more bullets into the bleeding man's head. Moments later the mysterious gunman was gone. James Pierson's ruthless execution was over in seconds.

Inside the warm house he had left only moments before, his pretty sixteen-year-old daughter, Cheryl, was curled up in bed, drowsily waiting for the alarm clock to ring. She had heard her father leave, but drifted back to sleep, only to be awakened again minutes later by the family's toy poodle. The dog was agitated and eager to be let outside.

There was nothing for Cheryl to do but to stumble sleepily out of bed and let her pet out. Rubbing at her eyes, and dressed in nightgown and knee socks, the teenager padded to the front door and pulled it open, then peered through the screen. The body of her father was lying in plain sight a few feet away, in a growing pool of crimson.

Stunned and horrified, the girl turned and ran to her room, where she quickly wriggled into a sweatsuit, then hurried back to her father's body. She bent over him for a moment, then straightened up and ran across the icy driveway to the home of neighbors, Michael and Alberta Kosser, for help. Kosser, an auto mechanic for the Brookhaven Highway Department, telephoned the Suffolk County Police Department and told them that his neighbor was hurt. He thought Pierson had slipped and fallen on the ice.

Then Kosser hurried outside with a towel and pressed it to his neighbor's body in a futile effort to staunch the blood that was flowing from Pierson's head and chest.

Within minutes a squad car from the Suffolk County Police Department pulled up and two uniform officers leaped out and hurried toward Kosser and the body that was still facedown on the frigid cement. Two emergency technicians arrived and turned Pierson over, preparing to apply mouth-to-mouth resuscitation. But it was too late. He was dead.

Police and emergency workers quickly determined that he wasn't killed in a fall. James Pierson was shot to death, ambushed a few feet from the front door of his house in the quiet little working-class community of Selden, on Long Island's North Shore. It was February 5, 1986.

By the time the first light of the new day was streaking the midwinter sky, the street in front of 293 Magnolia Drive was a beehive of activity. An ambulance from the Selden Volunteer Fire Department pulled up and braked to a stop. Uniform officers arrived in squad cars and cordoned off the driveway with yellow tape. Plain-clothes investigators and evidence technicians began painstakingly searching the scene for clues. A policeman found four .22-caliber shell casings a few inches from the body. Another empty shell casing was found near a tree a few feet away.

Reporters from newspapers and a local television station soon joined neighbors, who had gathered at a respectable distance from the taped-off crime scene. A policeman confided to one reporter that the shooting had the look of a contract killing. Cheryl had retreated inside her house, where she advised her ten-year-old sister JoAnn that they wouldn't be going to school that day. Cheryl said their father had fallen on the ice and hurt himself. Then the sisters walked to the kitchen window to watch the activity outside.

Kosser and one of the uniform officers drew the unpleasant task of informing the girls that their father was dead. Then Kosser took them to his house.

After photographs were taken and distances between the corpse and the car, curb, house, and other landmarks in the immediate area were carefully measured, the body was finally released to the Suffolk County coroner for autopsy.

The initial phase of the investigation into Pierson's violent and mysterious death seemed to create more questions than it answered. The slaying was carried out with such professional expertise that some homicide investigators initially wondered if the respected family man might have been the victim of a gangland assassination. But there was no indication of a motive that would tie the murder of the electrician to organized crime. He had no known association with professional criminals, and so far as could be immediately determined, he had lived an exemplary and honest life.

Most of Pierson's neighbors and friends knew him as a devoted parent to his children, including the girls and nineteen-year-old James, Jr. He showered them with gifts and attention. Pierson took his family to amusement parks and on hunting trips. And he coached his son's Little League baseball team when the boy was grade-school age. Recently, however, a rift had developed between him and his son. The dispute was so serious, in fact, that James, Jr., moved out of the house to stay with friends soon after he turned eighteen.

But the elder Pierson had been especially loving and attentive to the girls since the death almost exactly a year earlier of his wife, Cathleen. The woman lost a spunky and difficult struggle for life, undergoing two kidney transplants and months of agonizing treatment. She was thirty-eight when she died—of pneumonia—after two weeks in a coma.

Cathleen Pierson's lingering illness was extraordinarily difficult for her family, perhaps especially so for Cheryl. As the oldest daughter, she was thrust into the roles of surrogate parent to her younger sister and as a near full-time nurse and helper to her ailing mother.

Matters were made even worse when James Pierson, Sr., fell and broke most of the bones in both feet while he was installing electrical wiring in the attic of his house. Cheryl was barely fourteen at the time. Nevertheless, she had to care for her injured father as well as her dying mother, while looking after her little sister and doing her best to keep up with her schoolwork. There was never enough time for sleep.

Cheryl's father did his best to care for the children during his wife's fatal illness and after her death. His mother, Virginia Pierson, and his sister, Marilyn Adams, often helped out. But it was clear that the electrician wasn't completely comfortable in the enforced role of being both father and mother to his brood. From outward appearances, the Piersons were a tight-knit family who were devoted to each other and stuck together. But there was a fly in the ointment somewhere, and it was the job of police to dig it out.

Suffolk County police homicide officers began probing into the dead man's financial and professional background, as well as his family and other personal relationships.

Examination of Pierson's financial records disclosed that when life insurance policies were included, his net worth was at least $500,000, perhaps much more. It was a sizable sum for an electrician who was a foreman for an electronics company in the nearby town of Huntington, and had a family to support. But he was also a partner in a lucrative cable television company. Investigators, however, failed to turn up any evidence of disgruntled business associates or shady deals that might have led to a contract killing. Pierson had accumulated his comfortable nest egg absolutely legally, through hard work, money-making real estate deals, and other timely investments.

Detectives learned that he had been a delegate for the International Brotherhood of Electrical Workers. But there was no indication that there were any unsavory dealings involving either the parent union or the local.

The investigation turned to James, Jr., and the source of the discord between him and his father. Police learned that the trouble between father and son apparently revolved around differences that make people talk about the generation gap. At six feet, two inches tall, and a hard-bodied 250 pounds, the elder Pierson had close-cropped red hair that matched his temper, and a reputation for being aggressively boisterous. He kept about a dozen guns around the house, including handguns, rifles, and an Uzi. Neighbors and other acquaintances recalled that he liked to sit on his porch and shoot squirrels and birds.

Pierson didn't like his son's long hair, and even though his son was straight, he called the teenager "the fag" because he wore earrings. The youth sometimes played drums at night, and talked about becoming a rock musician. It was behavior and aspirations that the elder Pierson had difficulty relating to. He also criticized James, Jr., for not learning a trade, and had threatened to cut him out of his will.

James, Jr., seemed to be taking steps to reconcile their differences, however, when his father was murdered. He had visited amiably with his father at a family gathering on Christmas Day, quit his job at the Stony Brook Hospital, found a better-paying job at a factory, and was taking classes at the Wilfred Beauty School in the Selden Mall to become a hairstylist.

The murdered man's wake was held at the same funeral home where his wife's services were conducted almost exactly a year earlier. While Pierson's body was on view in an open casket, his oldest daughter sobbed quietly as she sat with her brother and her boyfriend, Robert "Rob" Cuccio, Jr. It snowed the day of the funeral, but more than 250 people crowded into the mortuary to listen to a priest read a eulogy written by Cheryl.

Entitled "Our Dad," Cheryl's statement recalled her father's strong will and outspokenness, but also noted that he was softhearted. "He did a great job as a mother and father this last past year . . ." she wrote. "He was our best friend, as well as our dad . . ." Long before the priest completed reading the eulogy, most of the mourners were in tears.

The pretty teenager's testimonial, it seemed, had come straight from the heart. And it had contained no hint of the other Cheryl Pierson, the one who would begin to emerge as police continued to press their investigation.

Detective James McCready was chief investigator in the case and wanted to know more about the trouble between the father and son. When McCready talked with James, Jr., a few days after the shooting, he asked him who did the killing, and when the boy said he didn't know, the detective asked, "You did, didn't you,

Jimmy?" The teenager responded that he had absolutely nothing to do with it.

In fact, McCready already knew that James, Jr., had a solid alibi, since he had clocked in at work before the shooting occurred.

James, Jr., pointed the finger of guilt at Cheryl. He said she had told him on Christmas Day, at a family gathering, that she wanted their father killed. A few minutes after everyone opened their presents, Cheryl told him she was upset because her father wouldn't let her go out with her boyfriend on New Year's Eve, he related. James, Jr., said he didn't believe at that time that she was serious.

At first glance the idea that the cute five-foot-two-inch teenager had engineered her father's death seemed preposterous. Cheryl appeared to be a loving daughter who had taken on family responsibilities far beyond her years and was especially fond of her father. Less than a year earlier he had thrown a big Sweet Sixteen party for her, and they danced together to the music of "Sixteen Candles."

Cheryl was a popular though average student at Newfield High School in nearby Coram. At the beginning of the school term the previous fall, her junior year, she was named a cocaptain of the junior varsity cheerleading squad. Her father attended many of the games and practices, and proudly watched his daughter perform. In return, she was Daddy's Girl. Since her mother's illness, she had been cast in the role of the woman of the house. She fixed her father's favorite foods, massaged his chest and back, sat on his lap, and watched sports with him on his bedroom TV.

But under continued questioning, James, Jr., told McCready that Cheryl had not only asked him once to help find a hit man to have their father killed, but on two other occasions queried him about his progress. Furthermore, he said, her boyfriend also asked him if he had found anyone yet to carry out the contract killing.

McCready picked up Rob a few minutes after the young man dropped Cheryl off at her house following a date watching a talent show at Newfield High School. The son of a retired New York City policeman who had worked as a detective in the Bronx, the handsome nineteen-year-old quickly confirmed that he and Cheryl had, indeed, approached James, Jr., about finding a hit man to kill Pierson.

A couple of hours after Rob had returned his girl-friend to her home, he returned to the house with police. It was after midnight, and everyone in the house had already gone to bed. Cheryl was awakened and taken into custody for questioning about arranging her father's murder.

Early that morning, during a grueling interrogation session that stretched from midnight to two-thirty A.M., Cheryl told McCready and a fellow homicide detective what they already knew or suspected. Her father had been sexually abusing her. And she had arranged for a fellow student named Sean Pica, who sat next to her in their homeroom, to carry out the contract killing. She claimed that she tried to call off the murder, but Sean went ahead with the plan anyway.

Speaking in halting words punctuated with sobs, the girl said her father began sex play with her when she was eleven years old, shortly after her mother became ill. The abuse progressed from wrestling games when her father would grab her between the legs or pinch her breasts, to fondling while they were watching television together under a blanket in his bedroom—and finally to sexual intercourse that began when she was thirteen.

She said that she could have probably continued to endure the abuse until she was old enough to move out of the house. But since she had begun dating Rob, her father had been spending more time with JoAnn, Cheryl told the detectives. And she was afraid that JoAnn would become the next target of his incestuous abuse.

Curiously, Pica became a player in the tragedy almost

by accident after Cheryl heard him talking with other
students in their homeroom at school about a Long Island waitress named Beverly Wallace who had paid hit
men $4000 to murder her husband because he abused
her. The story was being broadcast on local radio news
and talk shows, and was headlined in the newspapers.
Sean bragged to Cheryl that he could kill someone if he
was paid enough. She asked how much that would be.

One thousand dollars, she quoted him as responding.
It was a few days before Cheryl talked to Sean again and
said she had a job for him.

Sean didn't resemble the popular concept of a hit
man, any more than Cheryl looked the role of a daughter who would arrange her father's murder. A bony,
dark-complexioned sixteen-year-old, he still had braces
on his teeth and fuzz on his face. He was a Boy Scout
who was working on an Eagle badge. He was also handy
with tools, and was preparing to represent his school in
a carpentry competition.

Curiously, like Rob, Sean's father, Benjamin Pica, was
also a former New York City policemen. But unlike
Rob, who came from a close-knit family in Selden that
included a brother and a sister, and a mother and father
married for years, his parents were divorced. Sometime
after the divorce, the elder Pica married a policewoman
whom he worked with in the city. Sean lived in Selden
with his mother, a nurse; and a younger brother. An
older brother was in the Navy.

Sean was just leaving his house, on his way to school
in the morning, when police pulled up and hustled him
into an unmarked car. He was driven to police headquarters for questioning. He soon confessed to carrying
out the shooting. And he said he had initiated an earlier
unsuccessful attempt to murder his schoolmate's father
as well.

The first time Pierson was targeted for death, Sean
pitched a brick through a window of an unoccupied
house the widower owned across the street from the

family's house on 293 Magnolia Drive. He explained to the homicide officers that he planned to stab Pierson to death when the man came outside his house in response to the sounding of the burglar alarm. But the alarm didn't go off, so Sean put off the murder and started looking around for a gun.

He said that he finally bought a .22-caliber pump-action rifle at a Queens cemetery, where thieves and other no-goods gathered at night to sell or swap stolen goods. The day of the shooting, Sean got up before dawn, pulled on a pair of pants and a dark jacket, and loaded the rifle with five shells. Then he slipped off through a nearby woods and the chill winter darkness on his way to the Pierson house. He said he hid behind a tree with his rifle, until Cheryl's father walked out of the house about a half hour later.

After the shooting, Sean returned home, cleaned up, then drove his girlfriend and a couple of other schoolmates to the Selden Mall for breakfast. Finally, he drove the group to school.

Sean told police that he tossed the murder weapon into Mount Sinai Harbor on Long Island Sound. Even though he pointed out the exact location where he claimed he disposed of the rifle, however, police divers were unable to find it.

Weeks later, a teenage friend of Sean's told authorities that his pal had lied about buying the rifle at a stolen goods flea market. The teenager said he gave it to Sean for safekeeping after stealing it, and was unaware it would be used in a killing. Then he led the officers to a wooded area where the boys had used a tree for target practice. McCready recovered some of the expended shells and sent them to the ballistics laboratory. Tests disclosed they were fired from the same weapon used in the slaying of the Selden electrician.

Eight days after James Pierson, Sr., was shot to death in front of his house, his daughter, her boyfriend, and her classmate appeared in court to enter pleas for their reputed involvement in his murder.

Rob, whose slender, almost gaunt face was set off with a carefully trimmed mustache, was the first of the three teenage defendants to appear before the judge. He pleaded not guilty to a charge of conspiracy, based on his role making the payoff to Sean. His parents, who were in the courtroom with the families of the other defendants, immediately posted their son's $5000 bail.

Cheryl was the next to enter a plea. She entered the courtroom wearing sweatpants and her red high school jacket with the name "Wolverines" printed across the front. It was the nickname of the school's basketball team. The squad was having a bad season, but their pretty junior varsity cheerleader was having an even worse year. The frightened teenager's hands were cuffed behind her and she was crying. Her lawyer wiped the tears from her cheeks.

Family members had already found her an attorney, Paul Gianelli. He was an experienced criminal lawyer who knew his way around Suffolk County courtrooms. Cheryl's relatives had made a good choice. Gianelli told the judge that his client was more victim than defendant. And for the first time, publicly, he disclosed accusations that she had been beaten by her father as well as sexually abused.

"Many students have often seen her with black and blue marks from brutal beatings that she got. There was intercourse," Gianelli asserted. Cheryl pleaded not guilty to charges of second degree murder and conspiracy, and the judge set her bail at $50,000. It was a staggering amount of money, and the teenager's grandmother and aunt weren't in a position to post it immediately. With tears still streaming down her cheeks, and still in handcuffs, Cheryl was led out of the courtroom and returned to the Suffolk County Jail.

The last of the three to appear before the judge, Sean was described by the prosecutor as a contract killer who murdered for money. He pleaded not guilty to second degree murder and conspiracy, as Cheryl had. His bail was set at $100,000. Like Cheryl, the scrawny teenager was led back to the jail in handcuffs. He was still there four days later, on February 18, his seventeenth birthday.

Nine days after entering her not guilty plea, Cheryl was released from jail when friends of her father provided bail. She moved in with her father's sister, Marilyn, who had been appointed guardian. Sean was finally bailed out of jail in May, after his bail was reduced to $25,000. He went to live with his father and stepmother in nearby Valley Stream until his trial.

A few weeks after Cheryl was released from jail, she began bleeding and was rushed from her aunt's house to a hospital, where she miscarried. She had already confided to family members and her attorney that she was pregnant with her father's baby. Tissue and blood from the eight-week-old fetus and the placenta were sent to a high-tech laboratory in Westchester, where sophisticated genetic screening tests were conducted, to compare its molecules with molecules from blood and brain tissue kept from the autopsy on Cheryl's father. The DNA imprint didn't match. But similar tests showed a match with Rob's DNA. Cheryl's boyfriend, not her father, was responsible for her pregnancy.

Cheryl had admitted having sexual relations with Rob, although she insisted that they didn't become intimate until after they had dated for months—long after her father had begun forcing his attention on her. But it seemed that the only people who really knew for sure if her story of incest was true, or if Pierson had merely been a strict, perhaps sometimes brutal, disciplinarian, were Cheryl and her father. And he was dead.

Cheryl left her aunt's house and moved in with the Kossers a few days before the results of the paternity tests were determined. Mrs. Kosser, who was in the hospital when the shooting occurred, was one of Cheryl's mother's closest friends. She had a son and daughter, and both she and her husband had previously observed things in the Pierson home that worried them. They welcomed the troubled girl with open arms.

By that time, a Suffolk County grand jury had already returned second degree murder indictments against Cheryl and Sean. According to New York state criminal law at that time, sixteen-year-olds charged with murder were automatically treated as adults. Consequently, if convicted, they could face minimum prison terms of fifteen years. Sean's family had also found an attorney for him, Martin Efman. Like Gianelli, Efman was an experienced criminal lawyer.

Rob wasn't indicted. Prosecutors wanted his cooperation in the cases against his girlfriend and her former schoolmate. His testimony could be vital to prosecution efforts to establish a conspiracy link between Cheryl and Sean.

Rob told Assistant District Attorney Edward Jablonski that he had been seeing Cheryl for a long time when he began getting suspicious that her relationship with her father wasn't what it should be. He explained that it was months before her father allowed him to take her out on dates. Instead, he had to call at home, where he watched television with the family and didn't have an opportunity to be alone with her.

Rob said that when Cheryl paid too much attention to him on their curious in-home dates, her father reacted jealously. And the young man said he wasn't happy with the way that Pierson touched his daughter and hit her. Despite the eagle eye Pierson kept on his daughter, Rob said, he and Cheryl had already begun having sexual relations when he asked her around the time of the Christmas holidays if something bad was going on between her and her father. At first she denied there was anything wrong. But she finally admitted her father had been sexually molesting her since she was around twelve years old.

Cheryl told him even earlier that she wanted her father dead, Rob recalled. He said the first time she mentioned it to him was around the date of her Sweet Sixteen party, which he attended. And she told him about her conversation with Sean.

Rob said that the day after the murder, while several other people were in the house, Cheryl opened her father's wall safe, which was built into the living room closet, and took out some money. The next day he drove her to school, where Sean was paid $400 for the contract murder. He was promised the remaining $600 later.

While Cheryl and Sean continued free on bail and attempted to lead lives that were as normal as possible, the defense and prosecution were busy digging up evidence, witnesses, and jockeying for position in anticipation of the trial. Assistant D.A. Jablonski won a major skirmish when Suffolk Supreme Court justice Harvey W. Sherman ruled against a motion by Gianelli to separate the cases against the two teenagers. It appeared that when the trial occurred, the former schoolmates would face justice as co-defendants.

There was still a chance, however, that there would be no trial. Jablonski discussed a plea bargain deal with the two defense attorneys. He offered to accept pleas of guilty to scaled-down charges of manslaughter, but only if both defendants agreed to the deal. According to the plan, Sean would wind up with a six-year prison term, and Cheryl would be given a two-year prison sentence. Gianelli balked. Cheryl's lawyer wouldn't agree to any jail time for his client. If she was forced into sexual intercourse with her father over a period of years, she had already been punished enough, he insisted. There was no deal.

Judge Sherman set a tentative trial date for January 12, 1987. Then it was moved back a couple of months to March 24. Meanwhile, negotiations between the defense attorneys, the prosecutor, and the judge continued.

There was a surprise waiting for news reporters and other curious onlookers when they assembled at the yellow-brick courthouse in Riverhead on the bleak, frigid late-March morning that had been set for the beginning of the trial. The teenage defendants and their attorneys had agreed to a deal with the prosecutor after all. They were prepared to enter pleas of guilty to manslaughter.

Cheryl, wearing a white sweater and a gray skirt, with a dainty crucifix dangling from a chain around her neck, was the first of the defendants called before Judge Sherman. After eliciting her near-whispered confirmation that she was seventeen years old and was represented by Gianelli, the judge asked if she knew that she was about to plead guilty.

"Sure," she said.

Cheryl was trembling, although still on top of her emotions as she stood before the bench with her attorney. But she lost her control when Judge Sherman pointed out that after he had ordered and studied a probation report, and considered the possibility of treating her as a youthful offender, she could still face a possible prison sentence ranging from a maximum of six years to a minimum of two. Her shoulders slumped and she began sobbing.

The tears continued to flow as Jablonski began questioning her. Had she asked Sean Pica to kill her father?, the prosecutor queried. She said she had.

"Why did you want him to kill your father?" Jablonski asked.

Cheryl couldn't immediately reply. Tears were streaming down her cheeks, and her mouth opened as she struggled to speak. At last she succeeded. "He . . . was . . . sexually abusing me," she wailed.

Judge Sherman said he would announce a hearing date later, to determine her punishment. Still in tears, Cheryl lurched to the rear of the courtroom and into the comforting arms of her brother. She would remain free on bail, pending sentencing.

Then it was Sean's turn. His mother and father followed and stood on each side of him as he walked to the bench and stood before the judge.

"How do you plead?" the judge asked.

"Guilty," the boy replied in a voice that was even, and seemingly devoid of emotion.

The gray leather jacket Sean was wearing did little to hide his slight frame. Despite his studied calm, he still looked like the frightened teenager that he was. In response to continued questioning from the judge, Sean said he was eighteen years old, confirmed that Efman was his lawyer, and said he was aware that he was giving up his right to a trial by jury.

Judge Sherman told him that he had advised his attorney that he would consider youthful offender treatment, but that the youngster also faced the possibility of a jail term ranging from twenty-five years at the top to a minimum of eight and one-third years.

The potential prison sentence was considerably more severe than the possible penalty the court had outlined a few minutes earlier for Cheryl. But Sean was the triggerman in a killing that he had undertaken for pay. And there was no contention that he had ever been abused by the victim. Sean Pica hadn't even known James Pierson, Sr.

During questioning by Jablonski, Sean recounted the murder and confirmed that he had accepted $400 the next day, then after a time asked for more money, and permission to live rent free in the house he had tossed the brick through. Investigators had learned earlier that on the night of the victim's funeral, Sean demanded the additional money, the free house rent, and motorcycles for himself and his best pal.

Jablonski had no more questions. Nor did Judge Sherman. He announced sentencing for April 28. Sean was handcuffed and led from the courtroom to be driven to the Suffolk County Correctional Center.

When Sean returned a few days later for sentencing,

Efman addressed the court. It was the defense attorney's last chance to win leniency for his client. Efman insisted that the murder scheme wasn't Sean's. "This was not his idea. Money was not the motivating force. Someone gave his word to Sean Pica, and he had had that word broken to him in the past," the defense attorney declared. "This is not a murder for hire. This is not a murder for money. Sean made a commitment." Efman asked the judge to be merciful to his client.

Judge Sherman asked Sean if he had anything to say. "I just want to say I'm sorry that this happened," Sean replied.

The judge's sentencing statement was short, to the point, and stern. "I have no messages to send to society," he told the defendant. "But I do have a message for you—something I hope you'll think about during the time in prison. You are not being punished for the loyal assistance to a friend. You are being punished for asking for one thousand dollars, and executing him in ambush."

Judge Sherman ordered a term of from eight to twenty-four years in prison. For the last time Sean was handcuffed and led from the courtroom.

When Judge Sherman received the Suffolk County Probation Department report he had ordered on Cheryl, it carried a recommendation that she be sentenced as a youthful offender. Sentencing as a youthful offender would provide for a penalty ranging from probation to two years in prison.

Just two weeks before Cheryl's scheduled sentencing hearing, a segment about the Pierson case was broadcast on the popular television program, *20/20*. The presentation was generally sympathetic to her.

Suddenly, Cheryl Pierson's plight was in the thoughts of men and women around the country. Letters began streaming into Riverhead from sympathizers living in states hundreds of miles away, pleading with the judge to show mercy in his sentence decision. A distressing number of the women, and some of the men, had been victims of sexual and other physical and emotional abuse themselves when they were children. News and feature writers and columnists with newspapers in the Long Island and New York City area, as well as elsewhere, pounced on the story with renewed vigor. The consensus was that Cheryl had suffered enough.

Her boyfriend Rob wanted to marry Cheryl. His parents supported the young couple, and were looking forward to welcoming the girl into the family. It was clear that even though Cheryl had lost a big part of one family, she had gained another.

That was all well and good, but Cheryl's attorney, along with other legal professionals, were aware that Judge Sherman was unlikely to be swayed by emotion when he made his sentencing decision. And in many ways the sentencing hearing would take the place of the trial that never occurred, publicly answering some of the questions that were so troubling about the case.

Predictably, the courtroom was filled when Cheryl appeared on September 9 for the beginning of her sentencing hearing. She wore a white blouse and beige skirt with a pink ribbon tied around it. She was nevertheless beginning to lose the fresh high school cheerleader look. She had put on some weight, and her demeanor was understandably solemn.

Opening statements were brief. Gianelli pounced on the probation report. Noting that her incarceration was recommended in the report, he promised to show through witnesses "a rather vivid and realistic picture of the kind of life Cheryl Pierson was living several years before her father's death."

Jablonski announced that the prosecution wouldn't contest the girl's claim of incest. "No one here can answer that. The only person here who knows for sure is the person who had her father killed," he said. "And you have to ask yourself: Why?"

The prosecutor pointed out that incest is not unique.

But he questioned why Cheryl felt that it was necessary to take her father's life. "Why was her situation special?" he asked. "Why does she deserve probation, a mere pat on the head? Why was her situation different from all other incestuous situations?"

Alberta Kosser was the first witness called by Gianelli. She traced her friendship with Cheryl's mother, and she talked about Pierson's imperious manner in the home. She told of the children not being allowed to speak during meals, and about his rough treatment of the children.

She said she was concerned because Cheryl spent so much time in the bedroom with her father watching television, while Pierson's sick wife, Cathy, remained in the living room on the couch. Mrs. Kosser said that she once told Cheryl while they were in the kitchen together that she was a big girl and should watch television in her own room. Cheryl watched TV in her own room for a couple of nights, then resumed the old pattern, the witness testified.

Mrs. Kosser told about Cheryl sitting in her father's lap and rubbing his bare chest in front of company. She mentioned a conversation between Pierson and his daughter when he used an unnecessarily crude sexual term to warn her about attention from boys at school. And she said that once when Mrs. Pierson was in the hospital and the girls were having dinner at the Kosser home, JoAnn blurted out: "Cheryl slept with Daddy last night."

During cross-examination, Jablonski asked if she had ever queried Pierson about why Cheryl was in his bedroom at night. She said she did, and he told her that it was because the girl had nightmares.

Michael Kosser followed his wife to the witness stand, and when he was asked what he thought of his former neighbor, described him as crude. "He was always smacking the children. Pulling their hair, punching them. To me there was no reason for it," Kosser said.

Gianelli asked if Kosser was against striking a youngster.

"No, I am not," Kosser said.

The attorney asked what upset him about the physical violence. Kosser said that he wouldn't want to be punched the way Pierson hit his son. "Did you ever talk to James Pierson about it?" Gianelli inquired.

"Yes, I did," Kosser replied. "And he told me it was none of my fucking business."

The plain-spoken mechanic, who appeared as at ease and confident on the witness stand as if he were sitting at his own kitchen table, also told of a time in 1981 when Mrs. Pierson's stepfather dropped in at the Kosser house. Kosser said the man looked upset, and he asked what the trouble was.

"I hope I'm wrong. I think Jimmy and Cheryl—something is going on," the witness recalled his worried guest as saying. Kosser said the stepfather claimed he had walked in on them and Cheryl was under the covers, lying on top of her father.

"I made a purpose of watching after that," Kosser said.

Gianelli asked what he saw.

"He was always pinching, pulling her hair, fondling her, making remarks like, 'Doesn't she have a nice pair of tits?' He was rubbing her bottom." Kosser said Cheryl was fifteen or sixteen at that time.

Witness after witness trooped to the stand, talking of suspicions of incest, seeing evidence of physical abuse or overhearing crude sexual comments by Pierson about his daughter. But one after the other, with one glaring exception, each one of the witnesses admitted that they had not brought their suspicions to the attention of authorities. They either excused themselves by remarking that they had no proof or said they didn't think anyone would believe them.

Judy Ozarowski, another neighborhood friend of Cheryl's mother, told of a Fourth of July party when she overheard Pierson call to his daughter. "You. You little cunt, get over here," she quoted him as demanding.

MaryAnn Sargeant, a neighborhood and school friend of Cheryl told about the curious restrictions that Pierson imposed on his daughter's social life. More ominously, she testified that one time when the girls were talking on the telephone, Cheryl told her she had to hang up. The girl said Cheryl explained that she had to take a nap with her father.

Grace Sargeant, MaryAnn's mother, testified that she considered notifying the authorities once when Cheryl showed up with a black eye because she had bought a Valentine for a boy. But at her daughter's behest, Mrs. Sargeant didn't call police or social workers. And she didn't seek help for her daughter's girlfriend when MaryAnn came home one day and said that she had left the Pierson house because Cheryl's father came home.

"And I said, 'So what?'" the witness recalled. "And she [MaryAnn] said Cheryl had to take a nap with her father. And then I said, 'That's it!'" There was no question of the sincerity in the woman's voice when she told the court how she regretted not doing anything at that time. "That bothers me more than anything," she said.

Mrs. Sargeant testified that when her daughter telephoned her on the morning of the shooting and told her that Pierson was dead, she ran to the house and saw two police officers. "And when I saw them, I thought: 'Please God, don't let it be Cheryl because he went after JoAnn,'" she said.

Toni-Ann Macaluso, an attractive young woman who had once dated James, Jr., testified that she was at her boyfriend's house one time when Pierson was picking on his daughter. Describing Pierson as "a strong, very macho man," she said he was hitting Cheryl. "What's a matter? What's a matter? You can't take it? You can't take it?" she quoted him as saying.

"The only way he would stop was for her to give him a big hug and say, 'Oh Daddy, I love you,' and be all over him," the witness said. She told the court that she also saw Pierson lift his daughter over his head and slip his hand between her legs.

"In the vagina area?" Gianelli asked.

"Yes," she said.

A telephone installer who had once worked for Pierson in the cable television business, and also lived for a time in the rental house, told the court that the victim often beat his son. And he said he saw Cheryl with bruises and a swollen eye. "She told us her father hit her because a card fell out of a book," he said. It was another account of the Valentine card incident.

When the phone installer's wife testified, she was asked to describe Pierson. "He was loud, vulgar, and abusive with his mouth and his hands," she said.

Another woman, whose mother had married Mrs. Pierson's uncle, recalled Cheryl's father as having a terrible temper. She said that she saw him hit Cheryl so hard that the girl flew back against a wall. And she said he was a groper. "He felt free to grab my behind. I didn't like it. He scared me. On a sexual level," she explained. "He had no real regard for women."

More than a dozen adults were called by Gianelli to testify, but although many of them had witnessed behavior by Pierson toward his daughter that was clearly sexual, no one had sought help from police or other government agencies for the girl. Only a teenage girlfriend and former schoolmate of Cheryl had spoken up. And she was rejected by the professional she went to for help.

Diana Lynne Erbentraut said that after she began suspecting there was something wrong about the relationship between Cheryl and her father, she asked her friend about it. She said Cheryl looked at her, frightened. Diana went to her school guidance counselor for help. But she said the counselor told her she didn't have time for her then. So Diana told her father, and he advised her to try the guidance counselor again. The concerned schoolgirl told the counselor that she was worried Cheryl was beaten, and there was something seriously wrong with the father-daughter relationship.

"I cannot take your word for it," she quoted the counselor as telling her. "Cheryl will have to tell me about it." But Cheryl didn't.

If spectators were expecting to see a clone of the brutal man they had been hearing about when Cheryl's brother was called to the stand, they were badly mistaken. James Pierson, Sr., was a crude six-foot-two-inch bully who wore his red hair cropped close to his head. James, Jr. was a tall, slender, handsome young man with shoulder-length blond hair, whose speech and manner were civil and polished.

Under Gianelli's questioning, he told of a childhood that was filled with emotional and physical abuse from his father. Report card time was a horror. Even B-pluses could bring a beating. No matter what he did, he couldn't please his father.

Mealtime was an ordeal. He said that his father didn't allow the children to drink anything at meals until they had finished all their food. And they had to eat their food in even proportions, a bit of this, and a bit of that, until they finished. The children weren't allowed to talk at mealtime, and they were often slapped before the meal was over.

He said that when Cheryl was fourteen or fifteen, their father installed a special security system so that while he was lying in bed he could tell exactly where anyone inside the house was walking.

Gianelli asked how he responded when Cheryl told him that she wanted to have their father killed. He said he told her that he had gone through it, and to "Hang in there." The lawyer wanted to know if JoAnn was mentioned during the conversation.

"Yes," the young man replied. "Cheryl said that she couldn't leave JoAnn behind. I told her I went through the abuse. She went through the abuse, and it would be JoAnn's turn."

Although James, Jr., said he was thinking of physical abuse when he talked with his sister, his statement had a chilling effect on spectators in the courtroom. Even the prosecutor had said that he wouldn't contest Cheryl's claim of incest. And professionals in criminal justice and the social sciences have repeatedly warned that in homes where father-daughter incest occurs, when an older child grows up, the abuser's sexual attentions are frequently transferred to a younger child.

The witness said that Cheryl told him she would never leave their little sister behind. She vowed she would take JoAnn with her when she left, he related.

Continuing to respond to questions, James, Jr., testified that he wasn't worried about his father's safety after the conversations with his sister during the holiday period. "I just figured things were tense around the house. I went through the same thing," he explained. "A few times I also wanted him dead."

But when it was Jablonski's turn to cross-examine, he wasn't about to drop the matter of the witness's lack of concern over the elder Pierson's safety. He demanded to know if James, Jr., hadn't begun to take the matter seriously after Rob Cuccio talked with him about Cheryl's murder scheme.

James, Jr., said he still didn't believe they were serious about Cheryl wanting their father killed because he wouldn't let her go out on New Year's Eve. And in fact, the witness pointed out, their father had let her go out after all.

Jablonski asked if James, Jr., knew his father planned to cut him out of his will. The witness said he knew, and had told his father that he didn't care. The young man was calm and studied on the witness stand. He responded alike to angry accusations or sarcasm with replies that were courteous and audible.

When Jablonski asked him what he would have done

if he had known his father was sexually abusing his sister, the unflappable witness replied: "I probably would have killed my father myself." James, Jr. said he didn't know his father was sexually intimate with his sister until the night of her arrest, when she told him.

Responding to Jablonski's request to describe the estate left by his father, James, Jr. said it was worth about $600,000. That included the family house, which was valued at about $140,000; the rental house across the street, worth $110,000; another $25,000 house in upstate New York; eight life-insurance policies with a total value in excess of $130,000; and bank accounts totaling about $200,000. Most of the bank accounts were in the names of his sisters, he said.

James, Jr. was executor of the estate, and he told the court that he planned to give Cheryl a share larger than his own. He said her legal expenses would also be paid from the estate, and he planned to buy her a house. "I will provide for Cheryl whatever she needs," he said.

Cheryl's brother had been a strong witness for the defense, and his loyalty to his besieged sister was impressive.

But the former cheerleader, herself, was the most dramatic witness of the hearing, which was already taking longer than many trials. Cheryl, wearing a white blouse and gray skirt, was called to the witness stand at the beginning of the second week. Her fluffy shoulder-length, honey-brown hair was pulled back with barrettes. Although she had put on some weight and was beginning to lose a bit of the little girl look, her appearance was still one of vulnerability.

Peering alternately at her lawyer, the judge, and the spectators, Cheryl said her father first began fondling her after her mother became ill. During the drive to the hospital, she would lay her head on his lap and he would stroke her back and buttocks. At other times she would sit close to him and he would rub her legs and chest. She said she thought he was merely showing affection.

She talked about watching television with her father in his room, and of falling asleep in his bed at night while her sick mother slept on the living room couch. She said he became increasingly possessive as she got older, rummaging through her drawers and her purse. He used a personal phone he kept in the basement to listen in on her telephone conversations.

The girl said that he would pick on her, and she would have to lie down with him to make him happy. If she didn't cooperate, he would fly into a rage or pick a fight with his wife.

Cheryl's recital was controlled and free of intense emotion until Gianelli asked how she dealt with giving in to her father's demands. Then she began to cry, and said she would simply lie on the bed as he did what he wanted.

"When he was on top of me he used to breathe in my face," she said. "I used to put a pillow on my face and block it out until it was over."

Turning to other matters, Gianelli asked her about Valentine's Day two years before her father was killed. Cheryl said her father was driving her between their house and school when he found a Valentine card she had bought for a boy she had a crush on. Pierson exploded in anger and hit her in the face. She said he continued hitting her on the way home, then complained to his wife that Cheryl lied to him. It was the marks of that beating that the neighbors had testified about earlier.

Cheryl said her father began touching her once when her mother was dying in the hospital, and she told him: "I don't believe you! Your wife's in the hospital and she's in a coma, and you're touching me."

Her father was outraged, the girl said. "Don't you ever put a guilt trip on me again," she quoted him as warning her.

Cheryl said that she lay on her mother's side of the bed when she and her father were together there. And after her mother's death, Cheryl always felt that she was looking down at them. "I figured if she was in Heaven, she would be watching us," the teenager testified.

She said that her father's demand for sex increased once the household quieted down and guests left following her mother's death. He forced her into bed only two days after her mother's funeral. Cheryl claimed they were having sex about twice a day.

Gianelli turned to Pierson's relationship with JoAnn. Cheryl said that after school resumed, and she began leading cheers and going to games, she would return home and find her little sister with her head on her father's chest, watching television "like I used to do."

Cheryl recounted her conversations with Sean, first about the Beverly Wallace case, then about a $1000 murder contract on her father. "Did you think about what you were asking Sean to do?" Gianelli inquired.

"I thought my father wouldn't have sex with me anymore, that it would end," Cheryl responded. "It didn't seem serious. It was more like a game. . . ." She said that after Sean tossed the brick through the window of the rental house, she tried during different conversations—including one the day before the slaying—to get him to call off the murder plan.

Near the end of her testimony, Cheryl outlined her recollections of the morning of her father's murder. She recalled getting up and padding to the door to leave the dog out, then looking through the blinds and seeing her father lying in a pool of blood. She said that after the police officer told her and her sister that their father was dead, JoAnn hugged her. "Does this mean I can wear nail polish?" she said her sister asked.

Cheryl said that she had a job as a beautician, and was attending therapy twice a week.

Questioning by her own attorney was long and arduous, but Cheryl's cross-examination was expected to be the most difficult part of the ordeal. Before she was cross-examined, however, testimony was heard from Dr. Jean Goodwin, a professor of psychiatry at the Medical College of Wisconsin. Widely recognized for her expertise dealing with the sexual abuse of children, Dr. Goodwin talked with both Cheryl and James, Jr. and had flown to New York from Milwaukee for the hearing. She also interviewed Cheryl's personal therapist.

Dr. Goodwin told the court that she believed Cheryl was subjected to emotional, physical, and sexual abuse. And she said she believed that when the teenager set the wheels in motion for her father's murder, she was suffering from post-traumatic stress syndrome.

Post-traumatic stress syndrome was a condition that Americans had been hearing a lot of since the Vietnam War. The troubles of many veterans of fighting in Southeast Asia who returned to the United States and had difficulty adjusting to civilian life have been blamed on the syndrome. A generation earlier, psychiatrists, psychologists, and other mental health professionals who treated former American servicemen after World War II, talked of "shell shock" and "battle fatigue."

At first, descriptions of post-traumatic stress syndrome was usually applied to veterans who couldn't find or hold jobs, who had difficulty with marital and other personal relationships, beat their wives and children, or who got into other troubles with the law. It has been blamed in the courts by lawyers and mental health professionals for everything from murder, rape, and suicides to alcoholism, narcotics abuse, and bad credit ratings.

Gradually, post-traumatic stress syndrome began to be applied in the courts to nonveterans, including victims of domestic violence—wives or children submitted to sexual or other physical or emotional abuse. Now, Dr. Goodwin was telling the court that Cheryl had experienced the condition. She had observed the symptoms in Cheryl, or in her behavioral background, the psychiatrist testified.

She pointed out that Cheryl was easily startled, and once struck a roommate who touched her while she was sleeping. She said other phobias, as well as what she termed the "easy startle response," supported the diagnosis. She said that Cheryl was still terrified of being in the shower; afraid of the dark; complained of chronic anger and temper tantrums; and "repetitions of trauma she had in nightmares and flashbacks."

Dr. Goodwin pointed out that Cheryl's response to her father's sexual demands was typical of incest victims when she tried to mentally or emotionally distance herself from what was going on in her daily life and with her body. Placing the pillow over her face during sex with her father was one example, the witness cited.

She used the pillow incident to lead into the question of how serious Cheryl may have really been when she talked to Sean about killing her father. She talked of Cheryl trying to cope with her problem by not being able to feel what was real and what was not. "That explains her perplexity about the murder plot. Was it something she and Sean thought was really going to happen, or just something they were talking about, and the talking made her feel better?" the psychiatrist asked.

So, it seemed according to the testimony that by fantasizing, Cheryl was attempting to cope with her helplessness, feelings of guilt, frustrations, and all the other problems of being incestuously victimized by her father. Merely talking about killing James Pierson, Sr., made her feel better. The revenge fantasy was her release. And, of course, the girl had been telling authorities all along that she didn't think her schoolmate would really murder her father.

Dr. Goodwin further buttressed her contention by pointing out that when Cheryl asked her brother for help having their father killed, James, Jr. didn't take the matter seriously. "It is interesting that her brother regarded it not as a request, but rather as a cry for help," the witness pointed out. "In November she asked Sean Pica. In December she asked her brother. It is the same girl, and her brother knows her best. And he knows she's just letting off steam."

When Cheryl returned to the stand to be cross-examined, the prosecutor once again led her through her talks with Sean about murder; about her behavior on the morning of the shooting; about her sexual activity with her father and with her boyfriend; and about her pregnancy. The only time she cried, however, was during a period of particularly intense questioning about why on the two occasions when she admitted to concerned friends that her father hit her, she didn't also tell them about the sexual abuse.

"When you told them about the physical abuse, did you ask them not to say anything?" Jablonski demanded.

"Yes. But I didn't want to tell anyone," Cheryl replied.

"So you figured it would be better or easier to kill your father than to tell," the prosecutor accused.

"I figured if I wouldn't get caught, no one would ever know I was abused," Cheryl said.

The prosecutor pounced. "Now that you're caught, you just don't want to go to prison," he boomed in a half statement, half question.

Cheryl was crying. "I don't know," she sobbed.

She cried again during her attorney's redirect examination. It was important for Gianelli to establish why she hadn't told anyone else about the sexual abuse except her boyfriend Rob, before police interrogators confronted her. She said she was ashamed. Gianelli asked if when people point at her or whisper when she is around, if she is ashamed about the abuse or because she hired someone to kill her father.

"Even if my father weren't murdered," she sobbed,

"they would still point and whisper about the sexual abuse."

Cheryl's testimony was riveting and emotionally draining. Several other witnesses, including her boyfriend Rob, also testified, shedding further light on the case. But perhaps the most startling testimony was provided by a man whom few people in the packed courtroom had ever heard of before, until he took the stand.

Jay Fleckenstein had written to Gianelli from Tucson, Arizona, after seeing the *20/20* television broadcast about the case, and suggested that he had information that might be helpful. Beginning his testimony, the thirty-three-year-old witness explained that he was Cheryl's uncle through marriage. He and her mother lived in the same household when Cathleen Pierson was a teenager.

Fleckenstein said that the last time he saw Mrs. Pierson was December 1982, when he returned to Long Island for his father's funeral. He was accompanying Cathleen to the doctor's office when he asked her during casual conversation why she was still so sick, after having a kidney transplant.

"She said they [her kidneys] had deteriorated," Fleckenstein said, "because of the beatings James Pierson had given her."

There were audible gasps from the spectator section. But Fleckenstein had more shocks in store for the court. "I asked her why she was getting beaten, and she said that while James thought she was asleep, he was going into Cheryl's room."

The message seemed to be clear. The frail, sick woman had known that her husband was sexually abusing her daughter. And when she complained about it, the beating she received may have cost her life—or at the very least, hastened her death.

During closing arguments, Jablonski pleaded with the judge not to give Cheryl probation without jail time. He cautioned that leniency of that kind would send the wrong message to the public: that her conduct was being condoned.

"The biggest fear is that there is another person being abused right this minute. We fear a woman who is a victim of rape, unhappy by how she may be treated in a courtroom, might take the law into her own hands if all she receives is probation," the prosecutor declared.

At the conclusion of his statement, he conceded that Pierson was a terrible father. "I would have loved to prosecute James Pierson for that conduct," he asserted. But neither the D.A.'s office, the judge, or a jury got that opportunity, he pointed out. "She became the prosecutor, the judge, and the jury, and decided whether this man should live or die. She decided that all by herself, and then with other people," the prosecutor declared. Cheryl was in tears again.

Gianelli talked about the tragedy of Cheryl's mother going to her grave and leaving her daughter behind, unprotected from James Pierson, Sr., without calling on someone else for help. And he stressed Cheryl's fears that her little sister had already been pinpointed as the next victim.

Gianelli pleaded for probation for his client. "I'd like you to consider the kind of girl she is. Consider what simple incarceration will do to her. She's not a streetwise kid. She is an immature, shy, sheltered girl from the suburbs," the defense attorney asserted.

"At some point in her life she has to put this behind her and live a normal life . . . I ask you to be merciful."

It was an impassioned and eloquent plea, and it ended the grueling three-week sentencing hearing. Judge Sherman began working on his decision.

It was October 5, 1987, and James Pierson, Sr., had been dead almost two years when Cheryl, attorneys, family members, and other spectators reassembled in the courtroom. Cheryl was already in tears when she walked inside, and she looked like she had been crying most of the morning. But there was worse to come.

The judge hadn't yet entered the courtroom when the defense attorney and prosecutor walked out of his chambers carrying copies of his nine-page decision in their hands. His features grave, Gianelli slid into his chair beside Cheryl and whispered to her. "No. Oh no," she screamed. The color drained from her face, and she began to shake.

A few moments later the judge entered the court-room and she was called to stand before the bench. Cheryl lurched to her feet, wobbled to the front of the room, and stood unsteadily in front of the judge. Then her legs gave way, and bailiffs hurried toward her with a chair. Cheryl slumped into the seat.

When the judge asked if she had anything to say before sentence was passed, she couldn't immediately speak. She kept trying, and eventually succeeded in forcing the words out, one and two at a time. "I realize that what I did was wrong. And I . . . I'm . . . sorry!" Cheryl used the paper towel she had hastily scribbled a few notes on for her statement to swipe at the tears flowing down her cheeks.

Judge Sherman said that he had received more than a hundred letters from people asking him to treat her with leniency. Most of the letters were from victims of incest, other sexual abuse or domestic violence. He was still talking when Cheryl's rag-doll body slid onto the floor. The bailiffs lifted her back onto the chair, and one of them waved a vial of smelling salts under her nose.

She was conscious and sobbing when he announced: "Cheryl Pierson, I hereby sentence you to five years' probation. As part of that sentence, you are to serve six months in the county jail."

Cheryl's body wavered. "No, no, no," she cried.

Two bailiffs, supporting both her arms, quickly walked her from the courtroom. Her face was flushed and she was wailing, "I don't want to go to jail." Sheriff's deputies waited to handcuff her until she was outside. Slumped disconsolately between his parents, her boyfriend watched helplessly from the spectator seats. He also was in tears as family members helped him from the courthouse.

Cheryl's grandmother, who had said the girl should be jailed, was also watching. "That kid's got to learn to live with this disgrace," Virginia Pierson told reporters. But the jail sentence was no victory for her. "I hurt for both of them," she said. "My son because he's in the ground, and my granddaughter because she's got to go to jail."

The sentence was neither a total victory nor a total defeat for the prosecutor or for the defense attorney. "I was hoping like hell she would walk out with me," Gianelli told reporters after the sentencing. But he said he was pleased that it was a relatively short sentence. He described it as a bittersweet ending to a sad case. "She's a very, very fragile child," he said of his client. "One day of incarceration is going to hurt her. She is not prepared to undergo the indignity of jail."

Despite the judge's order, Cheryl wasn't expected to spend a full six months behind bars. She was given credit for the two weeks that she was locked up immediately after her arrest. And credit for good behavior could trim the time she was actually locked up by additional weeks, or months. Nevertheless, the teenager was devastated. Gianelli's remarks about her fragility hadn't been mere legal bombast.

Regardless of how many people sympathized with her, for the time being she had to spend her nights in a six-by-eight-foot cell. During the day she could roam a narrow area between cells with a few other young inmates, read at the institution library, or work at her jobs mopping floors and serving meals. She was placed in a special section of the correctional facility set aside for sixteen-to-nineteen-year-old females. A prisoner in a cell next to Cheryl's told reporters that the former cheerleader cried the first night she was locked up.

Meanwhile, supporters on the outside were working for an early release. One group of women held a candle-light vigil for her outside the jail. Cheryl received more than seven hundred letters from people who sympa-thized with her plight. Many of the letter writers were former incest victims, and some wrote that they wished they had shown the courage to do what she had done to end the abuse.

The teenager's boyfriend and his parents also contin-ued to show their support and love. Cheryl told report-ers she called Rob's parents "Mom" and "Dad."

Three days after Cheryl was jailed, Rob was sen-tenced as a youthful offender. According to terms of his agreement with the prosecution, he pleaded guilty to a scaled-down charge of criminal solicitation and was or-dered to spend five years on probation. Following his sentencing, he asked reporters outside the courthouse to help his girlfriend. "The silent majority is outraged that Cheryl is further being victimized by this system," he declared.

"It's not too late. Can't we shorten or suspend the sentence somehow?" he implored.

There was no question that the press was on the side of the imprisoned girl. The New York *Daily News* criti-cized Judge Sherman for not giving Cheryl probation, with a stipulation that if she violated the terms, she could then be sent to jail for as long as the jurist consid-ered proper. "Contract murder is an outrageous crime," the editorial asserted. "But there may be no crime worse than incest. None!"

Even New York's feisty and outspoken mayor Edward Koch complained that although the judge was right to send a message that murder was wrong, Cheryl shouldn't be imprisoned. He told reporters that jailing her with criminals was "heartless." And he revealed he had begun working on a plan utilizing the media to contact young victims of incest and inform them how they could find help. Victims' advocates complained that the judge's decision had reinforced the concept that those who suffered sexual abuse or other forms of family violence were at fault.

Cheryl wrote a letter from her jail cell to New York governor Mario Cuomo asking him to intercede and order her early release in time for Christmas. But there was no order of clemency from the governor.

Every day Cheryl was locked up, Rob visited her, and tied a yellow ribbon around an oak tree in front of his parents' house.

On January 19, 1988, 106 days after Cheryl was led from the courtroom, her boyfriend, brother, and a neighborhood friend were driven to the jail in a white stretch limousine. The sun hadn't yet risen when Cheryl walked out of the grim jailhouse in jeans and a sweatshirt with her first name emblazoned across the front to join hands with her boyfriend. The tiny cross she had worn during her sentencing hearing was once again dangling from her neck. And she was fifteen pounds lighter than when she was first locked up. They joined their friends in the limousine while a gaggle of reporters watched. Ear-splitting rock music blared from the stereo as they headed for a nearby diner to have breakfast.

Later, in front of the Cuccio house as Christmas music could be heard inside, Cheryl cut one of the yellow ribbons and posed for newspaper reporters. Then she and Rob went into his parents' house to celebrate a late Christmas and open the presents that were still wrapped under a brightly decorated tree.

"Rob adores that girl," Robert Cuccio, Sr. told a reporter for the New York *Post*. "She deserves some goodness. She's been through the horrors of Hell."

The elder Cuccio said his son proposed as soon as he had a few minutes alone with Cheryl, then gave her an engagement ring that had been "burning a hole in his pocket."

Approximately eight months later, on October 9, 1988, the couple were married in St. Louis de Montfort Roman Catholic Church in Sound Beach. James, Jr. walked the bride down the aisle and gave her away.

Chapter 9

Ten Faces of Evil

Ross Michael Carlson's parents doted on him. They bought him designer clothes; took him on expensive vacations; gave him three cars, including a Porsche, by the time he was nineteen; and were ready to hock their house so he could go to law school.

He thanked each of them with a bullet in the head!

In one of the most bizarre cases in the history of American criminal justice, Carlson never faced a jury of his peers, despite overwhelming evidence of his guilt, which included an eerie videotaped reenactment of the crime.

Why not? Because he spent years in a mental hospital while a battery of legal experts, psychologists, and psychiatrists debated his sanity and ability to stand trial. It was never determined who was guilty—Ross Carlson or one of ten tortured personalities that reputedly lived in his sick mind.

After six years of exhausting legal and medical haggling, the only real punishment was meted out to the people of Colorado, and to Carlson's grandparents in Minnesota. Colorado taxpayers were saddled with more than $2 million in court and legal costs, psychiatric and medical fees, and hospital bills. And medical and legal fees ate up most of the near half-million-dollar estate left by the murdered couple.

For more than a half decade, an incredible, surrealistic tragedy was played out in Colorado courts, jails, and mental hospitals, featuring Chief Deputy District Attorney Robert Chappell; Carlson's slick defense team of Walter Gerash and David Savitz; and a host of defense and state psychiatrists and psychologists. Even bankers got into the act during protracted bickering that revolved around the accused killer's use of his inheritance to pay defense attorneys and medical experts.

But the star, or stars, of the show were Carlson and ten strange personalities, who were reputedly contesting over control of his mind. Along with their host, the invader personalities not only played the lead roles, but also wrote the script and directed the other players.

"Ross Carlson presides over his own soap opera," Denver's *Rocky Mountain News* noted in a 1985 headline.

Public involvement in the grotesque "soap opera" began on the morning of Thursday, August 18, 1983. A construction worker showing up early for work spotted something strange in a field near a building site just outside Littleton, Colorado. It was an area of burgeoning tract houses for families fortunate enough to escape the growing congestion of Denver, about twelve miles northeast.

The curious workman casually approached what appeared to be two brightly colored objects reflecting the bright morning sun. The area was sometimes used as a lovers' lane by teenagers, and at first it appeared that it may have been blankets left behind after a night of romance. But there was nothing romantic about the two bodies sprawled in a shallow roadside ditch.

A man and a woman were lying facedown, each with their head on their folded arms. The man was dressed in neatly pressed blue slacks and a tan shirt. The woman wore a knee-length, blue evening gown. Aside from the incongruity of their location and dress, they seemed to be sleeping peacefully—except that the backs of their heads were pulpy messes, and their arms and the ground around them were covered with drying blood. They had been shot, execution style.

Sheriff's deputies from Douglas County, where the bodies were discovered, and from Arapahoe County, which began only a few hundred feet north of the site, responded to the construction worker's report. Douglas County sheriff's homicide investigators and the Douglas County chief deputy coroner quickly determined that the couple were slain in the exact positions in which they were found. Each was shot once with a rifle or pistol.

The victims were rapidly identified as Rod R. Carlson and his wife, Marilyn Ann Carlson. Both were thirty-seven years old, and both were schoolteachers at the same school in Littleton. Rod taught sixth-graders; his wife, first-graders. They had lived for about five years in a suburban development near the field where their bodies were found.

Neighbors, colleagues, students from school, and other acquaintances were shocked and disbelieving when news of the mysterious and violent deaths of the couple was publicly revealed. A door-to-door canvass of the neighborhood, and talks by homicide investigators with other teachers and school administrators, failed to turn up even a hint of possible enemies of the couple. And there was no evidence of any recent troubles either of the Carlsons might have been involved in that might be expected to lead to an alarming double murder.

The victims of the mysterious crime were respected as a clean-living, churchgoing couple who were devoted to their only child, Ross Michael Carlson. A handsome, blond, six-foot-tall, 150-pound nineteen-year-old, Ross was a freshman at Metropolitan State College in Denver, where he majored in psychology. Relatives and neighbors described him as friendly and an above-average student.

He seemed to be the kind of son who would make any

parent proud. The Carlsons were so proud of their son, in fact, that they had almost shamelessly indulged him with gifts and attention.

When police talked with the youth, he indicated that he was shocked by the dreadful crime. But he appeared curiously unemotional for someone who had so suddenly been orphaned.

Three days after the double slaying was discovered, the couple's missing medium-blue, four-door, 1980 Cadillac Seville was located in the parking lot of an Arapahoe County motel. Witnesses were quickly located who recalled seeing the car parked there since late Wednesday or early Thursday—just about the time of the murders. The contents of the car were removed and sent to the Colorado Bureau of Investigation's crime laboratory, while homicide detectives from both counties continued their probe of the slayings.

By that time, attention had already begun to focus on the son of the victims. Among other things, investigators learned that Ross Carlson was not exactly the Golden Boy that he may have seemed at first glance to be.

He wasn't as popular with classmates and other peers as he was with his parents. In high school he had been the frequent butt of jokes by classmates. Police, and later journalists, who talked with his acquaintances and former high school classmates were rewarded with descriptions such as "weird" and "strange."

More intriguing to investigators, however, was discovery that he had been arrested for trying to buy dynamite, and was currently serving a two-year term of probation. Police and court records showed that he was apprehended in September 1982, after writing to the author of an article in *Soldier of Fortune* magazine. He asked the writer to send him three sticks of dynamite for a project. The letter was signed J.N.T.

The magazine writer reported Carlson's request to authorities, who set up a sting meeting with the teenager in the parking lot of a shopping mall near his house. An undercover investigator from the Arapahoe County Sheriff's Department met him and claimed to have the dynamite and several blasting caps. Carlson paid the agreed-on fee of forty dollars, then asked the detective if he could get him a .38-caliber handgun and ten rounds of ammunition. That was when the police officer sprung his trap and arrested the teenager on charges of receiving stolen goods and illegal possession of incendiary devices.

Carlson told investigators three different stories about his motive for trying to buy dynamite. First, he said he wanted to use it to commit suicide. Then he said he wanted to blow up his parents' house because he believed it had structural defects. Finally, he claimed he had taken a class on terrorism and he tried to buy the explosives simply to satisfy his curiosity about how easy it would be to make the purchase.

Approximately two months after his arrest, Carlson pleaded guilty to the charge of illegally possessing incendiary devices, and the other count was dropped. In addition to being placed on probation, he was also ordered to undergo psychiatric evaluation. His parents arranged for regular weekly treatment.

Homicide investigators began fitting in new pieces to the puzzle of the double murder early in September after an eleven-year-old boy discovered a black suitcase while chasing down a lost football in a weed-covered field. The field was near a house where Ross Carlson often worked as a handyman to earn spending money.

The suitcase contained a .38-caliber Garcia-Rossi revolver, ammunition, a black leather holster, surgical gloves, a flashlight, some clothing, a woman's purse containing Marilyn Carlson's driver's license, and a wallet with a driver's license issued to a Ross "Karlson." Police forensics and ballistics experts had already determined that the Carlsons were killed with either an FIE derringer or a Garcia-Rossi revolver.

Retracing movements of the victim's son, detectives

learned that he and a friend had gone to dinner and a movie on the night of the murders. The friend told police that Ross left the movie theater at approximately nine-thirty P.M., after explaining that he had to close a "big deal." Ross returned about two hours later and cryptically announced, "It's done."

While they were driving home, Carlson insisted the radio dial be kept on a music station so he could sing along, his friend told police. And Ross asked him not to read local newspapers for a while.

A police canvass of houses near the murder scene had also turned up neighbors who said they heard gunshots between ten-thirty and eleven P.M. on the night of the double slaying. Once the information from Ross's buddy was put together with the report from the residents living near the field where the couple were shot, it pointed to the same suspect.

On September 18, exactly one month after the execution slaying of the Carlsons, police arrested their son for the murders. He was locked in the Douglas County Jail in Castle Rock and held without bail on twin charges of first degree murder.

A public defender was named by the court to provide legal representation for the youth, and a psychiatrist was appointed to help in his defense. It was the beginning of a complex and bizarre odyssey that would entangle the Colorado courts, the medical profession, and bankers in a frustrating six-year search for truth. About a month after his arrest, Carlson announced from his jail cell that he planned to plead innocent by reason of insanity.

At the same time, he petitioned the Douglas County District Court for release of a trust fund created for him by his parents, as well as other money and property from the estate, including their $400,000 house. He explained that he planned to use his inheritance to hire Gerash, one of the most highly respected, and expensive, criminal lawyers in the state.

Spokesmen for the United Bank of Denver, which

was executor of the trust, disclosed that the fund contained between $300,000 and $400,000. Gerash was reportedly asking $75,000 to $100,000 up front to represent the youth. And that was just for starters.

But bank officers weren't ready to immediately begin writing checks on the fund. They pointed out that Colorado criminal statutes prohibit convicted killers from inheriting the money or property of their victims. Consequently, if the bank released the money to Carlson and he was later found guilty, he would, in effect, have sidestepped the intent of the law and financially benefited from the murder of his parents.

The bank finally agreed to release a substantial portion of the trust fund to Carlson on November 25, after his grandparents in Minnesota formally threw their support behind his request. The suspect immediately hired Gerash, with Savitz as his associate. Savitz, a high-profile Denver lawyer, had represented the suspect in the legal tussle over the trust fund. And in compliance with a court order, Carlson repaid $5044 to the Public Defender's Office for representation prior to hiring his new defense team.

On December 19, Carlson, with Gerash at his side, appeared before Judge Richard Turelli in Douglas County District Court. He entered pleas to the first degree murder charges of not guilty by reason of insanity, and not guilty by reason of impaired mental condition.

Judge Turelli ordered the defendant to undergo a thirty-day mental evaluation, and scheduled a sanity hearing for April 12, 1984. If Carlson was found to be mentally competent to aid in his own defense at the hearing, then a mini-trial would be conducted to determine his sanity. If the judge at that proceeding determined that he was sane, he would at last face a murder trial for the slaying of his parents.

In March 1984, Savitz asked the court to have Carlson released on bail from the Douglas County Jail, where he had been held since his arrest, or transferred

to a psychiatric hospital. The lawyer claimed that his
client suffered from "a multiple personality disorder,"
which could not be treated adequately at the jail, was
depressed and suicidal, and was growing progressively
worse. Savitz said both a psychologist and a psychiatrist
had diagnosed and confirmed that Carlson suffered
from the mental condition.

Savitz told the court that his client's condition was
similar to the mental disorders described in the book
and movie, *Sybil,* and in the movie, *The Three Faces of
Eve.* He said mental health experts had identified at
least seven different male personalities that ranged in
age from six to forty-two, and shared the defendant's
mind. The lawyer told Judge Turelli that he was gravely
concerned about his client, and claimed corrections officers at the jail mocked Carlson and called him a fraud.

According to some mental health experts, young children who are subjected to severe sexual, physical or
psychological abuse sometimes create multiple personalities for themselves through a process of self-hypnosis.
It is reputedly a means of self-protection, which allows
one of the other personalities to deal with the problems
while the true psyche of the host child is submerged and
shielded from the distressful goings-on.

Savitz's petition was a startling development, but it
wasn't the first time that a criminal defendant had
claimed to be suffering from the exotic mental disorder.
Kenneth Bianchi, who teamed up with his sadistic
cousin, Angelo Buono, in a series of ghastly Los Angeles area murders that earned them the joint nickname
"Hillside Strangler," is one of the most notorious. He
tried to hoodwink the courts by claiming to suffer from
multiple personalities.

In 1978 the curly-haired killer was locked up in the
Whatcom County Jail in Bellingham, Washington, after
his arrest for two murders there when he watched the
movie *Sybil* on television and hatched his scheme to use
psychiatry to sidestep punishment. He even starred in

an intriguing PBS television documentary, *The Mind of a Murderer,* which played to the possibility that he was a reluctant victim of the perplexing mental aberration. Despite all his inspired posturing and impressive command of psychiatric gobbledygook, however, his outrageous sham didn't work. He was eventually forced to abandon his insanity defense and imprisoned for life.

Turelli may or may not have had Bianchi in mind when he ruled on the petition presented by Savitz and denied the transfer request. The judge pointed out that a sheriff's report indicated that Carlson showed "no current behavioral problems" in jail and that the defense attorney had failed to show that the defendant's needs could not be met at the local lockup.

The judge also denied a request by the defense for a change of venue, which would have switched the trial to another county. Carlson's attorneys cited extensive local publicity and the results of what they said was a scientific telephone survey they conducted which indicated that a majority of people in Douglas County not only knew about the case, but believed their client had murdered his parents and was faking mental illness.

Judge Turelli did, however, grant a defense request to postpone the April 12 sanity trial until June to give Gerash time to recover from a back injury. A week earlier, to the amusement of journalists and some other spectators, Gerash had appeared at a hearing laid out on his back on a stretcher, with his knees drawn up to his chest.

A week before the sanity trial was scheduled to begin, Gerash and Savitz asked for a competency hearing. They claimed that their client's mental condition was so badly deteriorated that they couldn't tell which of his many personalities they were dealing with.

They said he continuously switched personalities while they talked to him, and routinely slipped from one personality to another in the courtroom. One moment he was fearful, almost on the verge of tears, then logical and cool. Sometimes he was aggressive, even violent. Worse, they explained, one personality seemed unable to remember what had happened while another personality was in control. The judge granted the request, and set the hearing date for June 6.

The state countered with a request that Turelli be replaced by another judge for the hearing. Chief Deputy District Attorney Robert Chappell intimated that he might call Judge Turelli to the stand during the hearing as a witness for the prosecution. Denying defense objections, Turelli granted Chappell's request.

If observers following the labyrinthian case in the press were attracted to the case because it was strange and unusual, they were in for a treat. It was about to become even more bizarre. The courtroom would be turned into a legal and psychological circus, with the defendant and his many alternate personalities as the ringmasters.

And predictably, each side produced its own mental health experts: with professional witnesses for the defense contending that the accused killer suffered multiple personality disorder; and their counterparts testifying for the prosecution that they believed he was a fake who was manufacturing phony symptoms.

With former Colorado Supreme Court justice Edward C. Day presiding at the competency hearing, Carlson's attorneys opened by launching a surprise attack on the dead victims, charging that their client was a scapegoat for an entire family that was mentally ill.

Testifying for the defense, psychiatrist Robert H. Fairbairn cited several incidents he claimed was abusive treatment by Carlson's parents that probably helped cause him, as a child, to begin creating at least seven different personalities.

"It is my opinion that this young man was the scapegoat of a sick family, and whatever pressures were on the family were attributed to him," Dr. Fairbairn told the court. The psychiatrist described a number of incidents of child abuse which he said the defendant had revealed to him.

Citing one example, he said the defendant's father reputedly swung at him several times with a hammer when he forgot to take out the garbage, causing the emergence of "Black," one of the most violent of Carlson's multiple personalities. "Black" was said to have taken the hammer away from the elder Carlson on several occasions. Dr. Fairbairn told the court that the most recent of the hammer incidents occurred only six months before the slayings.

The witness also testified that when the defendant was about two years old, someone rubbed a dirty diaper in his face after a toilet training accident. Ross told the psychiatrist he believed it was his father. "I think that is a very sad, violent assault on a little boy, and suggests a punitive, sadistic style of child-rearing, which approaches the concept of child abuse," Dr. Fairbairn observed. Later testimony would indicate that the multiple personality problem began at about that time.

Another time, when the little boy smashed his finger in a car door, his father reputedly told him, "Big boys don't cry," the witness recalled. Dr. Fairbairn said of the parental admonishment, "It hints to me at the unreasonable, dogmatic posture of the father, the demands they made of the child not to cry—a rather typical, I think, misguided demand of many parents."

The suspect also told the psychiatrist that when he was about six years old and his crayons melted in a dryer after he left them in a pocket of his clothes, he was struck with a "spoon, fist, belt, whatever." Dr. Fairbairn called that punishment for such a common mistake among children "pathological" and "evidence of a sick household."

And the youth told his psychiatrist that Rod Carlson sometimes threatened to move the family to a nudist colony. Ross said he was a very modest child, and recalled struggling desperately when his father once held him naked in front of a window. "That tells me that there may be a sadistic type of behavior in the father. The parent is getting pleasure and amusement out of the embarrassment and pain of the child," Dr. Fairbairn explained.

The psychiatrist also said two recent incidents supported the contention that the defendant's personalities cannot remember what happens when one is submerged and another is in control—the key to the argument that he was incapable of following legal proceedings, therefore making him incompetent to cooperate in his own defense.

One of the incidents occurred when the defendant shaved off his eyebrows while he was in jail. One personality reputedly did the shaving, but another, said to be in control later, could not remember having removed the eyebrows. Dr. Fairbairn said that the second personality, whom he identified as "Justin," was very vain about his appearance and was infuriated by the loss of the eyebrows.

Describing the second incident, Dr. Fairbairn said that after he gave the defendant a present for his twentieth birthday, spent behind bars at the jail, he received two "thank you" notes.

The psychiatrist said he believed that one of the notes was written by "Justin." Penned on blue stationery, it was polite and impersonal. The other was written on lined yellow legal notepaper and was more personal and revealing. Dr. Fairbairn said he believed the second note may have been written by a combination of "Justin"; forty-two-year-old "Steve," and six-year-old "Blue."

"Black" emerged during an April interview, the witness added, violently ripping loose a wrist strap that bound the defendant to his chair. The psychiatrist said he was terrified of "Black," who had suddenly replaced the whining six-year-old. "It was as if he grew before my eyes, and he began to growl and breathe rather like a gorilla," Dr. Fairbairn testified.

The psychiatrist told the court that he was skeptical of the multiple personality claims before his interviews with the defendant. But now, after what he had heard and witnessed, he was convinced that the young man was not faking. Dr. Fairbairn said a pretender would attempt to offer evidence of insanity. But Carlson had been reluctant to provide that kind of evidence, even refusing to produce various personalities when the psychiatrist asked to talk to them.

In additional comments to the court, Gerash added to the picture of his client's reputedly tortured childhood. He said the youngster was lonely and felt unwanted. And he said Mrs. Carlson was four months pregnant when she was married, causing many problems among the couple's traditional relatives.

The Carlsons were still attending college when they married, but despite many difficulties, graduated with high marks and moved to Colorado in 1969 to begin a new life with their only child. However, either consciously or unconsciously, both parents resented young Ross, and in their frustration, had abused him. Consequently, the boy retreated into his own mind by way of an elaborate system of multiple personalities, the lawyer said.

According to various experts, Carlson's known multiple personalities—which had eventually grown to ten—included:

• Steve. An articulate designer of women's fashions, he was one of the most commonly encountered personalities. In his early forties, he appeared to be smart, logical, and about as entertaining as a lump of cold mashed potatoes. He showed an impressive ability to sketch drawings of buildings and bridges, and under other circumstances might have developed into a promising architect.

- Justin. He vied with Steve for center stage as one of the most frequent personalities to emerge. He appeared to be in his twenties, was outgoing, extremely polite, and liked to live it up with other handsome people who appreciated beautiful clothes, gourmet food, and fine wines. But he could be extremely shallow. Sometimes he signed his name "Justin Time." It may have been Justin who signed the letter to the *Soldier of Fortune* magazine writer, Savitz suggested.

- Black. He was as mean, violent, and tough as an oil field bully. Carlson told Dr. Fairbairn and Gerash that the only way to stop Black was with "thirty men and a bullet." Black was known to emerge screaming like a gorilla, and he showed up when weaker personalities felt threatened. Despite the host personality's remark about facing down Black only with overwhelming force, he wasn't really that invulnerable. He could be easily chased off and replaced by another personality simply by asking him a mathematical question.

- Blue. He was a six-year-old crybaby who couldn't learn the alphabet. He depended on other personalities, whom he referred to as "Biggers," to protect him.

- Gray. About twelve to fourteen years old, he was constantly depressed and was suicidal. When Gray appeared during the competency hearing, the defendant usually stared blankly into space.

- Stacey. He was an eighteen-year-old athlete who loved weight-lifting and had a black belt in karate. It was apparently Stacey who emerged to spark a team of fellow patients to a rousing basketball victory at the Colorado State Hospital while the defendant was undergoing psychological testing. A few days earlier a recreational therapist had watched Carlson in an incredibly clumsy basketball-shooting performance.

- Michael. A seventeen-year-old, he didn't emerge often and his characteristics were not well known.

- Norman. Incredibly foul-mouthed, he was apparently an adolescent street punk. But he appeared to be all mouth and bluster, and he didn't exhibit the overt threats of physical violence of his ominous companion personality, Black.

- Antichrist. As illustrated by his name, Antichrist seemed to be pure evil. He may have been a malicious meld of Black and Norman, or of Black and the real Ross. Carlson claimed at least once that it was the demonic Antichrist who murdered his parents.

- Unknown. This apparently was a personality just developing at the time of the competency hearing, and some experts believed it might represent a merging of Justin and Steve. The personality was later identified by the name Holden, and was unable to remember anything that happened before 1985.

"Right now, there is no Ross Carlson," Gerash told Justice Day at the hearing. In later remarks outside the courtroom, the lawyer told reporters, "I don't know which personalities killed the Carlsons." He said, however, that he suspected it was "Black."

Gerash also gave the court a psychiatrist's report relating the events leading up to the deaths of the schoolteachers. The information had been provided to Dr. Fairbairn by the defendant.

Justice Day called the report "one of the most detailed accounts of a person's actions from suppertime to bedtime that I've ever read." The jurist declared that the recounting of events contained explicit details of the last evening of the murdered couple's lives, right down to the "bang, bang" of the gun.

It revealed, among other shocking things, how the defendant had lured his parents to the murder site by

claiming he wanted them to see a mailbox he had built
for a neighbor. Then he forced them to empty their
pockets and to lie down before he killed them.

"I pulled out a gun," he told the psychiatrist during
an interview at the Colorado State Hospital at Pueblo.
"Things were speeding up like I had been shot out of a
cannon. My mind was doing two hundred miles an hour.
I seemed to be watching it. I am big on movies. I was
watching it from another place. I saw my shoulder. The
camera concentrated on my shoulder."

He told the psychiatrist that he shot his father first,
"then Mother, bang, bang." The young man quoted his
mother as saying, "I don't want to live. This is hell. Go
ahead and shoot me."

Dr. John Elder, another defense psychiatrist, said he
believed Carlson's parents may have allowed themselves
to be killed without a struggle because of "extreme re-
morse" over their early mistreatment of their son. He
added that the defendant killed his parents out of "his
extreme rage."

Another defense witness was a California clinical psychologist who said that he had examined thirty-seven
people with multiple personality disorders. He stated
that the accused killer was a textbook example of the
condition and could not be faking.

"In such cases as this, I ask myself, 'Could I do this?
With twenty years of experience with multiples, could I
fake one?' I'm telling you, I couldn't. I know I couldn't
do it, and I doubt that any sane person could," he testified.

But Gerash's final witness, called on the eleventh and
final day of the hearing, perhaps was the most impressive. And he was neither a legal expert nor a mental
health professional.

He was a thirty-six-year-old neighbor of the Carlsons,
who recalled a curious incident that had occurred five or
six years earlier. He said that young Ross Carlson
mowed his lawn one day, then showed up several hours

later to mow it again. It seemed at the time that when the boy showed up at the neighbor's house the second time, he had somehow forgotten he had already mowed the lawn and been paid for his work.

The witness said the boy was furious when he saw the lawn had already been mowed. And young Carlson accused his neighbor of doing the job himself to save money.

"There you have it," said Gerash afterward. "Amnesia—the key to this case. Amnesia from one personality to another, and the reason why we cannot communicate with our client so that he can help us defend him."

Assistant District Attorney Chappell's first witness was a psychologist from the state mental hospital, who said she suspected Carlson was indeed faking illness to escape punishment for killing his parents.

She said Carlson acted certain ways when he knew he was being observed, and others when he thought he was not being watched. "I did not see any disturbances in his thinking," she declared.

Another state witness said Carlson showed many inconsistencies during five hours of direct observations and lengthy videotapings. "He said the right words to give him a diagnosis of a multiple personality," but he "changes his story from time to time."

Prosecutors also pointed out that Carlson received high grades at Metro State College, that he majored in psychology, and had enrolled in a course on trusts and estates. They suggested that he killed his parents, not out of rage, but simply to obtain the money from the trust fund they had set up for him.

As the competency hearing dragged on inside the courtroom, friends and neighbors called a press conference to defend the dead couple against the accusations that they were cruel and abusive parents. Meeting at the Littleton home of hosts Dick and Lee Fritz, six friends of the teachers told reporters that the Carlsons were good neighbors, devoted churchgoers, and loving parents.

"If they had a fault," Dick Fritz said, "it was that they loved their son too much, that they were too indulgent. They were doting parents."

The couple's friends pointed out that when Ross had trouble learning to read in the first grade, his parents hired a tutor for him. He went along on their expensive vacations, and when he decided he wanted to see what the *Love Boat* was like after watching the popular television series, they took him on a costly Caribbean cruise.

The neighbors recalled that the couple bought their pampered son designer clothes, took him to expensive restaurants, and began buying him his own cars as soon as he was old enough to drive. At the time they were murdered, the doting couple was even preparing to close on a second mortgage on their house to finance their son's college education.

"You name it, Ross had it," said Bill Cathey, Rod Carlson's best friend. ". . . All this talk about child abuse and stuff—you can't believe it." He complained that the youth was now using the inheritance, which the Carlsons had worked so hard to provide for him, to smear their reputations.

Fritz said he thought Ross Carlson's problems started much earlier than the dynamite incident. He recalled when Carlson, in his early teens, was walking through a neighborhood park, and Fritz saw him with a group of boys with a football. The boys were maliciously mocking and teasing him. "I felt for him. They were making a fool out of him," Fritz said.

"I do know he was not popular with his peers," the neighbor explained. "It started with traits I saw in him when he was a little boy. . . . I'm sure there were times when he was unhappy, but I don't think the cause of it was his parents."

The Fritzes said that despite whatever problems Ross may have had as a boy and later, he appeared to be a normal child with a normal relationship with his parents. He was a friend of the Fritzes' son, the couple pointed out, and as a child sometimes spent the night at their house.

The competency hearing ended on June 20, eleven days after it had begun. Justice Day said he would announce his decision the next day. If Day found Carlson incompetent and incapable of going through the sanity trial, the youth would be confined to a mental hospital and treated there until hospital officials pronounced him cured. Only then would a sanity trial be held.

On June 21, a few weeks short of a year after the cold-blooded slaying of Rod and Marilyn Carlson, their son was ruled to be mentally incompetent to stand trial for the murders.

Justice Day explained that a combination of defense testimony as well as his own observations led to the decision. The judge cited the lawn-mowing and eyebrow-shaving incidents as important factors in helping him make up his mind. He added that credentials and experience of the defense's psychologists and psychiatrists were also more impressive than those testifying for the prosecution.

The jurist ordered Carlson transferred from the Douglas County Jail to the Colorado Department of Institutions, where doctors would attempt to fuse his warring personalities into one—his own. Mental health experts estimated it might take as long as three years to fuse the personalities, and somehow arrived at seventy-eight percent as the chances of success. But before he could be formally judged as cured of insanity and capable of helping in his own defense, psychiatrists would have to determine that he was not a danger to himself or others.

Although it appeared that Carlson was the winner of an important round in the legal jousting, he wasn't happy with the judge's order that ultimately led to his commitment at the Colorado State Hospital in Pueblo.

Savitz said his client was afraid that his personalities would be fused into one and he would get better. But then he wouldn't have the necessary personalities to help him survive, the lawyer explained.

A week later the defense attorneys asked for a delay in sending Carlson to the state mental hospital, claiming they had serious doubts he would receive proper treatment there.

"How can we expect the hospital to treat Ross Carlson competently and fairly when doctors there don't believe he's sick in the first place?" Gerash asked the judge.

The lawyer added that the staff at the hospital lacked the necessary experience to deal with such a complex case. He and his colleague asked that Carlson's transfer be postponed until a satisfactory alternate plan could be worked out for his treatment. But Justice Day stuck with his decision at the earlier hearing, and Carlson was transferred to the state mental hospital in early November 1984, despite the protests of his counsel.

As Carlson's attorneys had predicted, however, he was warehoused for almost a year at the hospital, receiving little or no treatment. On May 28 he observed his twenty-first birthday in the dining hall by staring into space, urinating in his pants, and pouring a cup of water on his head.

Justice Day was furious when he learned about the treatment lapse. And in early October 1985, he presided at a hearing aimed at determining what was behind the foot-dragging. He didn't like the explanations he heard, and wound up lashing into bankers, lawyers, and psychiatrists, whose shenanigans were becoming as complicated as the bizarre struggle for dominance reputedly going on in Carlson's head.

The justice blamed self-serving and devious obstructions for causing the young man to remain waiting for help in a locked room at the mental hospital, as independent experts warned that the longer treatment was postponed, the more difficult a cure would be.

Justice Day complained that doctors operating the state hospital continued to insist the defendant was faking, and therefore were not making any efforts to treat him. And Dr. Barry Quinn, an outside psychologist and expert in multiple personality disorders, selected to head the effort to fuse the personalities, had seen the patient only a few times because he wasn't sure how, or if, he would be paid his $75-an-hour fee.

Bankers who controlled the balance of the dead couple's estate refused to pay fees for Quinn or for other experts because, if the young man were cured, he would have to stand trial. If that happened and he was found guilty, the remainder of the estate should go to the youth's grandparents.

Justice Day threatened the United Bank of Denver, trustees for the estate, with a civil lawsuit if they did not pay the psychologist's fee. But a year later the Colorado Supreme Court ruled that the jurist had no authority to order an independent psychologist to treat Carlson. The high court declared that state psychologists and psychiatrists were good enough.

It seemed that there would be no end to the interminable debate over the ten personalities of Ross Carlson, his mental condition and treatment. In 1987, after another lengthy hearing in Douglas County District Court, Senior Judge Robert Kingsley ruled that Carlson was still incompetent to stand trial. And he repeated Judge Day's order of three years earlier for mental health professionals at the state hospital to provide treatment to fuse Carlson's multiple personalities.

During one of the court hearings, attorneys watched six hours of videotaped interviews between the patient and a psychologist, which included a vivid discussion of the murders. Carlson sprawled on the floor of the interview room at one point, to describe the position of his parents as he had shot each of them in the head.

"I was watching but I was getting shot," he explained. "I see a man in blue . . . I see a weapon, a black handgun. I see me on the ground. I'm laying next to me." Then, he said, he watched from the ground as the man in blue fired the gun.

After four or five years of legal jousting, prosecutors weren't any more tolerant of the multiple personality claims than they had been at the beginning of the exhausting proceeding. And they scoffed at the defendant's penchant for undergoing curious personality changes as he watched activities from the defense table. They had their own private names for Carlson's many personalities, including Sleepy, Dopey, and Grumpy. Convinced that the young man was deliberately·manipulating the courts, they sometimes referred to him simply as Ross the Boss.

At a hearing in early January 1989, Gerash petitioned the court for dismissal of the double murder charges against his client. The lawyer complained that his client had been incarcerated for six years and was still not competent to stand trial, despite the expenditure of vast sums of taxpayers' money.

"The six years he's spent in jail are equivalent to a mid-level manslaughter sentence of thirteen or fourteen years, with time off for good behavior. A good share of his twenties have been spent incarcerated, and he still hasn't been convicted."

Expert witnesses for the defense told the court that Carlson's condition had actually worsened, and that he believed evil men and cyborgs were invading his brain. Savitz said that during one telephone conversation his client "talked about men and cyborgs coming into the back door to hit him over the head with mallets, crush his brain, and steal his secrets." The attorneys described their client as "delusional" and "paranoid."

But chief prosecutor Chappell and doctors at the state hospital countered by pointing out that Carlson had continually refused to cooperate in efforts to treat him, and seemed content to sit in his room with a computer and a stereo.

Dr. Martin Orne, a University of Pennsylvania psychiatrist hired by the state hospital in Denver as part of a two-member team to evaluate Carlson and recommend a treatment program for him, complained at an earlier hearing that the patient wouldn't cooperate. "Stop treating him as a special case," the psychiatrist said. "I wouldn't want to take his computer away from him. But I would make [its use] contingent upon cooperating with the staff."

Dr. Orne suggested that one of the reasons Carlson might be refusing to cooperate was because he would probably have to stand trial someday for the murder of his parents.

Dr. Michael Weissberg, a University of Colorado psychiatrist and the head of the two-man team hired to recommend the treatment program, said he didn't believe the accused killer was afflicted with multiple personality disorder. But he said that the diagnosis wasn't the issue: the question was whether or not Carlson could help his attorneys work in his own defense. Answering that question, Dr. Weissberg declared:

"There is no question in my mind that this guy is competent. I've never seen somebody who is so capable. . . ."

The psychiatrist said that when he attempted to talk with Carlson, the defendant wouldn't cooperate and produced letters from his lawyers spelling out the reasons for his refusal. Weissberg said that very act demonstrated that Carlson had the ability to work with his defense team.

Judge Kingsley refused to dismiss the charges, and in October 1989 declared that the patient was fit to appear at the long-delayed sanity trial. Referring to his earlier ruling of incompetency, the jurist cited an old saying in making his latest finding. "Fool me once, shame on you. Fool me twice, shame on me."

The former chief judge of the Denver District Court pointed out that he had good reason to change his mind about the defendant's competency, after the 1987 hearing. He explained that he watched a videotape of Carlson refusing to communicate and rocking back and forth on a chair while a psychiatrist was trying to interview him. Finally, the judge said, Carlson threw himself onto the floor and was carried out by two attendants who held him under the armpits "as though he was a dead man." The judge said that when he asked the attendants what Carlson did after he was out of camera range, "I was told he got right up, called his lawyer on the phone and talked for thirty minutes."

Prosecutors had complained for years that Carlson cooperated with psychiatrists and psychologists for the defense, and clammed up when confronted with mental health professionals who were asked by the state to evaluate or talk with him. Both Dr. Weissberg and Dr. Orne had testified that they couldn't develop a program to treat Carlson because he wouldn't cooperate.

According to Colorado state criminal statutes, the defense could not appeal the judge's order setting up Carlson's long-awaited trial to determine if he was sane at the time of the double murder. Consequently, the sanity trial was scheduled to begin on December 5. A date for the murder trial was also set to begin on January 2, 1989, in the event that the verdict in the earlier trial indicated he was sane at the time of the slayings.

But no one had counted on a curious twist of fate that had nothing to do with state law, courts, and judge's rulings. It was a totally unexpected and ironically final development that would bring a surprising and abrupt end to the frustrating case.

On a Saturday night in early November, less than a month after Carlson had moved his computer and stereo out of his room at the state hospital and taken up quarters in the Douglas County Jail, he began vomiting up blood in his cell. He was rushed to a hospital, where he was diagnosed to be suffering from lymphoblastic leukemia, an especially virulent form of the cancer. He was transferred to the University of Colorado Hospital's Cancer Center in Denver for chemotherapy treatments.

Initially Carlson fought the chemotherapy, as he had fought psychiatric treatment. He claimed that he wouldn't cooperate because one of his personalities objected to a wrist cuff which, along with another on one ankle, shackled him to the bed. He agreed to submit to treatment after the restraint technique was altered. According to the new plan, he was shackled by both ankles, but his wrists were freed. And sheriff's deputies periodically released him from the ankle cuffs so that he could use the bathroom.

Late on a Sunday night he asked a female Douglas County Sheriff's Department deputy to free his ankles so that he could use the bathroom. He jumped her as she undid the last shackle on his leg, and twisted her revolver out of its holster. As they wrestled on the floor, she screamed for help and managed to shove her fingers into the trigger guard to prevent him from discharging the weapon until three doctors ran into the room and helped her overpower him.

After talking with Carlson, Savitz later claimed that his client was not trying to escape, but planned to kill himself by sticking the barrel of the weapon in his mouth and firing it. He said the young man was depressed by his illness and lack of close emotional support at the hospital from relatives and friends. Carlson's version of his motive for grabbing the revolver may or may not have been true. Even if it was true, however, his narrow brush with death by suicide turned out to be only a temporary reprieve.

The end came quickly for the troubled young parricide. As his health continued to rapidly worsen, he was transferred to the hospital's intensive care unit, and on Thanksgiving Day 1989, he was pronounced dead of natural causes. The perplexing ten faces of evil died with their host.

Chapter 10

Lethal Lovers

The Charles Manson–inspired slaughter of five people at the Sharon Tate–Roman Polanski mansion in Beverly Hills was still fresh in the minds of Americans when a new horror was uncovered at the home of Frank and Mary Columbo in the comfortable northwest Chicago suburb of Elk Grove Village.

The horribly mutilated bodies of the couple and their thirteen-year-old son Michael were discovered by Elk Grove Village police officers who were attempting to check out a stolen car report.

Chicago police had recovered the Columbos' brown Thunderbird from a street in the South Side black ghetto, where it had been stripped of tires, CB radio, and everything else that could be easily carried away.

But as soon as suburban police officers eased into the neatly kept $65,000 brick bi-level, ranch-style house through a door left ajar, they realized that they were dealing with a crime much more serious and complex than mere car theft. The interior of the ten-room house looked like an abattoir.

The body of forty-three-year-old Frank Columbo was lying on the floor of the living room, surrounded by a gory mess of blood, tissue, and shattered teeth. His skull was smashed, he had been repeatedly stabbed, his throat was slit, and he was shot four times, through each cheek, his mouth—and execution style, behind the left ear. Overturned furniture and blood splatters that streaked the nearby wall added further evidence of the fury and intensity of the murderous assault.

Even the brutality of the attack with gun, knife, and bludgeon, however, hadn't satisfied the killer, or killers. Further humiliation had been heaped on the victim by grinding out lighted cigarettes on his bare chest. Columbo was dressed only in his trousers and socks. His shoes, shirt, glasses, and watch were in the bedroom, indicating that he may have been roused from bed by the intruders.

His forty-one-year-old wife of twenty years had died an equally cruel and grotesque death. The attractive blond woman's body was lying just outside the door of a hallway bathroom a short distance from her husband. Her skull had also been smashed with a heavy object, she had been shot between the eyes, her throat was slit, and she was repeatedly stabbed.

Mrs. Columbo's nightgown and robe were ripped open and her underpants were pulled to her ankles. Despite an early report in the press that she had been raped, an autopsy would later fail to turn up any indications of sexual assault. Investigators concluded she was surprised by her killers while she was seated in the bathroom reading a newspaper and smoking a cigarette.

Michael Columbo's body was found in an upstairs bedroom, still dressed in his bloody nightclothes. The boy had been shot between the eyes and bludgeoned on the head. His face, neck and body was speckled with nearly a hundred stab wounds. Curiously, although some of the wounds were deep, many of the cuts had barely broken through the skin.

A pair of sewing scissors, a knife, and the heavy base of a bowling trophy, all stained with blood, were recovered inside the house. Police later told news reporters that many of the slashes on the arms of the victims appeared to be defensive wounds, indicating they put up a struggle before they were killed. Based on the furious fight for life that apparently occurred, a homicide investigator said he believed there were at least two intruders.

Entry was gained by activating an automatic garage door, then forcing a lock on another door leading to the family room, detectives determined.

The only living creature in the house left unmolested by the intruders was the family poodle, Gigi. And she was terrified. The little dog cowered and whimpered in a blood-soaked corner of the living room as a grim-faced team of police detectives and crime scene technicians gathered evidence.

Homicide investigators quickly learned from neighbors that the only family member to escape the dreadful slaughter was the couple's pretty, brown-haired, brown-eyed daughter, Patricia Ann. The willowy nineteen-year-old had moved out of her family's house more than two years earlier to live with her married boyfriend, Frank DeLuca, Jr., his wife Marilyn, four daughters and a son, in the nearby town of Lombard. Then Patty and her sweetheart moved into their own apartment.

The young woman, known to her neighbors there as "Trish," was flamboyantly sexy. She piled on her makeup and pranced around the apartment complex in a revealing thigh-high miniskirt and go-go boots while boasting to neighbors that she was a model for Frederick's of Hollywood. She also liked extremely short, tight-fitting shorts and filmy blouses, which she wore in the winter with a long fur-trimmed coat that she allowed to flap open and show off her shapely legs. She confided to one man that she was from Georgia and planned to open a modeling agency. She seemed to be always busy, but made time to baby-sit a few times for some young parents who lived in nearby apartments.

Patty was tall and slender, with the stunning figure of a showgirl. Her lover was short, swarthy, and bony, but knew how to charm the ladies. He dressed neatly, often

choosing leisure suits, and wore boots or shoes with
high heels that made him look taller. Neighbors would
later tell reporters that Patty gave the impression she
and the older man she lived with were married.

When she was notified that her immediate family had
been wiped out by mysterious killers, Patty handled the
bad news with remarkable calm. She helpfully suggested
that police look around for teenagers high on drugs.
And she remarked casually to a neighbor that the tragedy reminded her of the dreadful Manson slayings in
California, except that no one had written messages in
blood on the walls of her family's home.

In Elk Grove Village, jittery neighbors of the victims
also talked guardedly about a Mansonlike massacre, and
nervously waited for the next shoe to fall. Several people who never owned guns before bought pistols and
began traveling to local shooting ranges to practice their
marksmanship. Some bought dogs. Many of them, like
the Columbos more than ten years earlier, had fled
there from Chicago to escape the escalating violence of
big-city life.

There appeared to be some precedent for linking the
feral madness of the crime with the work of drugged-up
killers.

The slaughter at the neatly kept house on East
Brantwood was discovered on May 7, 1976, barely six
years after fanatic members of Manson's drugged-up
hippie clan shocked the nation with their grisly string of
helter-skelter murders in California.

And Chicagoans would never forget the miniholo-
caust wreaked by Texas drifter Richard Benjamin Speck
when he stumbled into a dormitory housing nine student nurses on Chicago's South Side, then strangled and
stabbed eight of the girls to death, and raped one during
a drug- and alcohol-induced frenzy. Only one of the
nurses escaped the massacre, by rolling under a bed and
hiding.

For a time early in the investigation, the possibility

that the Columbos might have been murdered by a gang of home invaders, who either tricked their way inside the house or simply barged in through an unlocked door, seemed to be one of the more popular explanations for the murders. Several criminal gangs were active in the Chicago suburbs at that time, forcing their way into private houses to rob and brutalize the inhabitants.

Valuables like those usually stolen by burglars or other thieves were left untouched inside the house, however. Although the house had been ransacked, Columbo's will and $4000 was still inside the safe, which wasn't broken into, and the television, radios, silver, expensive jewelry, and other valuables were not taken. Even Columbo's rifle was overlooked, and expensive diamond rings were left on his wife's fingers. About the only objects police were able to confirm as having been taken were two citizens band (CB) radios, two handguns, the heavy base of a glass floor lamp, and the two family cars. The second car was found abandoned on Chicago's West Side a few days after discovery of the bodies.

But some investigators pointed to the cigarette burns on Columbo's chest, the scores of shallow stab and slash wounds, and what they believed at that time to have been the woman's rape, as possible indications they were tortured in efforts to make them reveal the location of the wall safe. The thieves may have gotten high on narcotics, and the planned robbery turned into a sex assault, torture, and murder, the detectives reasoned.

Officers from the Chicago Police Department's Central Investigation Unit joined in the investigation to look into the possibilities of the involvement of a home invader gang.

Deputy Chief William Kohnke of the Elk Grove Village Police Department suggested, however, that the victim overkill may have been an attempt to make the slayings look more bizarre and send investigators off on the wrong track.

Even Dr. Robert J. Stein, who performed the autopsies for the office of Cook County coroner Andrew Toman, commented on the wounds—many of which did not appear to be designed to kill. "There certainly appeared to be a lot of hate on display there," he told reporters.

Elk Grove Village police and Cook County Sheriff's Department officers who joined in the investigation of the Columbo killings didn't immediately discount any possibilities. Nevertheless, there appeared to be other motives that were equally as promising as either a random or planned home invasion by a gang of drugged-up bandits.

Rumors quickly began circulating about Columbo's possible involvement with drug or loan-sharking activities and Chicago's powerful and fitfully violent organized-crime family. Investigators found a wall safe in the recreation room and notes indicating that at one time he may have kept $30,000 or more in cash there. Surnames matching those of several locally known hoodlums were also found jotted down in his personal telephone book. And an anonymous telephone caller tipped off authorities that Columbo may have been a silent partner in an area cartage company and a day labor firm.

His financial records indicated he had been living surprisingly well for a family man whose annual salary was around $25,000. Investigators learned that in addition to owning his house, two cars, and a motorcycle, he had recently had new siding put on the house, bought a mink cape for his wife, and she was talking to friends about planning a vacation in Hawaii.

Another anonymous tip came in the form of a typewritten letter to Elk Grove Village police a week after the slayings. The writer identified a man named in the note as a drug dealer and a dangerous person, and

claimed he had been overheard talking with two well-
known contract killers about settling a score with Frank
Columbo. The reputed drug dealer was seen on the
West Side near the area where one of the Columbo cars
was abandoned, the mysterious tipster added.

Neighbors, friends, and relatives who knew Columbo
hotly defended him as an honest man and a good citizen, however. And Patty telephoned a Chicago newspaper reporter to complain about stories suggesting her
father had links to organized crime. Between sobs she
insisted that he was an honest, hardworking man who
wouldn't even lie. She added that she feared for her
own safety, had changed the locks on her doors, and
kept a German shepherd. She was identified in the reporter's article as a model and cosmetician.

Cook County State's Attorney investigators nevertheless quickly called several reputed organized crime figures, as well as friends, business associates, and fellow
members of the Columbos' bowling team, to appear before a special grand jury. The investigative panel sub-
poenaed the calling records for the Columbo house, the
two businesses, and some other individuals tied to the
inquiry, from the Illinois Bell Telephone Company.

But the Mob, as it's known in Chicago, or the Mafia,
which seems to be preferred in most of the rest of the
country, had a history and reputation of not physically
involving women and children in their wars and other
disagreements. And judging from everything investigators could dig up on Frank Columbo, he was every bit as
honest and hardworking as his neighbors and daughter
insisted he was. He had earned a comfortable living for
himself and his family for years, as Chicago district ship-
ping manager for Western Auto, a chain of auto acces-
sory stores. The grand jury probe failed to turn up even
a hint that the dead man had criminal connections.

In fact the only serious brush with the law by any
member of the family involved Patty. A few months after she moved in with DeLuca, police arrested her for

deceptive practices involving a credit card. Her embar-
rassed father bailed her out, and she was eventually
placed on probation.

As homicide investigators pondered possible motives,
results of the autopsy were revealed, indicating that the
victims were slain about midnight on Tuesday, May 4,
two or three hours after returning home from dining at
a restaurant in nearby Arlington Heights. The bodies
were alone in the house with the traumatized poodle for
three days before they were found. Ballistics tests
showed that the bullet wounds were inflicted with a .32-
caliber handgun.

Police also heard from Michael J. Dunkle. A nephew
of Mrs. Columbo, Dunkle told them he had telephoned
the house from the Greyhound bus station in the Loop,
Chicago's central business district, between six and
seven A.M. on May 5. The young man from Omaha, who
often passed through the city on business trips between
Nebraska and Ohio, told police the telephone was answered by a woman he believed to be his aunt. He said
she sounded nervous, and quickly broke off the conversation without inviting him to the house as she usually
did.

The information was troubling, because detectives
had determined that the Columbos were killed several
hours before Dunkle reported telephoning his aunt.
Consequently, there were tough new questions to be
answered in an already perplexing investigation: Had
the killers remained in the house for six hours? Did they
leave, then return to the scene of the crime? Or was
there some other explanation for the curious development?

When detectives began looking for enemies of the
victims, they found two, close to home. Columbo had
been feuding with his headstrong daughter and her
older lover ever since the May-December pair had
started dating nearly three years earlier, when Patty was
sixteen and DeLuca was thirty-six. She met her boy-

friend when she began working at the cosmetics counter in the Walgreens drugstore he managed in an Elk Grove Village shopping center.

A one-time model daughter who was the pride of her parents and a loving big sister to her brother, Patty seemed to turn against her mother and father almost overnight after meeting DeLuca. She fought with her father over her demands to be allowed to drop out of her junior year at Elk Grove Village High School so she could work full time at the store. She kept her own hours, and she called her parents filthy names when they tried to enforce rules of behavior. Finally she moved in with her lover, and was written almost completely out of the family's will.

The relationship between the parents and the lovers deteriorated so badly that Columbo finally asked his daughter and her boyfriend to come to the house for a peace conference. The younger couple never showed up, and the furious father tracked them down in the drugstore parking lot.

Angry words were exchanged, and the enraged parent leaped from his car, waving a rifle. It was unloaded, but only he knew that. Patty shrieked and ran for cover as her father and her lover grappled. The fight ended in a spray of blood and flying teeth when the husky Columbo smashed the rifle butt down on DeLuca's mouth.

Patty reported the fight to police, and her father was picked up at his home and arrested. He spent the rest of the night in jail, held on charges of assault. After his release, he bought Patricia a car, as an apparent peace offering. When she and DeLuca refused to drop the charges, he angrily took the car back. The charges were eventually dismissed when DeLuca failed to follow through on his complaint.

Columbo meanwhile rewrote his will, cutting his wayward daughter's inheritance from more than $100,000 to $5000. He left the bulk of his approximate $250,000 estate to his son. If Michael died, however, his sister would become the primary beneficiary to the estate, which included an additional $80,000 in life insurance.

While her father was trying to figure out how the family's relationship with the only daughter could have gone so terribly wrong, Patty began looking around for a hit man to kill her parents. A girlfriend introduced her to twenty-four-year-old Lanyon R. Mitchell, who had formerly worked as a clerk in the Cook County Sheriff's Department as part of a federal employment program. He introduced her to his friend, Roman Sobczynski, a thirty-four-year-old civil service recruiter for Cook County's Personnel Department, and also a former Cook County sheriff's deputy. Patty was convinced that the pair were tight with the Mob, and decided she had found her hit men.

But the two pals were outrageous impostors. Mitchell, whose friends called him "Lannie," was a car salesman, and Sobczynski was a petty bureaucrat. They were more interested in getting the vengeful teenager with the slender body, long legs, and big breasts in bed than killing anyone. Patty said she would pay them $50,000 from her inheritance, and they could have all the sex they wanted if they would murder her parents. But she specified that they would have to be satisfied with anal lovemaking, however, because she was reserving everything else for DeLuca. Then she started making her advance payments on the contract.

While his girlfriend was taking care of the arrangements for the murders, DeLuca began confiding to friends that he expected to be coming into a large amount of money soon and planned to buy a boat. There would also be enough to pay for a divorce, already filed in DuPage County Circuit Court, to marry Patty and set themselves up properly in a new love nest, the loose-lipped ladies' man boasted.

Patty meanwhile provided the two bogus hit men with dossiers on each of her family members, which included precise information on their appearance, personal habits, frequent travel movements, and schedules. Even their places of birth, hair color and style, height, weight, the color of their eyes, and their hobbies were listed. She noted that her mother had been married before, in Georgia. And she wrote that her brother's hobbies were a motorcycle club and CB clubs.

Partial descriptions of the family cars were also provided, although Patty didn't know the years of manufacture or license plate numbers. She even described the family poodle and warned that it bites.

Color photographs of her parents and brother and a carefully detailed hand-drawn floor plan of the house were included with the material. But the bogus hit men stalled. Although Patty continued to participate in the sexual romps they demanded, they came up with one excuse after another for not carrying out the hit. Most often they complained that she hadn't put up front money.

In response, Patty became increasingly insistent that they carry out their part of the bargain. She wheedled, complained, and threatened. Once she pulled a loaded derringer from her purse and waved it at Mitchell. "See how easy it is to kill someone," she said. "All you have to do is pull the trigger." She called Mitchell "chicken-shit Lannie."

Mitchell would later testify that at one time, "She told us we had to do it before Christmas and it would be a Christmas present from her."

After five months of the perilous game-playing, the two con men at last realized that they were dealing with a sincere and dangerous woman. They began making themselves scarce, and refused to return her telephone calls.

The bogus contract killers weren't the only people who had the idea that Patty might be dangerous or less than a model daughter. Her parents had become so worried about the turn their lives had taken that they changed the locks on their doors and dropped their list-

ing from the telephone directory. And after a man tried
to get into Mrs. Columbo's car one time when she was
stopped at a traffic sign, her husband bought her a pistol
to keep in the vehicle. He bought another for himself,
which he kept in a nightstand drawer in the master bedroom.

After the murders, Patty clashed angrily with surviving members of the extended family over her rapid
move to have her parents and brother cremated. Many
of the family members were traditional Roman Catho-
lics and were upset by the decision, which conflicted
with their religious beliefs about the dead. But the day
after the bodies were discovered, Patty talked with the
family's parish priest, the Reverend J. Ward Morrison of
the Queen of the Rosary Parish, and he obtained church
permission for her to go ahead with the cremation. She
told him that her parents had lived as a close family and
she wanted them buried that way.

The Reverend Morrison later presented the eulogy
for the couple and son who had faithfully attended his
church for eleven years. "The resurrection of Christ is
an absolute fact," he intoned. "Tonight, you need it.
Tonight, Frank and Michael and Mary want it." Plain-
clothes officers from the Elk Grove Village Police Department kept a vigil inside and outside the chapel,
watching for strangers who might be attending the
wake.

The writer of a news story in the *Chicago Tribune*
noted sympathetically that the last surviving member of
the Frank Columbo family greeted other mourners at
the Galewood Funeral Home with "a weak smile," and
"summoned the strength to kneel at the three caskets. . . ."

A day or two later, Michael's fellow seventh graders
at the Tom Lively Junior High School began planning to
plant a tree with a commemorative plaque in his name.
Eighth graders sponsored a dance to raise money for
another plaque. And the Western Auto sales company

announced they would pay a $5000 reward for apprehension of the killer of their longtime employee.

By the time the wake and funeral were held, rumors pointing the finger of blame at Patty and her lover as the likely killers were already being whispered around the suburbs. A few days after the services, Patty's girlfriend had a talk with her father. She said Patty had been trying to find someone to murder the Columbos. And she told him about conversations she had with Mitchell dealing with the same subject. The young woman's father notified Elk Grove Village police and arranged for his daughter to tell them her story. After repeating her account, the nervous nineteen-year-old was placed under twenty-four-hour police guard.

Police questioned Mitchell, then Sobczynski. On Saturday night, May 15, less than two weeks after the shocking multiple slaying, Patty was arrested and accused of being responsible for the deaths of her parents and brother. DeLuca was taken into protective custody but was not immediately charged.

Police were armed with a search warrant, but Patty made them wait outside her apartment for almost ten minutes while she called them filthy names before she let them in. She continued cursing while they conducted their search. DeLuca had moved out of the apartment and back in with his family a couple of days earlier after the management of the building filed a civil suit against him seeking more than $2000 in back rent and attorney fees.

Patty's derringer was found during the search, but its small caliber ruled it out as one of the possible murder weapons. Among other possessions confiscated as possible evidence were homemade stag films starring the small but wiry DeLuca with another attractive woman a few years older than Patty. There were also photographs of the leggy teenager.

Curious neighbors watched a short time later as village police dragged the small pond at the apartment complex with a huge magnet, looking for weapons, the missing lamp base, and anything else the suspect may have dropped from her apartment window overlooking the water, as officers waited outside her door. The magnet stirred up too much mud, however, and was replaced by police scuba divers. The search was still unsuccessful, and a couple of months later divers from the Chicago Fire Department searched an area of the Des Plaines River in the Robinson Woods Forest Preserve after a prosecution witness said the gun and a knife used in the killings might be there. Again the effort failed to turn up the missing gun or other evidence. The pistol was never recovered.

The night of her arrest, Patty gave a nine-page statement to police and to an assistant state's attorney, admitting that the previous October she had plotted her family's murder and taken Mitchell on a dry run to the house. She wanted the hit men to rough up her father because he had beaten her boyfriend, she added.

"To begin with, my father was the only one I wanted hit, but they said if he went, my mother would have to go too," she told her interrogators. "I said, 'Okay,' as long as my brother was not hurt."

Patty said the men told her they would plant a bomb in Columbo's car while her family was out bowling. But she claimed she later called off the contract because her father changed his attitude toward DeLuca.

But she couldn't get in touch with the men to cancel the contract, she explained. Patty said she and DeLuca were together on the night of the murders, but insisted neither of them had anything to do with the killings.

"Frank didn't know," she said. "I never told him about the contract."

When homicide investigator Raymond Rose of the Elk Grove Police Department confronted her with the dossier, she admitted she had written it. "But I don't think they did it," she said of the bogus hit men. Rose also showed Patty some nude pictures of herself in vari-

ous poses with her German shepherd, Duke, that police
had taken from the apartment. She was unfazed, however. She had different feelings about morality than he
did, she told him. The stunning teenager explained that
she and her lover had sent their names and descriptions
to swingers magazines for listing because they wanted to
swap sexual partners.

She also asserted in the statement.that her father had
put out a murder contract on DeLuca. She quoted her
father as saying there would "be no marriage because
there would be no Frank DeLuca."

Patty was locked in the Cook County Jail in Chicago
and held without bond on three counts of murder and
one count of conspiracy to murder. DeLuca was locked
in another section of the old jail, and the couple continued to express their love for each other through messages delivered by inmates. Patty was later transferred
to the Cermak Memorial Hospital at the jail complex to
undergo court-ordered psychiatric evaluation to determine her fitness to stand trial.

Two days after her arrest, she asked to talk with homicide investigators. During the conversation at the
Women's Center at the jail, she claimed that while she
was in a courthouse lockup she had seen a vision of her
murdered family that indicated she might have been involved in the murders, after all. Calling on her memo-
ries of the miraculous occurrence, she said she saw
herself at the scene, and recalled a pair of scissors with
blood on them. And she described the way her murdered family members were dressed and the positions
they were lying in.

Detective Gene Gargano of the Cook County Sheriff's Department later testified about the conversation at
a court hearing. "I felt that I was there. I'm confused. I
see someone there with me. I believe I was there and I
did it," he quoted her as saying.

Police meanwhile were continuing to collect statements and other evidence linking the star-crossed lovers

to the slayings. Mitchell and Sobczynski quickly admitted their pretense and agreed to testify against the couple. Mitchell, who was married shortly after breaking off his relationship with Patty, told interrogators that she once took him on a dry run to her parents' home. She went inside the house by herself and wound up in a nasty quarrel when her mother and aunt showed up unexpectedly.

Mitchell and Sobczynski had never planned to go through with the murders. Mitchell told investigators he hadn't believed Patty was serious about having her parents killed.

Two of DeLuca's former fellow employees at the drugstore also chipped in information damaging to his accounts to authorities. They told investigators that DeLuca had boasted to them on May 5 that "the hits went down last night."

Other investigators were busy as well, and a forensic anthropologist concluded that a glove print lifted from the steering wheel of one of the Columbo cars was made by someone with a missing left index finger and the tip of another finger. The short but athletic DeLuca, who was a star halfback on Chicago's Austin High School football team as a teenager, then played college football for the Purdue University "Boilermakers," had mutilated his hand in a sky-diving mishap.

DeLuca continued to claim that he and Patty had nothing to do with the slayings and were together the night the slaughter occurred. Each of the lovers was the other's alibi. DeLuca, in an effort to clear himself, agreed to a police request to take a lie detector test. The results were inconclusive, but the pharmacist was released from protective custody.

Mitchell also took a polygraph test and passed. At his own request he was held in protective custody in the witness quarters at the Cook County Jail. After a weekend there, however, he was released and State's Attorneys officers made arrangements for his protection outside the jail.

A few weeks later, after considering evidence and listening to testimony, two separate Cook County grand juries returned criminal indictments against both DeLuca and his girlfriend.

The first grand jury indictments named Patty on murder and conspiracy charges similar to those she was already held on. The panel added an additional charge, however, of solicitation to murder, accusing her of attempting to get Mitchell to kill her family. Patty, who was being represented by assistant public defenders William Murphy and William Swano, was eventually granted $250,000 bail. But she had no money, and remained in custody. DeLuca sat in the spectator section during her hearings to give her moral support, and brought her cigarettes.

He remained free until about the middle of July, when he was arrested after another Cook County grand jury indicted him on three charges of murder and one count of conspiracy to murder in the Columbo slayings. He was taken into custody on a Saturday night at his apartment in the Chicago suburb of Villa Park.

Gargano testified months later during preliminary court hearings that when DeLuca was interrogated shortly after his arrest, the druggist admitted he had gotten fed up with the foot-dragging of the counterfeit hit men. "These guys are just jagging us around, we'll just have to do the job ourse," the witness testified.

The sheriff's investigator said that when he asked the suspect if he meant "ourselves," DeLuca snapped: "You said it. I didn't."

DeLuca then began fishing for information from his interrogator, according to the detective. "Hypothetically speaking, if this guy and this girl did commit three murders, what would be the penalty?" the suspect was quoted as asking. DeLuca also asked if he and his girlfriend could be sent to the same prison if they were convicted of the crime. Then he inquired about the possibility of helping their chances of being sent to the same institution, possibly a mental hospital, if they pleaded guilty, Gargano testified.

The detective testified that DeLuca said he thought Columbo had targeted him with a murder contract, that Michael had stared suspiciously at him in the drugstore, and Patty thought someone had followed her car. The druggist stated that he and his girlfriend responded by keeping a loaded gun in their apartment, the lawman said.

Appearing fidgety and looking unsure of himself, DeLuca pleaded innocent at his arraignment, and told the court that he was unable to pay attorneys because he had lost his pharmacy job and was saddled with $800 monthly child-support payments. He claimed he was a pauper. Presiding judge Richard J. Fitzgerald appointed the same two public defenders who were helping Patty, to represent her lover. Bail was also set at $250,000 for DeLuca. Like his girlfriend, he was unable to raise the money and remained behind bars.

During a hearing on a bond reduction plea by defense attorneys, the lovers stood together holding hands, while DeLuca's ex-wife watched from the spectator area. The lawyers had previously asked that Patty's bail be pared to $40,000, and at the hearing were seeking a reduction to $20,000 for DeLuca. They pointed out that his now divorced wife and five children depended on him for support. Assistant State's Attorney Algis Baliunas opposed a reduction because of the seriousness of the crime. Judge Philip Romiti reserved a decision on both requests until he had time to study and consider the matter.

Four days later, as the lovers once again stood together before him with their hands linked, Judge Romiti rejected both bond reduction motions. He said he wasn't prepared to take the risk that the defendants might not show up at subsequent court proceedings. As

DeLuca's former wife watched once more from the spectator seats, DeLuca took the opportunity to give his girlfriend an affectionate peck on the cheek, before they were led from the courtroom back to their cells.

Patty's pint-sized paramour behaved at times toward his codefendant like a lovestruck teenager. During one hearing when a sheriff's deputy brought her a coat after she complained of being cold, DeLuca quickly helped her put it on.

On September 1 he wrote a letter to Chief Criminal Court judge Richard J. Fitzgerald seeking the judge's permission for him to marry Patty.

Inmates sometimes marry each other or outsiders at the Cook County Jail, but the judge was aware that a wedding between DeLuca and his sweetheart could potentially lead to problems with their prosecution. Spouses cannot be required to testify against each other. After consulting with State's Attorney officers, however, Judge Fitzgerald gave his permission for the couple to marry.

But there was no wedding. A spokesman with the Cook County Marriage License Bureau pointed out to inquiring reporters that they picked up marriage requests from inmates three or four times a year. The next pickup wasn't planned until December or January. The marriage plans fizzled out.

Near the end of March 1977, only a few days before the trial was scheduled to begin, one of the most sensational developments of an already lurid and melodramatic case was publicly revealed. DeLuca was accused of arranging to have his ex-wife bail out a cellmate so that the man could carry out a twin murder contract. Twenty-nine-year-old Clifford X. Childs told authorities that DeLuca offered to pay his bail and thousands of dollars in cash to murder a man and a woman who had formerly worked with the pharmacist and planned to testify against him.

Childs, who was in jail, accused of an armed robbe

spree with two companions on Chicago's South Side, also told investigators that DeLuca had confided details of the triple slaying to him. Police records revealed that the accused bandit had serious previous troubles with the law, and served three years in prison for carrying a concealed weapon. He had also been given probation in New Jersey on charges of forgery and selling drugs.

DeLuca's former coworkers were immediately placed under an around-the-clock police guard. Childs was taken into protective custody, and authorities said he would be called in the murder trial as a prosecution witness. The accused stickup man had already spent twenty-one months in jail awaiting trial, including about seven months sharing a two-man cell with DeLuca before he was bailed out on February 24. He listed Mrs. DeLuca's home in suburban Addison as his address on documents for the $4250 bond.

At a hurriedly scheduled court hearing, DeLuca's bail was ordered doubled to $500,000. Baliunas described the defendant as a desperate man in the successful request for higher bond. The prosecutor asserted that discovery of the alleged contract killing scheme had demonstrated that DeLuca was a threat to the community.

After disclosure of the latest shocking development in the case, Patty's attorneys renewed their efforts to get her trial separated from DeLuca's, citing information about the reputed jailhouse murder solicitation. But their motion was rejected, and when the trial at last opened, the two lovers faced justice together.

Judge R. Eugene Pincham, newly elected to the Circuit Court bench after years as one of Chicago's most formidable defense attorneys, was named to preside over his first high-profile murder trial. Baliunas, a coolheaded thirty-two-year-old veteran of the State's Attor-
's Office, headed the prosecution, with help from
ty-seven-year-old Patricia Bobb and Terry Sullivan.
rphy and Swano had been joined by Larry Acker

on Patty's defense team. New attorneys, both former public defenders, had been especially appointed by the court to represent DeLuca. Michael P. Toomin, who had become a local private practice attorney, and Stanton Bloom, who had moved to Phoenix, Arizona, were named to handle the former pharmacist's defense.

A jury of six men and six women was selected to hear the sensational torture murder case, in the seventh-floor courtroom of the old Criminal Courts Building on Chicago's South Side.

The judge had already ruled during pretrial proceedings against allowing fifteen homemade pornographic films, reputedly featuring DeLuca, into evidence. But the prosecution was armed with more than a dozen photographs of DeLuca and a naked Patty with her dog, Duke, that could possibly be presented as evidence if either of the defendants chose to testify.

During opening remarks, the prosecution told the jury that the couple were furious over Patty's father's interference in their love affair and hatched an unsuccessful plot to have him murdered. But when the men they thought were contract killers turned out to be phonies, they slipped on gloves to avoid leaving fingerprints and carried off the slayings themselves.

Defense attorney Swano recounted his client's story that she had complained to the bogus hit men about her father's attack on DeLuca. And when Columbo suddenly changed his attitude and agreed to their marriage, Patty tried to contact the counterfeit contract killers to call them off, but couldn't find them.

The defense lawyer claimed his client went shopping, then returned home and was in bed in her apartment at about eleven P.M., the approximate time prosecutors had concluded the murders occurred. He also told the jury about Dunkle's early morning telephone call. The nephew's testimony would show that Mary Columbo was still alive several hours after the prosecution claimed the slayings were committed, Swano asserted.

Assistant State's Attorney Bobb had successfully argued to Judge Pincham earlier that statements about Patty's sexual behavior should be accepted into evidence because the defendant's morals were relevant to the case. Consequently, the trial quickly began living up to its billing for salaciousness when Mitchell was called to testify.

Named by the grand jury as an unindicted coconspirator, and testifying with partial immunity, Mitchell admitted that he and his pal had posed as hit men to impress the sexy teenager. Some of his earthy street language, such as a remark that Patty "wanted it in the ass," brought shocked gasps from spectators who were not quite prepared for such explicit detail or talk.

The out-of-work used car salesman said he sparked her interest while they were dancing at a party he hosted for his friend Sobczynski and his jacket flapped open so that she could see the .38-caliber pistol he was carrying. "She looked impressed and asked why I was carrying it," he explained.

"I told her I was with Roman and he was heavy. I told her if she took care of Roman, there would be favors for her," he testified. Mitchell said that he offered Patty $100 to be his pal's date. She responded that she would "fuck his eyes out," Mitchell said.

As the jittery witness told his story of sex, betrayal, and murder schemes, the young woman the press was alternately describing as a Farrah Fawcett look-alike and a brunette with a face like a Barbie doll, sat quietly at the witness stand, alternately glaring at him and shaking her head from side to side. Occasionally she leaned over to whisper to one of her attorneys.

"Her parents were bugging her and giving her and Frank a hard time, and she wished that they could be killed, dead, and gone," Mitchell continued.

When they told her that they wanted money up front, he said she asked: "What do you want me to do, put my ass on the table?"

"We said, 'Yes . . . How about tonight?' "

Mitchell said that later while she, the men, and another young woman were on their way to a motel for a sex orgy, Patty asked him where she could get an unmarked gun and bullets. He eventually bought bullets for her, and she later told him DeLuca had been practicing with them in a field, the witness continued.

A friend permitted him and Sobczynski to use his house for sex sessions with the defendant, Mitchell continued. The two counterfeit killers strung her along for about five months, while she grew progressively more impatient. She once told Sobczynski "that either I do it or she's going to get someone else or she'd do it herself," he testified. Mitchell quoted Patty as saying she would pay $50,000 from her inheritance for the murders.

Patty's previously immobile face took on a look of wide-eyed disbelief and she shook her head from side to side when the witness testified she wanted her brother killed along with their parents. Mitchell said she explained that after Michael grew up, he might put two and two together and figure out that his sister and her boyfriend were behind the slayings. Moments later, however, Patty continued staring at the bright yellow eagle atop the American flag at the front of the courtroom, as she did throughout much of the trial.

During spirited cross-examination by Murphy, Mitchell conceded he lied under oath when he was being questioned by homicide investigators a few days after the murders were discovered. He agreed that he didn't tell the detectives at that time about the sexual romps he and his pal were engaging in with Patty because he didn't want to damage his friendship with Sobczynski.

Mitchell asserted that he posed as a hit man because he wanted the county job recruiter's help getting an appointment as a deputy sheriff. "I never wanted to string her along . . . I just wanted a job," he said. "I wanted to be friends with him for a job." His pal was only looking for sex, he said.

After the debacle on the dry run to the Columbo house, when Patty was surprised by her mother and aunt, Mitchell used the opportunity to bolster his boast of being a hit man. He said he warned her, "If you ever pull another stunt like that, you can kiss Frankie baby good-bye."

Responding to Murphy's questions, the witness agreed that he once lied to a former girlfriend, claiming to be $3000 in debt to a mobster in order to con her out of fifty dollars.

"You'd lie for sex, wouldn't you?" Murphy asked.

"Yes, sir," the witness responded.

"You'd lie for money, wouldn't you?" the lawyer continued.

"Yes, sir," Mitchell replied.

"You'd lie to get a job, wouldn't you?"

"Yes, sir," Mitchell agreed.

But when Murphy asked the auto salesman if he would lie to sell a car, Mitchell hedged. "That's a different theory, sir . . ." he stammered. "I'd stretch the truth."

There was no hedging or talk of stretching the truth when Murphy asked the witness if he would lie to stay out of jail. Mitchell replied with a firm, "No, sir!"

As his friend had done, Sobczynski also testified under a grant of immunity from prosecution. The former deputy sheriff said that he gave Patty a .32-caliber revolver after she told him she wanted a gun for protection because she was afraid her father was going to have her boyfriend killed. Sobczynski said that he began worrying about the gun later, however, and told her he wanted it back because it had been used in a robbery and could be traced. He quoted her as telling him it was too late—she had tossed it into Lake Michigan.

Sobczynski testified that as part of the subterfuge, he introduced Patty to several of his friends who bragged that they were bigshots and powerful men in the Chicago area.

Wearing the same gray three-piece suit and boots he wore throughout most of the trial, DeLuca showed no emotion. Occasionally, as testimony continued, he rubbed his chin between the thumb and a knuckle of one hand, or would turn and study Patty, who was seated beside him a few feet away.

The ex-lawman also testified he telephoned Patty a few weeks before the slayings and told her that he wanted DeLuca to come up with some money. He said that he and his pal wanted the druggist to take the cash from the pharmacy.

However, some of the most chilling testimony of the proceeding was provided by DeLuca's two former coworkers, and the onetime jail inmate he was alleged to have tried to hire to murder them. Even then, in a move to protect Patty's right to a fair trial, Judge Pincham ruled out some statements quoting DeLuca that placed her in the house. The jury never heard reputed remarks from her lover stating they they were both covered with blood, or about the actions of "Pat and I" at the murder scene.

Mrs. Joy Heysek testified that he told her before the murders he planned to have Patty's family killed, but the hit men let him down and he was going to have to do the job himself. She said that when she arrived at work on the morning of May 5, she noticed one of his hands was cut and scratched. When she asked him what had happened, he replied: "I took them all down last night." Frank Columbo had put up a tough fight, she added.

"He said he shot Mr. Columbo in the back of the head. The bullet came out and took his teeth with it," the woman stated.

DeLuca added to his revelations about the torture murders when she met him in the drugstore lunchroom two days after the bodies were discovered, according to the witness. "He said they found Mr. and Mrs. Columbo but they can't find Michael," she stated. "Then he started laughing. I looked at him in disbelief."

Speaking in such a frail voice that she could barely be heard, Mrs. Heysek testified that she carried on a romance with DeLuca from 1970 to 1973, and when he began confiding details of the murder plot to her, he threatened to injure her children if she passed on the information to police. He warned "he would have my son run over on his bike, my daughter beaten up and raped, and have me beat up so badly that no one would ever recognize me," the thirty-seven-year-old witness said.

During cross-examination by Bloom, DeLuca's former lover said that one time about ten days before the slayings, she began dialing the Columbos' telephone number to warn them, but changed her mind and hung up.

"You didn't think they'd believe you, is that it?" the defense attorney asked.

"Yes," she responded in a near whisper.

Bert Green, who had worked with DeLuca as assistant store manager, testified that when he arrived at work on the morning of May 5, he encountered his boss coming out of the basement incinerator room. Green said he could see the glow from the fire, and DeLuca explained he had been burning the clothing he had worn the night before.

Between gulps of Maalox and skim milk swallowed every half hour for an ulcer, the slight twenty-eight-year-old recounted a grim conversation with the former store manager. DeLuca was nervous and talking rapidly, and had a series of small lacerations on his hands which he explained he suffered when the lamp shattered as he hit Columbo on the head with it, according to the witness's account.

"He told me that the hits went down last night. . . ." Green testified. DeLuca said the house was left in a mess and he was covered head to toe with blood, the frail man continued.

DeLuca told him that when he shot Columbo through the back of his head, it blew out four of the victim's teeth, Green said. "Now his teeth are like mine," he quoted his former boss as saying.

"He said the old man was a tough old bird and he had to smash a lamp over his head. He said the old man asked him: 'Who are you? Why are you doing this to me?' "

When testimony resumed and DeLuca's ex-cellmate took the stand, Patty leaned back in her chair, idly fiddled with a tiny silver crucifix dangling from her neck, and occasionally glanced at her co-defendant as if to gauge his reaction. DeLuca stared straight ahead, at the witness. Childs was the third witness to tell the jury he had played the drugstore Lothario for a fool by posing as a hit man. He testified that DeLuca told him he wanted the witnesses killed because they could put him in the penitentiary.

Childs said he went along with the hit man story simply because he needed bail to get out of jail, but never planned to go ahead with the slayings. He told the court that DeLuca offered him $40,000 to carry out the executions, and provided him with a dossier that included maps and descriptions of the man and woman targeted for death. The defendant's ex-wife paid his bail, and after he got out, gave him $1300 in cash and the keys to DeLuca's car, he said.

The ex-convict also said his former cellmate admitted killing the Columbos. "Frank told me he shot the whole family," Childs testified.

DeLuca bragged that he had concocted a perfect scheme to cover his tracks, according to the witness's account. Speaking audibly and confidently, Childs quoted the defendant as saying he set up alibis for the night of the murder, disposed of the gun, burned his bloody clothes, and tore up the house to make it look like the work of home invaders. DeLuca claimed furthermore that he maneuvered to throw the suspicion on blacks, Childs said he was told. He claimed that DeLuca explained that he abandoned one of the family cars in a black area of Chicago's West Side and left money and other valuables inside. He expected blacks to "bust in the car, steal the stuff and the car, and take the weight for the home invasion," the witness continued.

In response to questions, Childs said prosecutors had agreed to recommend to his trial judge that the charges against him be reduced to robbery and that he be let off with a minimum sentence in return for his testimony.

On June 21, about a month into the trial, Patty observed her twenty-first birthday. Her lawyers gave her a birthday card, perfume, and a devil's food cake with white icing, which she shared with some of the officers of the court during a brief observance in an anteroom.

The conclusion of testimony in the prosecution's case became another birthday present of sorts when Judge Pincham ruled against the state's efforts to introduce evidence about Frank Columbo's will. The jurist pointed out that prosecutors hadn't shown that Patty knew the details of the document.

During the first weeks of the proceeding, prosecutors had called dozens of witnesses and submitted more than two hundred pieces of evidence. One of the most shockingly grisly items was a blood-smeared T-shirt worn by Michael. The only bit of evidence that appeared to provide a direct link between Patty and the murder scene was a single strand of hair found on the boy's body. A crime lab expert said the hair probably came from Patty, although he couldn't testify with total certainty that it did.

As lawyers prepared to present the defense, the big question in the minds of trial watchers concerned the possibility of testimony by the defendants. Interest was especially focused on whether or not Patty would be called on in an effort to refute some of the damaging testimony by prosecution witnesses.

Legally knowledgeable observers were aware that although Patty's direct testimony might help her defense, she could face fearsome cross-examination and open the door to questioning about some of the more lurid aspects of the case if she were called to the witness stand. One of her lawyers confided to the press that the defense team hadn't yet made up their minds, and said if she did testify, it would be late in the proceedings.

Defense attorneys opened fire the next day with the testimony of a convicted bank robber who was locked up for a time on the same jail tier as Childs. Clifford Jackson-Bey had been transported to Chicago for the trial from the federal penitentiary at Marion, Illinois, where he was serving three concurrent fifteen-year sentences on federal charges of bank robbery and intimidation. He also faced serving fifteen to eighteen years in a state prison on a robbery conviction.

The witness testified that Childs told him that he was scheming to hoodwink State's Attorney's officers into arranging for a lenient sentence on the robbery charges by concocting a story that DeLuca had tried to recruit him as a contract killer.

Childs had confided that whenever DeLuca was taken from their cell for court appearances, he read police reports and other documents on the case that his jailmate had left behind, Bey said. DeLuca was entitled to have the information in order to help him prepare his defense, and Childs believed he could learn enough about the case by reading them to make his story believable, according to the testimony.

"I've got some heavy armed robbery charges, but I think I can kill two birds with one stone," Childs was quoted as saying. "I'm going to see what I can do about getting around going to the joint on these charges."

During cross-examination, Baliunas indicated that DeLuca had loaned nearly $5000 to Childs as bond money, and asked the witness if he would loan $5000 to the accused stickup man.

"I wouldn't loan Clifford X. Childs a wrestling jacket for a mosquito," Bey responded.

Dunkle was also called to testify about the telephone call he made to the Columbo home on May 5, several hours after the prosecution contended the murders occurred. He talked with his aunt for about five minutes and she sounded nervous, he said.

The personnel officer of a suburban company where Patty had applied for a job was another witness called to bolster the defense's contention that someone else committed the murders. Mrs. Danielle McDonald of the Myercord Corp., in the northwest suburban town of Carol Stream, told the court she interviewed the defendant for a job as a purchasing secretary at 8:40 A.M. on May 5. Patty was described as being composed and impressive during the interview, which occurred only a few hours after the prosecution claimed her family was slaughtered.

Despite the shocking things already said during the proceeding about Patty's hatred for her father, her outrageous sexual behavior and foul mouth, it seemed difficult to believe that the slender young woman seated at the defense table could have been so cool and in control of her emotions so soon after overseeing or participating in the horrible slaughter of her parents and brother.

Mrs. McDonald, who was permitted to testify earlier in the trial while the prosecution was still presenting its case, because of scheduling difficulties, said she was so impressed with the job applicant that she thought the interview was worthwhile following up.

"I thought she conducted herself very well. She was very calm and relaxed. She answered all my questions and she was outgoing and energetic," the witness said.

During cross-examination, Assistant State's Attorney Bobb brought out the fact that Patty had lied during the interview, and represented herself as twenty-five years old and married. When the attorney asked if the witness had any idea where Patty was on the night before the interview, Mrs. McDonald replied that she didn't.

One of the strongest defense witnesses for DeLuca was his ex-wife, Marilyn. During questioning by defense attorneys, she said she had dinner with her former husband at her home the night after the murders, and didn't notice any cuts on his hands.

Mrs. DeLuca, whose divorce from the defendant became final in May 1976, also told the court that her motivation for bailing Childs out of jail was money. She was promised a profit from the loan to the accused stickup man, when he collected on a workmen's compensation case, Mrs. DeLuca explained. She said she used some of her former husband's holiday and bonus pay and sold stock they jointly owned to raise $4000. The witness said she was supporting her family with help from state aid for dependent children. There had never been any evidence that Mrs. DeLuca knew of the alleged plan to have witnesses killed.

Her former husband spent his thirty-ninth birthday, Tuesday, June 28, on the witness stand. Patty's attorneys had decided against calling her to testify, and she tearfully but stubbornly refused their urging to leave the courtroom while her co-defendant was being questioned. Patty showed more emotion while she was insisting that she stand by her man than she had during some of the most grisly testimony about the terrible injuries inflicted on her parents. Judge Pincham, who was also observing his birthday, had given her the option of leaving or remaining.

DeLuca got sick a short time before being called to testify, but the judge rejected a motion by defense attorneys to delay the trial. And in sharp contrast to his co-defendant, who appeared cool and self-assured, when the gaunt pharmacist was sworn in, he looked frail, pale, and tense.

During friendly questioning by Bloom, DeLuca

strongly denied that he had murdered the Columbos. And he denied that he had tried to put murder contracts out on his former girlfriend or the assistant manager at the drug store.

He claimed that he was window shopping at a suburban shopping center in the early evening on the night of the murders, and later telephoned his assistant manager at the drugstore at about eleven P.M. before going to bed.

When it was the prosecution's turn to cross-examine, Baliunas put DeLuca through a withering five-and-a-half-hour barrage of tough questions, many of them posed in the form of accusations. Baliunas's boss, State's Attorney Bernard Carey, later told reporters that the feisty prosecutor virtually squeezed a confession out of the defendant on the witness stand. DeLuca admitted that he and Patty had given Sobczynski the go-ahead to murder her father, but said he did so only because he thought Columbo was trying to have him killed. And he said they tried to call off the contract.

Another witness, named in court as the man who provided the apartment used by the counterfeit hit men for their sexual trysts with Patty, refused twenty times to answer questions. The jury was absent from the courtroom while he was on the witness stand.

The panel was permitted back into the courtroom while Deputy Chief Kohnke read into the court record the anonymous letter Elk Grove Village Police received shortly after the killings. Police had traced the mysterious tipster.

When the seventy-five-year-old woman identified by investigators as the author of the mystery letter was called to testify, her appearance on the witness stand provided some of the few moments of levity in the lengthy and arduous trial. The cantankerous gray-haired witness told the court she wrote the letter to stir up trouble for her neighbor, whom she didn't like. Merceita Genoer explained that she had lived in the same block on Chicago's West Side all her life, and claimed her neighbor was trying to drive the old-timers out. Providing a bird's-eye view of Chicago political life, she explained, "He'd send the building inspectors against us. And we didn't like that because all they ever wanted was payoffs."

Attorneys asked how she had expected to benefit from writing the poison pen letter. "Well, he was very harassed, very nervous, very upset, and that's just what I wanted," the spunky witness retorted. The courtroom erupted in laughter. Even the defendants, who had flashed few smiles during the grueling ten-week ordeal, joined in the chuckles. State investigators said that the poor man was in fact a law-abiding citizen.

During summations, Baliunas followed up his excellent cross-examination of DeLuca with another premier performance. He reminded the jury that nearly all the injuries on Michael's body were light puncture wounds, which he said had to have been inflicted by someone with "some type of sick, twisted motivation." The lack of force used in making the cuts was "consistent with a woman," he said. Baliunas also pointed to the absence of any evidence indicating forced entry to the house as an indication that Patty had helped her lover get inside.

"You know, there's just one thing about this case that's interesting," the prosecutor told the panel. "Patricia Columbo and Frank DeLuca used just about everybody. And in the final analysis, they used each other. Don't let them use you and sail out of this courtroom over the charred remains of Frank Peter Columbo." Then the prosecutor repeated his plea as he described the death of each of the victims.

Defense attorneys asserted that the prosecution's case was contrived, and insisted that someone else could have been responsible for the murders. "There is not one iota of evidence that would place Patricia Columbo in the house," Murphy declared. "The state's case is full of mysteries, full of reasonable doubts."

After listening to more than seven hours of closing arguments, the jury deliberated only two hours and took ten votes before notifying court officers that verdicts had been reached. A few minutes before midnight on Friday, July 1, Judge Pincham's court clerk read the verdicts. Both defendants were found guilty on all counts of murder, conspiracy, and solicitation to commit murder.

The faces of the lovers were set in grim frowns as they listened to the verdict, and Patty let her head droop, peering at the floor. After sheriff's deputies led her and DeLuca from the courtroom, she hugged him, leaned her head on his shoulder and sobbed. Judge Pincham set August 1 as the sentencing date. Although the Illinois criminal codes carried the death penalty, life in prison was the maximum term that could be imposed because the slayings were committed before the state's new capital punishment law was passed.

Several jurors interviewed by reporters credited Baliunas's methodically brilliant closing argument with removing all doubt in their minds over the guilt of the defendants. After they were dismissed by Judge Pincham, the jurors left together on a bus laughing and waving to reporters. The exhausted panelists were going home just in time for the big holiday weekend.

On August 8, one week after the originally scheduled date, the convicted killers appeared before Judge Pincham for sentencing. Given an opportunity to make presentencing statements, both continued to insist on their innocence.

Standing at the defense table, Patty declared: "There is one thing the court cannot take away from me—my father and my mother and my baby brother know that wasn't us in the house that night or that morning, or whenever it was, and that's all that matters."

DeLuca told the court: "Patricia and I are innocent. I will stand on my testimony on the witness stand because that was the truth."

The judge sentenced the lovers to prison terms totaling from two hundred to three hundred years on the first degree murder convictions. He also ordered a twenty-to-fifty-year term for Patty, and a ten-to-fifty-year term for DeLuca on the convictions for solicitation to commit murder. The sentences were ordered to run concurrently. Despite the mind-boggling centuries-long sentences, however, according to regulations at that time the lovers would be eligible to apply for parole as early as 1984.

A violent thunderstorm swept over Chicago, and a power failure extinguished the lights and plunged the courtroom into a depressing gloom as the sentences were pronounced. The lethal lovers appeared subdued, and listened to the sentence without changing their expressions. Patty's shoulders were hunched forward, and when she was led from the room, her distinctive splay-footed walk was more noticeable than it had ever been. She looked like anything but the sexy fashion model she had once claimed to be. Beside her, DeLuca appeared wan and tired.

It was another seven weeks before the convicted multiple murderers were ordered transferred to custody of Illinois State Correctional authorities to begin serving the life terms. Patty was driven to the Dwight Women's Correctional Center, and DeLuca was sent to the reception center at the penitentiary in Joilet, where he would await a decision on a permanent prison assignment.

The judge rejected a plea by Patty for a delay to give her time to be interviewed by representatives of Northeastern Illinois University. She said she planned to take their correspondence school courses while imprisoned.

Acting on a request from the state, Judge Pincham also ordered DeLuca to pay $33,201 in trial costs, including $32,769 in fees for his court-appointed attorneys, since DeLuca had $26,000 in a pension fund from his former employer.

After his testimony against DeLuca, the robbery charges against Childs were dismissed by the state, but it wasn't long before he was in trouble again. He was arrested with a companion following a gunfight with police that broke out when officers attempted to question the pair about a gas station robbery. After Childs was taken into custody, police opened the trunk of the car he was driving and found a twenty-one-year-old man inside. He told officers Childs forced him into the trunk at gunpoint after stealing the car to use in the gas station stickup.

Less than a year after conclusion of the Columbo-DeLuca trial, Childs pleaded guilty to charges of armed robbery, kidnapping, and attempted murder. He was sentenced to a ten-year prison term.

But the courts and the public hadn't yet heard the last of Patty, or of her reputed involvement in sensational sexual escapades. Scandal seemed to follow her wherever she went. In 1979, after spending about two years behind bars at Dwight, some of her fellow women inmates accused her of recruiting them for deviate sex orgies performed for high-ranking male prison officials.

Some prison authorities dismissed the lurid accusations to the press as merely the handiwork of jealous inmates who resented Patty's beauty and her job as a clerk for one of the men named in the complaint. But they conceded she had enjoyed privileges not usually available to convicted killers. A woman guard was even quoted as saying she worked at the prison for a week before she realized that the pretty young woman called "Trish" by convict pals was an inmate and not a civilian employee of the prison.

State Corrections Department officials launched an immediate investigation. Several inmates who complained about the reputed orgies took lie detector tests and passed. Illinois Corrections Director Douglas Franzen revealed that investigators were told that sex parties were held in the basement, in offices, and in various other areas of the prison where a bit of privacy was available. Sometimes more than one inmate was present, and at other times only one woman and one male prison employee reputedly partied, he said. Franzen added that the women were not given money, drugs or liquor, but may have received better job assignments for participating.

In the wake of the scandal, Patty lost her secretarial job and was transferred to solitary confinement for thirty days pending investigation of the matter, and the woman warden and the two male officials named in the accusations resigned. The John Howard Association, a prisoners' advocate group, demanded reforms. Prison officials described Patty as hurt and bewildered by her latest portrayal as a sexual libertine and procuress. Murphy, one of her former trial attorneys, who was still representing her in appeals, told reporters she denied knowledge of prison sex parties and was upset because she believed her boss was falsely accused.

By 1980, Patty had been cleared of the nasty accusations, the storm had subsided, and she was earning A's and B's while working on a two-year associate of arts degree and looking forward to her first bid for parole in 1984. She and her former lover, who also appeared before a parole board then, were turned down. But as prisoner C77200, Patty was still insisting that she didn't engineer or participate in the murder of her family.